DEVELOPING A CRITICAL PEDAGOGY OF MIGRATION STUDIES

Ethics, Politics and Practice in the Classroom

Teresa Piacentini

First published in Great Britain in 2025 by

Bristol University Press
University of Bristol
1-9 Old Park Hill
Bristol
BS2 8BB
UK
t: +44 (0)117 374 6645
e: bup-info@bristol.ac.uk

Details of international sales and distribution partners are available at bristoluniversitypress.co.uk

© Bristol University Press 2025

British Library Cataloguing in Publication Data
A catalogue record for this book is available from the British Library

ISBN 978-1-5292-2713-0 hardcover
ISBN 978-1-5292-2714-7 paperback
ISBN 978-1-5292-2715-4 ePub
ISBN 978-1-5292-2716-1 ePdf

The right of Teresa Piacentini to be identified as author of this work has been asserted by her in accordance with the Copyright, Designs and Patents Act 1988.

All rights reserved: no part of this publication may be reproduced, stored in a retrieval system, or transmitted in any form or by any means, electronic, mechanical, photocopying, recording, or otherwise without the prior permission of Bristol University Press.

Every reasonable effort has been made to obtain permission to reproduce copyrighted material. If, however, anyone knows of an oversight, please contact the publisher.

The statements and opinions contained within this publication are solely those of the author and not of the University of Bristol or Bristol University Press. The University of Bristol and Bristol University Press disclaim responsibility for any injury to persons or property resulting from any material published in this publication.

Bristol University Press works to counter discrimination on grounds of gender, race, disability, age and sexuality.

Cover design: Lyn Davies Design
Front cover image: Socksy/ Ruth Black

Contents

List of Case Studies		iv
Acknowledgements		v
1	Critical Pedagogy and Pedagogic Discomfort	1
2	The 'Political Now'	24
3	The Ethical Classroom	46
4	The Political Classroom	72
5	Migration Literacies	97
6	Impact and Refusal	120
7	Connections	141
Notes		162
References		164
Index		180

List of Case Studies

2.1	Windrush	34
2.2	The *Gilets Noirs*	35
2.3	'Do not come'	37
3.1	The ethics of breaking free of the classroom	51
3.2	Responding to emotions and safety in the classroom	55
3.3	Ethically creating space for knowledge holders	60
3.4	Working with empirics/counter-empirics	62
4.1	The Asylum University	81
4.2	'Immigrants, we get the job done'	90
5.1	IOM and WAKA Well	105
6.1	RISE: Refugees, Survivors and eX-detainees	126
6.2	'Curating Discomfort'	130
6.3	A manifesto for a critical pedagogy of migration	136
7.1	Collaborating ethically: Example 1	146
7.2	Collaborating ethically: Example 2	147

Acknowledgements

The ideas presented in this book would not have come to fruition had I not started working with people seeking asylum at a time of radical change to UK immigration legislation in 2000. Through this work, I have learned what it means to endure and sometimes be broken by, but also survive and resist the brutal UK asylum regime from hundreds of people seeking refuge and the many community organizations and activists tirelessly fighting for asylum rights. I acknowledge your experiences, stories, journeys, desperation, hope and strength. You are with me in every classroom and every conversation about migration as part of my fight for social justice. I will keep telling your stories. Thank you to the many friends and colleagues for their support along this journey. Special thanks go to Ali Fraser, Stephen Ashe and Matt Dawson for their kindness and for listening, particularly during times when I struggled to articulate my thoughts. To my fellow world*ing* classroom collaborators and co-conspirators, Gareth Mulvey, Kolar Aparna, Joris Schapendonk, Pinar Aksu and Annika Joy; our collective efforts have achieved something remarkable, and I continue to learn from each of you. To those comrades who participated in the June 2018 workshop that laid the foundation for many of the ideas in this book; I hope I have done our critical conversations justice. Special thanks to Eiri Ohtani, Dylan Fotoohi, Zoë Holliday, Gary Christie and Colin Clark for your wisdom, critical questioning and intellectual generosity. Thank you to the students I have had the privilege of teaching and learning with over the years. Your insightful questions, invaluable experiences, activism, willingness to learn and knack for challenging my thinking have greatly contributed to my practice. Thank you to Victoria Pittman and Anna Richardson of Bristol University Press and Dawn Preston of Newgen Publishing UK; your belief in this project, along with your support, guidance and patience throughout every stage, have been so important. Deep thanks also to the anonymous reviewers for engaging so thoughtfully with the proposal and manuscript, offering suggestions and feedback that really sharpened my thinking. To my family: remembering my Dad Andrea, whose own immigrant story shaped so much of who I am today; thank you to my wonderful Mum Rosemary, who showed me that learning is indeed is a lifelong pursuit; and to my amazing, brilliant and loving sisters. I am especially indebted to Maria for her calm writing assistance and guidance, and to Laura for her unwavering emotional and intellectual support at every step. This book would not have happened without your steady and unfaltering belief in me. To Marshall, thank you for everything: for the emotional and physical space I have needed to do this work; for keeping home life ticking over; and for all those cups of tea that I might not have properly thanked you for at the time! Finally, to Andrea and Luca, my wonderful, beautiful kids; you are my inspiration and beacons of hope for a better, more socially just world. This book is for you.

1

Critical Pedagogy and Pedagogic Discomfort

Introduction

We are living in difficult times. Migration is a highly politicized and hotly debated topic, ramped up by increasing border violence and racist and xenophobic rhetoric, and driven by 'solutions-focused' approaches to managing the movement of certain racialized people. Practices and logics of detention, deportation, pushbacks, building migrant barges and camps, and offshoring have all become increasingly mainstreamed as 'migration management' policies in response to these seemingly 'unprecedented times'. Teaching about migration in the current political times feels urgent, messy and frustrating. It is also hard intellectual and emotional work. However, we need to unravel the notion that the current conjuncture is new and unprecedented, and instead understand it as deeply steeped in histories of colonialism. We need to recognize the many ways in which contemporary and historical politics shape the classroom, and why this is vital in our pursuit of challenging existing norms and fostering meaningful, transformative change. We also need to contend with the deep, complex ethics, politics and emotions surrounding how we talk, think and learn about migration. These concerns also feel urgent and pressing. They are also immediately relevant to a wide range of disciplines in which migration topics are taught, each bringing their own grammars and vocabularies, orthodoxies, and normative assumptions. How do we understand today in the context of the past? And how do we connect this teaching and learning to our relationships with, and understandings of, ethics, politics, power, racism, inequalities and injustice in the classroom and beyond? *Developing a Critical Pedagogy of Migration Studies: Ethics, Politics and Practice in the Classroom* (hereafter, *Developing a Critical Pedagogy of Migration*) is a book about these very questions. It is about developing theoretically informed critical-pedagogical approaches to learning about migration and making links between three interrelated areas of analysis – ethics, politics and practice – and it urges us, as teachers, students and practitioners, to take these links seriously. It is important to highlight that migration studies, as a field, encompasses a broad and diverse array of disciplines, including sociology, political science, anthropology, geography, law, economics, human rights, health studies, disability studies, development studies, journalism, languages, postcolonial studies and more; it combines their insights into its approaches and integrates their knowledges and methods (Scholten et al, 2022); and the hope of this book is that it has broad appeal to these many disciplinary perspectives.

The idea for *Developing a Critical Pedagogy of Migration* can be traced to several learning moments from my own practice as a sociologist teaching and researching about migration. The first relates to patterns I have noticed emerging in student feedback in recent years. Student feedback generally reveals an evolving sociological imagination, students describe feeling unsettled by thinking sociologically about social issues and their 'lives changed' as they begin to see the world in transformative ways. However, in the past few years, there has been a small but steady creep of feedback telling me that there is 'too much focus on social justice' in the content and calling for 'less bias', 'more objectivity' and 'more neutrality' of their lecturers. This signals two things: first, that despite, as Sean Cameron Golden (2023) suggests, the 'personal as political' and 'the myth of neutrality' being commonly recognized concepts in education, there are still expectations that the lecturer should strive to be a figure of neutrality and that learning should be an apolitical process; and, second, that discussions about what constitutes 'debate' and the value of 'both sides' arguments in the current conjuncture signal a creep of the so-called 'culture wars' that have come to characterize the present moment into the classroom. This has led me to reflect on several questions: why might there be this failure, or reluctance, to see and accept how the politics that shapes our lives also shapes our decisions to enter teaching and how we do our jobs, including curriculum design, how we frame and structure debates, and how we engage with those debates? Why is the presence of political positioning and the declaration of that politics unsettling or discomforting for students and indeed teachers? And if so-called 'culture wars' have indeed found their way into the classroom, how might we address this in our teaching practice?

The second moment comes from thinking reflexively about how, through a sustained focus on racialized people to explore questions of social identities and structural inequalities, I have been in danger of uncritically reproducing patterns of othering in my teaching. This has come to light through student work where I noticed slippages between the experiences of 'Muslim minorities' and 'migrants', with one label becoming synonymous for the other, as well as an ease with which students would describe and analyse Muslim people as a migrant population. This brought to my mind

Ambalavaner Sivanandan's (2009) important words from his speech 'Catching history on the wing'. He spoke there about the relationship between the liberal intelligentsia and their discourse that informs popular racism and influences government policy, so that 'any Muslim could be a terrorist, any Black migrant could be a Muslim, if not an economic refugee, or an "unjustified" asylum seeker' (Sivanandan, 2009: 97). I thought I had 'done the work', but I also had to reckon with whether I had got it wrong and instead been adding 'to the cacophony of negativity tied to identity markers' (Lichty and Palamaro-Munsell, 2017: 319) by uncritically reproducing a subjugated 'other'.

The third moment is related: a reckoning with the highly mobile tropes that dominate much of how we talk about migration and racialized populations. I emphasize the limitations of the depoliticized concept of 'integration' when discussing the harsh brutality of the UK asylum process and the 'hostile environment'. To challenge these narratives, I employ counter-stories to disrupt reductive or stereotypical dominant narratives (Blaisdell, 2021), revealing the knowledge embedded in the experiences of surviving the UK asylum system. These stories are treated as expert knowledge of oppression and resistance (Lenette, 2019). I guide students to reframe 'integration' by considering its embedded connection to segregation within these counter-narratives. This approach helps centre discussions on power and border governance in the context of 'integration', survival, settlement and resistance. It also encourages the historical contextualization of integration as a continuation of colonial governance. In our classroom discussions, we explore whose experiences are given prominence in 'integration research', whose stories are shared and from whose perspective, and whose experiences hold value. We analyse the effects of segregated immigration regimes using counter-stories as a means of both intellectual and emotional understanding. While these discussions stimulate engaging classroom conversations, student coursework often reveals a persistence of dominant policy and research narratives. 'Integration' is reproduced as a depoliticized and de-historicized 'solution' or panacea, with counter-stories sometimes relegated to the illustrative rather than considered as serious knowledge. This underscores the importance of looking beyond conventional categories of knowledge, as emphasized by Oliver Bakewell (2008). When policy-relevant research determines so much of how we talk and think about what counts in migration work, this also applies to what we recognize as knowledge and how we go about teaching beyond the categories.

The fourth moment relates less to a 'moment' and more to an ongoing decolonizing of my practice through growing awareness of the politics of knowledge production and how this contributes to what postcolonial theorist Gayatri Chakravorty Spivak (1992) calls epistemic violence. Epistemic violence occurs through the imposition of dominant knowledge systems, particularly in the context of colonialism and postcolonial power relations. It involves the suppression, erasure or devaluation of indigenous or marginalized knowledge, ways of knowing and ways of being in the world. I have begun the work of filling the omissions that I knew were there in my own teaching practice, thinking more critically about how the knowledge I work with is produced, circulated and legitimized. I also understand this as a way to do some decolonizing work by showing how the privileging of certain knowledge silences others and shapes what has come to count as, and be elevated to, 'canonical knowledge'. This has opened possibilities to move from a largely accepted and ultimately safe way of knowing to new ways of knowing, effectively placing the canon in its place (Dennis, 2018). Counter-stories and working closely with activists and communities within and outwith the classroom have again offered me ways to replace and undo the dominant majoritarian narratives that prevail in policy-focused migration research, with its negative and deficit-focused connotations.

The fifth and final moment occurred during a one-day workshop I had organized in 2018 with academics, community organizations and students to discuss and explore together how we critically teach about migration in the 'political now', work that was to come to be foundational to many of the ideas in this book. One participant, Twimukye Macline Mushaka, a long-standing community activist in Scotland and Uganda, asked me during a coffee break, "Where are the other people who look like me?". Twimukye is also a woman of refugee background I have known since the early 2000s when I began working as a community interpreter in Glasgow. When I asked what she meant, she told me: "Teresa, you know who I mean! I mean people with experience of the asylum system, people who are refugees, people of colour!". I had invited people currently in the asylum system to be part of this workshop, but she was right, people with refugee experience were not represented in a significant way. I was trying to dismantle how we talk and think about migration through 'learning with' approaches, but in their absence, they remained the object of study. Had I fallen prey to what Zimbabwean writer and poet Tawona Sitholé (2022) calls the 'disease of expertise'? Had I tried hard enough to centre their experience as knowledge? Had I, in the end, limited its 'usefulness' as illustrative testimony, only to be valued once put through the academic filter?

These moments collectively represent my realization of my role in upholding the structures I aim to critique and dismantle. This awakening is humbling and discomforting. It is not only about recognizing our shortcomings and implementing corrective measures but also about identifying spaces for dismantling practices and teaching as a space of possibilities and 'what ifs' (Boda et al, 2022). It is only through critical reflection on my teaching practice that I have come to realize that this discomfort is also liberatory and necessary for change to happen. It has led me to approach knowledge differently, reflect deeply on the ethics and politics of knowledge production, and adopt different knowledge practices in my teaching, learning and research. So, what does all this mean for our teaching practice? How do we make room for the different politics we all bring to the classroom? How do we understand the now through the lens of history? How do we explore the many interconnected and multidisciplinary ways in which social, political and cultural issues manifest in our everyday lives? How do we achieve our teaching and learning goals of troubling dominant narratives while attending to the diverse body of students before us? How do we connect the outside to inside the classroom? Where is the space for meaningful dialogue? What strategies can we develop in the classroom that will help us dismantle and disrupt? How do we embrace discomfort? How do we understand the relationship between theory and action, not just knowing the world but changing the world? How can we change ways of knowing as part of changing the world? Such questions are deeply embedded and foundational to the critical pedagogy tradition, and these are some of the questions that this book will seek to address.

Developing a Critical Pedagogy of Migration has two main aims. First, it is an invitation to think about teaching practice: it offers an in-depth and theoretically grounded discussion of critical pedagogy approaches, their connection to the various fields from which migration studies originate and the disciplines where migration is a topic of intellectual focus, and their ethical and political consequences; and it provides a deep dive into the affective investments and emotional imperatives of doing this work, as well as the subsequent complexities for interrupting and disrupting. Second, this book is action-oriented. Across the chapters, it offers practical guidance through various pedagogical devices, such as problem posing and reflective tasks, talking points, teachable moments, case studies, and teaching activities. These devices are offered as ways to think more concretely about disruption and transformation in our teaching practice. Taking these two aims together, the book explores how critical pedagogy can inform and transform cross-disciplinary and multidisciplinary teaching practices about migration by encouraging teachers and students to consider ethics, politics and the broader impact of their pedagogical approaches. Fundamentally critical pedagogy questions the myth of the neutrality of education, aims to redress all the biases that have informed ways of teaching and knowing in our societies, and centres education for transformative change. The remainder of this chapter sets the stage for exploring the work of key thinkers in critical pedagogy. It then identifies the key ideas this book engages with and interventions it seeks to make. These are woven throughout this book, helping shape the story of how we can build better critical-pedagogical approaches to teaching migration.

Introducing critical pedagogy

> **Reflective task**
>
> As bell hooks (2009: 9) wrote, 'critical thinking involves first discovering the who, what, when, where, and how of things – finding the answers to those eternal questions of the inquisitive child – and then utilizing that knowledge in a manner that enables you to determine what matters most'. What are your thoughts on this statement? What happens if we begin our first discussions together as teachers and students with this question about deciding what does indeed matter the most?

The tradition of critical pedagogy can be traced back to Brazilian educator and activist Paulo Freire and his path-breaking work, *Pedagogy of the Oppressed* (Freire, 1970). This book revolutionized the concept of critical literacy by shifting its focus from the mere acquisition of skills (literacy as reading/writing) to thinking about literacy more broadly as a tool for raising consciousness. In contrast to traditional teaching models that treat students as passive recipients of knowledge, Freire (1970, 1973) advocated for a problem-posing approach rooted in critical thinking and dialogue, with the teacher and student positioned as equals engaged in a process of mutual learning and reflection, emphasizing 'a democratic way for students to take part in the contention over knowledge and the shape of society' (Shor, 1992: 35). Freire describes this as a dialogical process: learning shifts from teacher *to* student to teacher *with* student; both are subjects in this process; and both are 'com[ing] to see the world not as a static reality, but as reality in process, in transformation' (Freire, 1970: 71). The classroom is considered an important site where oppressive systems can be challenged because classroom 'knowledge, values, desires, and social relations are always implicated in power' (Giroux, 2020: 5). Critical pedagogy is an invitation to question what we think we know as situated knowledge. Freire describes this process of decoding text and context as reading the world to read the word: 'reading the world always precedes reading the word, and reading the word implies continually reading the world' (Freire and Macedo, 1987: 35). He urges us to critically examine our positionalities, values and systems of power as a process of unlearning through *conscientização* ('conscientization') (Freire, 1970: 27), which is at the core of a transformative educational experience. This involves the exploration and questioning of dominant social narratives and deeply ingrained common-sense assumptions by challenging the notion that the current situation is natural or inevitable, both within our own lives and in broader social contexts. A Freirean approach to critical pedagogy through conscientization emphasizes the importance of praxis (Tejeda et al, 2003: 14). Praxis involves reflection and dialogue followed by actively working towards transforming social realities. In the case of the classroom, through reflection, students confront the ethical and political consequences of the status quo and become ethically and politically motivated to struggle in the interest of greater social justice (McLaren, 1995). For conscientization to take hold, this responsiveness demands a doing of some 'thing' as we face the deepest and most important problems of our times. Through this unsettling process of unlearning and by fostering a deeper understanding of the social structures and power dynamics that shape our lives, conscientization and critical pedagogy serve as catalysts for meaningful transformation. Education is therefore viewed as both a project of freedom and a provocation to critically engage with the world to those who dare to teach (Freire, 1998, 1999).

Freire's ideas have been taken up enthusiastically by the American Canadian public intellectual Henry Giroux, widely recognized as one of the foremost theorists of critical pedagogy in the US (Besley, 2012). Whereas Freire's focus was primarily on the liberatory and transformative potential of education, Giroux extends these ideas, highlighting the limitations imposed by the capitalist economy that puts brakes on the transformative potential of education (Giroux, 1989, 2003, 2022). Giroux has written prolifically about the problematic relationship between pedagogy and the corporatization of education. His work underscores education as a fundamentally civic and political endeavour that must be deeply rooted in civic engagement, critical consciousness and social responsibility to confront and overcome systemic inequalities and injustices (Giroux, 2020). The classroom becomes a battleground, a complex and uneven terrain where experiences, knowledge and power are shaped by different and often unequal contexts (Giroux, 2022). One of his most significant contributions is his relentless insistence on infusing critical pedagogy with a language of possibility for social justice, resistance and hope (Giroux, 1981, 1997, 2022). He is a strong advocate for the fundamental social role of education to develop what he characterizes as a pedagogy of resistance (Giroux, 2022) and for an educated hope. This is the 'precondition for imagining a future that does not replicate the nightmares of the present, for not making the present the future' (Giroux, 2023: 59), and is necessary so we can 'imagine otherwise in order to act in other ways' (Giroux, 2020: 141). This is underpinned by a political and ethical commitment to move our thinking from 'what is' to 'what if' (Boda et al, 2022). However, this educated hope requires time. It requires a connection between the personal and the social, and between the knowledge and the everyday lives and experiences, histories and resources that students and teachers bring to the classroom. Importantly, as bell hooks (1994) argues, these should not be excluded or considered as deficits or as inferior forms of knowledge or types of social relationships.

As Carole Azumah Dennis (2018) argues, the pedagogical and the political are a continuity that exceeds the confines of the school, college or university to intervene in the reinvention of the world. Education therefore occurs in various other domains, such as mainstream media and the digital sphere. This highlights another of Giroux's key contributions: the conceptualization of public pedagogy and the idea of multiple sites of literacies, where connections between personal life and broader societal issues can be made, and where they can also be shut down (Giroux, 2000, 2020). A public pedagogy involves the analysis of the domains of cultural education, public space, popular culture, cultural institutions and political struggle as sites beyond the classroom where learning takes place and knowledge is generated. This prompts us to question who has control over the production of knowledge, values and classroom practices, and to consider the location of knowledge itself (Giroux, 2020). Drawing from cultural studies and the work of Stuart Hall and Antonio Gramsci, Giroux demonstrates how popular culture and various media formats serve as a political and pedagogical arena for negotiation, struggle, domination and contestation over identities and ideologies, thus expanding critical pedagogy beyond the confines of the institution. Public pedagogy recognizes that through multimedia platforms, many of us live in 'second-hand worlds' (through what C. Wright Mills called the 'cultural apparatus', a term Giroux also adopts), aware of so much more than we have personally experienced or confronted. This, Giroux argues, is a crucial link between knowledge and everyday life, influencing what social realities we engage with or choose to ignore. This also translates into the classroom choices about the knowledges we select as important and those considered less so.

While pessimism today seems more pronounced, and it feels harder and harder to find hope, resistance cannot be limited to any one sphere or to the classroom alone (Giroux, 2003, 2022). In today's media-saturated world, public pedagogy requires critical media literacies to help us become discerning consumers of information in our interactions with news, information and each other, despite the feelings of threat or discomfort that may be evoked (Giroux, 2022). Giroux (2020: 201) argues that we must be vigilant of manufactured illiteracy as 'a tool of political repression' that discourages critical thinking and questioning, preventing individuals from challenging existing power structures and hindering their ability to recognize how power operates in society, thus producing a manufactured ignorance (see also Giroux, 2022). Critically engaging with multiple sites of literacies is pedagogically significant because it provides us with opportunities for building the literacies we need to read the world (Bargallie et al, 2023). Manufactured illiteracy and manufactured ignorance are important ideas which remind us that just because the digital realm is a site of possibility, this does not automatically lead to social justice. The media, particularly in the realm of migration, often perpetuate hate, violence, racism and the spread of misinformation and false stories. A public pedagogy is a recognition that knowledge is confronted, generated and consumed within these domains, which are shaped by power relations and political and economic structures, and critical media literacies help us manage the risk of succumbing to populism and assuming the existence of objective knowledge. Affect must surely be central to our capacity to even imagine the 'what if' of a pedagogy of possibility and indeed to any desire itself for disruption, transformation and transgression, all central aims of critical pedagogy (Yoon, 2005). While Giroux's ideas do address affect, emotions, confusingly perhaps, tend to be placed in the background (Zembylas, 2013a). We can turn to the work of trailblazing African American public intellectual and scholar bell hooks to place emotions at the centre of critical pedagogy.

Teaching to Transgress by bell hooks (1994) is one of the classics of critical pedagogy that continues a commitment to the practice of liberatory conscientization, though under changed circumstances. A revolutionary feminist writer, activist and cultural theorist, hooks drew deeply on her own experience of racially segregated schooling and writes about the role of (in)formal education in creating spaces for social change and the transgressive possibilities of education. She too was profoundly influenced by Paulo Freire, and her contributions to critical pedagogy are many; three are underlined here. First, she centres emotions, arguing that emotions in the classroom enhance our intellectual endeavour by keeping us 'aware and alert' (hooks, 1994: 155). Education is adventurous, she says; the classroom is an exciting place of serious academic engagement, and everyone's contributions are valued as pedagogic resources. However, we can also feel there the widest range of emotions, such as pain and suffering, anger and frustration, discomfort, and joy. Second, she reminds us that, more than ever before, educators are compelled to confront the biases, positionalities and politics that shape teaching practices, and to create new ways of knowing and sharing of knowledge (hooks, 1994, 2009). While typically considered essential components of rigorous research design, such concerns about our subjectivities have received less attention in the context of the classroom but are nonetheless vital if we are committed to teaching to transgress. Doing this reflexive work may be uncomfortable and produce unpredictable situations, and this discomfort is productive of change. Third, hooks (2003) emphasizes the importance of building community. One way to achieve this is through confessional narratives: 'the sharing of, and actively listening to, first-hand experiences in the classroom, and connecting them to academic knowledge as a method to expand and enhance our capacity to know and claim a knowledge base from which we can speak in the classroom' (hooks, 1994: 148). This approach emphasizes teaching 'from where you are' and understanding the unique perspectives and experiences of the students in the classroom. Building community is, she argues, part of cultivating a radical openness to new knowledge, including decisions about the curricula, content and language we use, though recognizing how they can also become tools of colonization, and to our collective pursuit of knowledge (hooks, 2003). Discussions about power, agency and history should not separate identity and experiences, and hooks highlights the value of voice and its strategic use in speaking freely, positioning students as speaking individuals deserving of a voice. In the end, she offers to us an engaged and radical pedagogy of love and vulnerability, centred on conversation, where power and knowledge are given and shared, ideas are always circulating, and conversations exploring different ideas and positionalities give way to serious thought (hooks, 2003, 2009).

> **Reflective task**
>
> Take a moment to think about the dynamics in your classroom. Who are the expert voices in the classroom? As teachers, are we open to critical review of what we think constitutes knowledge? Reflect on specific instances where you have revised your own understanding due to critical review. Consider the knowledge held by scholars, community members, experts in the field and those with diverse cultural backgrounds. How can you bring these external sources of knowledge into your classroom? Now consider building the curriculum. Are you open to the expertise of others, including your students, to review and enhance the content and approach of your teaching materials? Are you prepared to be a lifelong learner, continually seeking to expand your understanding and adapt your teaching methods?

Critical pedagogy is about building literacies of power in the classroom, but we must remain vigilant to its limitations and assumptions. For example, hooks (2009) acknowledges and critiques the significant lack of attention to gender and the explicit male bias in Freire's portrayal of oppressed individuals, particularly the limited binary of peasant–workers. Other scholars, such as Kathleen Weiler (2005) and Elizabeth Ellsworth (1989), emphasize the need for a more comprehensive understanding of oppression in Freire's thinking that includes gender dynamics. While Freire (2021) himself acknowledged this critique in his later writings and interviews, hooks (1994) has also reflected on how her perspective would have been different if he had not taken the feminist critique seriously. Our vigilance must extend to how we do this work of critical pedagogy and our role in sustaining power imbalances. Teachers should not assume that they are exempt from normative ways of seeing or that they are the sole arbiters of unveiling biases. There is an assumption in Freire's framework of critical pedagogy that the teacher remains largely at the centre of consciousness-raising activity, dismissing an alternative reality that many students come to the classroom with oppositional voices already formulated within various anti-racism and other movements (Ellsworth, 1989: 311). Students do not necessarily rely on teachers to interpret their goals, and hooks' advocacy of confessional narratives is helpful in this regard. However, most often, it is the teacher who designs the module, the class content and the assessments, and who remains the producer of representations that are given more weight in the classroom (Routley, 2016). Moreover, our decisions codify the knowledge, skills and attitudes that we, as teachers, hold to be important and often also reflect what the 'university' holds to be important (Gebrial, 2018: 25). How we curate knowledge and how we develop our pedagogic practices may in themselves contribute to inequities in the classroom rather than dismantle these. Therefore, we need to be mindful of work required to reject any sense of unearned power conferred systemically, as this will only sustain the status quo, and we must take responsibility for the knowledge that is both privileged and reproduced in the classroom (Lichty and Palamaro-Munsell, 2017).

From theory to practice: locating power in the classroom

- How can we critically assess and challenge the limitations of critical pedagogy, including the teacher's role and knowledge privilege in the classroom?
- Do we address power dynamics in our classroom, and if not, what are the reasons?
- How can we reconfigure power dynamics in the classroom to facilitate the active participation of students and communities, drawing from their experiences and activism?

Design a 'power-mapping' exercise where students visually represent perceived power dynamics in the classroom. After the exercise, talk about power imbalances and how they impact learning. Encourage students to come up with ideas and practical ways to address these dynamics.

Assign students a writing task in which they critically reflect on their own position in the classroom power structure. Ask them to explore their roles as learners and contributors to knowledge production, and to propose ways to challenge and reconfigure these roles.

- How can we collaboratively create a curriculum that challenges power structures, fosters empathy and advances social justice?
- How can we critically assess and modify our teaching materials and assessments to address embedded assumptions, privileges and exclusions?

- How do we balance institutional expectations with social justice goals while incorporating space for reflective learning on 'how we got here' and 'where we could go next' within critical pedagogy approaches?

Assign students the task of critically analysing existing curriculum materials and assessments. Ask them to identify implicit biases, exclusions or stereotypes, and propose practical changes or alternative materials to address these issues. Encourage them to engage in open discussions about their findings.

Create a space for students to collaboratively design a roadmap for incorporating reflective learning on institutional expectations and social justice goals within the curriculum. Encourage them to generate new ideas and practical ways to balance these objectives, considering the real-world constraints they may encounter.

Power, safety and unlearning with critical pedagogy

From a critical pedagogy perspective, experiences are foundational for learning, and their meaningful nature is what makes them a valuable resource to develop broader ways of knowing. This holds relevance not only for course materials but also for helping 'students locate themselves in the concrete conditions of their daily lives while furthering their understanding of the limits often imposed by such conditions' (Giroux, 2020: 181). We can, as hooks advocates with confessional narratives, take the initiative and engage in what may be perceived as risky behaviour by linking our personal experiences to the curriculum. Vulnerability plays a significant role here. Michalinos Zembylas (2012), an expert on social justice pedagogies, offers the idea of mutual vulnerability as a pedagogical principle that recognizes the interdependence of individuals and the importance of assuming critical responsibility towards oneself and others in a community. Embracing the mutual vulnerability that comes from sharing can help dismantle hierarchical structures within the classroom because, as hooks also suggests, sharing through personal narratives can contribute to the formation of a learning community based on cooperation and deep listening. Such an approach challenges conventional notions of a 'safe space' and pushes against the stifling of classroom discussions through conformity with convention. Instead of equating safety to the common-sense assumption of everyone agreeing or having equal time to speak, hooks (2009: 87) suggests that 'if we rather think of safety as knowing how to cope in situations of risk, then we open up the possibility that we can be safe even in situations where there is disagreement and even conflict'.

In the critical classroom committed to disruption and transformation, the questions we should be asking instead are: safe from what? Safe from whom?

Safe for whom? How do we cope with discomfort and risk? Providing a space for difference and diversity in the classroom, hooks (1989: 71) argues, 'requires that we shift old paradigms, allowing for complexity'. She emphasizes that the supposedly neutral classroom setting can in fact be unsafe for certain students, as it may suppress reflection, conflict, diverse perspectives and the validation of a wide range of experiences (hooks, 1994). We must be critical of simplistic narratives equating safety with inclusion. Others agree, arguing that: the pursuit of absolute safety in the classroom becomes untenable, counterproductive and therefore pointless (Wagner, 2005); the promotion of a completely safe and discomfort-free environment is contradictory to the goals of transformation and social justice (Davis and Steyn, 2012); and in-class conflict does not have to only be destructive but can also be productive of understanding social injustice and generative of social change (Hogue et al, 1998). Feeling tension and discomfort should not automatically be equated with feeling unsafe. Moreover, we should bring our expectations to the classroom that our views may, and can, be challenged and questioned. Writing about the Rhodes Must Fall movement, Dalia Gebrial (2018) has shown that bringing unfamiliar language and thought into public spaces can be difficult and fraught but necessary to upset the status quo and redress, confront, challenge and dismantle entrenched social and structural inequalities. Through the critical pedagogy lens, when we problematize safety and rethink discomfort as productive, we create spaces for critical dialogue, for dissent, for the exploration of complex and controversial topics, and for imagining the world differently.

Discomfort also arises from changes to our teaching approaches. Repetition, as Kevin Kumashiro (2002) suggests, can be comforting and familiar because it aligns with established norms, expectations and orthodoxies. This is not to be mistaken for repetition in the sense of rote learning but repetition in the sense of repeating in an uncritical way what it means to learn and what constitutes learning across teaching, supervising students and doing research. Repetition also relates to the unquestioned or unchallenged grammar of a discipline and uncritical reliance on certain disciplinary literacies. For example, consider how we might talk about migration from a political science, sociological, anthropological, human rights or critical geography perspective. What are the normative assumptions? Are there differences or similarities between and across disciplines? Critical pedagogy invites us to question and challenge these norms, and to learn 'to teach intentionally while learning to recognize the hidden ways we often teach unintentionally' (Kumashiro, 2002: 84). Unlearning repetition in practical terms can mean a number of things: creating opportunities for meaningful dialogue and collaboration among students; designing learning experiences that encourage us to question, analyse and challenge dominant narratives and structures; providing opportunities for students to engage with diverse perspectives and apply theoretical frameworks to real-world issues; involving students in curriculum design and decision-making processes; allowing some flexibility in assignments and assessment methods; and engaging with community-based learning.

From theory to practice: creatively designing curricula within the limits of the university

I want to suggest two approaches to how we might creatively design curricula within institutional confines. First is the living syllabus. Offering a creative and collaborative way of reading the world to read the word, a 'live' syllabus is a dynamic teaching document that goes beyond a static course outline. It must have the basics in place to cover the foundational learning that is needed to then build upon, but it adapts throughout the course based on students' continuing needs, evolving ideas and emerging topics. It serves as a repository of multi-format knowledge sources, such as academic materials, policy papers, videos, blogs and more, as well as digital tools and collaborative platforms that can be easily shared to enable real-time communication and foster creative exchanges between teachers and students, and among students themselves. Second, is the collaborative syllabus. Initially providing foundational content because students are not yet experts in course design, this approach integrates student choice into lecture design. For example, you could ask students to select topics for the later weeks in the semester from a list that you feel equipped to guide them through. These can be topics that connect classroom learning to real-world experiences and multiple literacies, promoting a collaborative learning relationship and balancing power dynamics in the classroom. You can also integrate a 'live' element encouraging students to research materials they can share between themselves.

Curating a living and/or collaborative syllabus is a first step, and as teachers, we must cultivate critical thinking that aims to transform consciousness. When using these approaches explore with students:

- What is it we seek to disrupt with this collaborative knowledge building?
- How will this approach challenge dominant narratives?
- How might we use these materials and resources for change?

In practical terms, achieving a balance between the philosophies underpinning critical pedagogies and the institutional confines, challenges and demands within which we teach is challenging. Even when we try to be creative, it can feel very difficult and frustrating, disempowering even, to push against the pressures of standardized course structures and assessment requirements, and the pressure of research, all of which limit the resources available for innovative and student-centred teaching practices. Time pressures to have course material ready well in advance of teaching make it feel impossible to genuinely co-design the curriculum. These pressures also create further inequities for precarious and marginalized staff, who often experience the heaviest teaching demands and workloads. Complicating matters further, the patterns of pedagogy we encounter in higher education (HE) are often deeply rooted in the broader secondary educational system. Challenging these entrenched habits and structures, and building new ones, also requires building community. It demands a collective commitment to transformative change from various people, including administrators, academics and students. Institutional confines extend beyond practical concerns for how we teach to also shaping the kinds of knowledge we turn to.

Is the university the place for radical pedagogies?

The Western university has historically privileged certain forms of knowledge while marginalizing and suppressing others, perpetuating hierarchies of power and reinforcing dominant narratives (Tejeda et al, 2003). This includes acknowledging the role of scientific racism and colonialism in pedagogical practices, and shaping knowledge production and the racialized 'other' as objects of study. By interrogating the historical narratives of the 'unshakably colonial university' (Bhambra et al, 2018: 6), we can challenge the biases and assumptions that underpin disciplinary knowledge and open space for alternative perspectives and epistemologies. A decolonizing pedagogy is not just about adding a token week on race or diversity; it is a fundamental rethinking of how knowledge is produced, transmitted and evaluated.

Reflective task

Decolonizing pedagogy requires engaging with diverse perspectives, challenging dominant narratives and creating space for multiple ways of knowing and being (Dennis, 2018; Zembylas, 2018). The Decolonizing the Curriculum movement maps directly onto critical pedagogy as a means to redress what counts as knowledge, how knowledge is ordered and who it works for. But are we clear on where we stand in relation to the decolonizing movement and what it means to our teaching practice? Some initial questions we can ask ourselves include: to what extent are our curricula informed by global perspectives? To what extent do we bring the wide range of

> student perspectives into the learning context and make space for students to bring their different experiences into the co-construction of curriculum content? What space do we make for the knowledge of community partners in our classroom? Where do we know from and why does that matter? How do we understand decolonizing as connected to the fight for social justice?

Decolonizing the curriculum is, as John Holmwood (2018) argues, intricately and intrinsically connected to fight for social justice, exposing the 'hidden curriculum' that encompasses a range of implicit norms, values, beliefs and practices within academic life and that are 'deeply wedded to imperial histories' (Giroux and Penna, 1979: 22). Such a pedagogy problem-poses ahistorical memories of people, events and practices of remembrance. The decolonizing turn requires a cross-disciplinary critical examination and reckoning with how topics like migration have been historically framed and taught in ways that may reinforce stereotypes, biases and power imbalances through their historical decoupling from colonial legacies and imperial ties, their reliance on idioms of colonial governance, and their role in the research–policy pipeline that shapes migration knowledge. Moreover, failure to centre questions of race and colonialism leads to a (politically and ideologically) race-blind and power-blind pedagogy of migration that reinforces colonial thinking. A decolonizing pedagogy is also a pedagogy of discomfort (Zembylas, 2018).

Critical pedagogy embraces transgression and seeks to work for social justice by challenging the dominant cultural narratives; it is activist in its very nature. Activist scholars Colette Cann and Eric DeMeulenaere (2020) have identified four dimensions to an anti-oppressive activist pedagogy that neatly aligns with the key tenets of critical pedagogy discussed earlier. The first relates to purpose: is justice prioritized? Is it ideological? Is it disruptive? Is it about scope beyond the confines of the classroom? The second relates to content and representations of students in the content, that is, in the stories being told, and how to ensure that we do not exploit voices. The third is about identity: how it is defined and how a reflexivity that moves beyond a politics of declaration, following Sarah Ahmed, can be nurtured. The last dimension relates to process: how we interact in the classroom; and how we build community, trust and an openness to share our discomfort in the knowledge that this is an emancipatory experience. Kathryn Gaianguest (1998) suggests that teachers with radical sympathies should work together to develop strategic methods of changing oppressive aspects of our colleges and universities, and that teachers need to be as concerned with the process of teaching as they are with the content of their teaching, which can help build community. This agenda drives much of what *Developing a Critical*

Pedagogy of Migration is about, and the remainder of this chapter sets out the interrelated key ideas and interventions guiding us through its pages.

Key ideas and key interventions

Key idea: critical pedagogy is a necessary confrontation with neutrality and power in the classroom

Teaching as political and as rejecting neutrality concerns itself with shaping an emancipated future for learning (Golden, 2023). Clinging to any notion of neutrality in education is another way to mask and obscure, disavow even, the political nature of education, and to deny the imposition of particular perspectives, as any quest for objectivity camouflages the asymmetric power relations within and outside of the classroom. As Karen Kopelson (2003: 117) warns, there is a problematic supposition that objectivity is somehow 'good' and subjectivity is somehow 'bad', and that anything political or opinionated is not only 'biased' but also to be avoided at all costs. By extension, this would suggest that our political and ethical involvement in the 'what' and 'how' we teach should be absent. However, we are people from somewhere bringing views from somewhere, and as critical teachers, we are, as hooks (2009: 27) argues, outwardly, loudly and explicitly saying that we are seeking to further the interest of social justice. We cannot assume the suspension of beliefs or a desire to do so. Moreover, no curriculum is devoid of ideology and power relations; it cannot be separated from how subjectivities are formed, desires are mobilized, experiences are legitimated, why some knowledge is considered acceptable when other forms are excluded and why certain knowledge serves specific social, economic, cultural and political interests. Every teaching decision entails judgements about what indeed matters the most, and this always presupposes a particular notion of the future (Giroux, 2020), as well as shapes how students perceive learning about the world and their place in it. Doing anti-oppressive teaching and research are two sides of the same coin in this regard: they both require us to confront enduring power inequalities and consider how what we 'do' avoids the reproduction of inequalities. This idea has been explored in this chapter and is woven throughout the book, and the ethical and political implications and consequences will be the focus in Chapters 3 and 4.

Key idea: interrogating migration knowledge requires developing critical literacies, but this is just the beginning

As students and teachers, we are encouraged to be aware of how a particular text influences us, how it positions us and whose interests are being served by its content (Leland and Harste, 2000). Critical literacy goes beyond surface-level understanding of texts, including written, visual or spoken forms of communication. It involves developing habits of thought, reading, writing and speaking that delve into deep meanings, root causes, social contexts, ideologies and personal consequences (Shor, 1992, 2019). Critical literacy helps us understand the power dynamics that exist within migration contexts, revealing the influence of political, economic and social structures on the experiences of migrants and governance structures. By being critically literate and by examining the politicized use of language and rhetorical techniques, such as metaphors, metonyms, hyperbole, sensationalism, misinformation, comparisons and repetition, we can gain a deeper understanding of how power operates and of how language shapes our perceptions and thoughts about the world. Critical literacy is an important tool for challenging these political tactics, dismantling deeply ingrained assumptions about knowledge and transforming pedagogical practices that may perpetuate oppression and exclusion. However, we need more to develop a critical pedagogy of migration. The concept of *'migration literacies'* and reckoning with the grammar of migration is offered as providing conditions that make it possible to build on critical literacies, and this is explored in Chapter 5.

Key idea: learning is not limited to the classroom, and knowledge comes in multiple forms

The critical classroom is a messy place that engages head on with changing politics, positionalities and social realities. It is an ethical project of intervention on the politics of oppression. As teachers, we need to think about how we respond with action, not with silence, to the pressing questions of today. Our role is not limited to teaching so students acquire information but extends to helping them understand what building knowledge means and altering their perceptions of education so they see it as a space for disruption and transformation. This can also entail a refusal and rejection of dominant narratives and so-called 'canonical knowledge'. All learning is firmly located in relationships and environments that extend well beyond the classroom, and the ethics and politics of these dynamics are in play before we open the classroom doors and step inside. Adopting a more expansive view of where knowledge comes from, the form it can take, who the experts are and what knowledge counts, we can identify ways of doing epistemic justice and develop a radical openness to ways of knowing and relating. These ideas will be explored in Chapters 3, 4, 6 and 7.

Key intervention: the 'political now' can only be located in its historical context

Reading the world to read the word requires taking seriously social, cultural, historical and political contextualization. Teaching migration today is pressing and urgent; it is a field of study that is dynamic and constantly changing. Indeed, in the UK alone, trying to keep up with the breakneck speed of legislative change feels like a pedagogic impossibility. However, to fully understand where we are today, we need to embed our analysis firmly in its historical context. Failure to do so seriously limits our understandings of how we have got here. It also limits possibilities to 'do migration work otherwise' because we not only fail to name the damage and harm caused by history but also reinforce the exceptionalism of the current conjuncture. Teaching migration without locating it in the historical oppression of border governance and the context of colonial legacies and imperial ties is a cross-disciplinary and sector problem we need to confront and change. Chapter 2 explores the 'political now' in depth, though it is thematically interwoven throughout the pages of this the book.

Key intervention: discomfort is a welcome and necessary way to 'do good harm'

How we understand our social worlds and the social, cultural and political practices contained therein is shaped by emotions, memories, beliefs, values and meanings that are reproduced in scholarly material and in public pedagogy. When these are challenged, they necessarily produce unease or discomfort (Zembylas and Papamichael, 2017). The critical classroom, then, as a confrontation with the limitations of our own knowledge and possible loss of our authority, requires us all to move out of our comfort zones (Zembylas and McGlynn, 2012: 57), and in this sense, it involves both intellectual work and an embodied and emotional response to (un)learning and knowledge production. This book proposes that discomfort takes centre stage in thinking more deeply about the ways we say and see things, or the ways we do not, and how such decisions make us feel. The argument for discomfort as productive and generative of transformation is that where students expect comfort, the possibility for growth through critical thinking is stunted (Davis and Steyn, 2012), and that expecting comfort reveals a privilege that shuts down debate and reproduces inequalities. Instead, when teachers and students examine the various ways power, knowledge and ethics shape their actions, recognizing the discomfort experienced means we can no longer endorse such norms. Moreover, critical learning should be painful, in that it should cause upset and discomfort. It should do harm because it is an inevitable, necessary and vital part of education for social justice. Across *Developing a Critical Pedagogy of Migration*, we will be exploring discomfort as effect, outcome and driver of alternative ways of knowing and relating, as well as how, through '*doing good harm*', discomfort is productive of change. Chapter 3 explores pedagogies of discomfort in greater detail, but throughout this book, we will be exploring precisely what 'doing good harm' can mean in practice, how it manifests and how it is experienced in relation to the ethics, politics and practice of teaching migration.

Key intervention: building better migration literacies are necessary to disrupt and transform learning

Drawing from the insights of critical literacy and racial literacy, I propose the conceptualization of migration literacies as a pedagogical device to build deeper and more nuanced understandings of the pervasive grammar of migration governance in shaping how we teach and learn about migration. The pedagogical device of migration literacies is directly connected to what kinds of knowledge are produced and how the field is semantically organized in terms of the subjects of interest to states and policy makers, and consequently to funding bodies and academics, as well as the concepts used, the narratives prioritized, the problems identified and the solutions proposed, alongside the perspectives that are privileged as a result. This produces a grammar of migration with underlying structures that finds its way into the classroom and influences our comprehension and emotional engagement with migration matters. In addition to drawing on critical literacy, migration literacies are informed by racial literacy, with its focus on understanding and confronting the ways in which race and racism operate overtly and systemically in everyday life and within power structures, as well as understanding racial privilege, implicit bias and the historical and contemporary manifestations of racism. Racial literacy centres on understanding the historical precedence of colonialism in how lives are lived today. It steadfastly places the past in the present, connects the self to society and knowledge to power, and fine-tunes our reading of the world through the lens of race (Bargallie et al, 2023; Schulz et al, 2023). Migration literacies also expand on Antoine Pécoud's (2015) invaluable work on international migration narratives (IMNs), folding in an engagement with the embedded racial, colonial and governance histories that shape how we talk about racialized migration as a phenomenon of governance and as a problem requiring a solution. The question to be explored here is the extent to which we contribute to replicating these structures, and therefore injustices, in how we teach about migration. Following Alana Lentin's (2020) call for more and better racial literacy, *Developing a Critical Pedagogy of Migration* argues for more and better migration literacies, and Chapter 5 explores how we can develop this.

Concluding this chapter, the following are suggested talking points to begin those critical reflections on the dynamics of knowledge production, representation and power in learning contexts connecting the personal to the political and the present to the past.

Talking points

- What is the nature and influence of knowledge in our learning spaces, and how is it shaped by power, values and privilege?
- Whose voices are heard or silenced in these spaces?
- Can we establish equitable knowledge-producing spaces that recognize and address power dynamics, ensuring better representation of diverse experiences?
- How do HE structures either perpetuate or challenge inequities in knowledge production?
- What actions can we take to challenge dominant narratives and power structures in knowledge production, promoting social justice and anti-oppressive action in the process?

Structure of the book

The aim of *Developing a Critical Pedagogy of Migration* is to be transformative in reshaping how we teach and learn about migration. The book is presented in seven substantive chapters. This chapter has introduced the key tenets of critical pedagogy through the work of Paulo Freire, Henry Giroux and bell hooks. It has explored what we mean by public pedagogy, engaged pedagogy and educated hope, emphasizing the activist, radical, decolonizing and anti-oppressive potential of critical pedagogy. The chapter has also begun the work of building the vocabularies and concepts that shape the book, introducing two new conceptualizations: '*doing good harm*', as, in pursuing transformative education it is necessary to disrupt established systems and beliefs, even if this initially causes discomfort or resistance; and *migration literacies*, referring to the need to tune into the centrality of migration governance as a form of grammar and semantic structuring of how migration is understood politically in public opinion, in media discourse and in the classroom.

Chapter 2 explains the notion of the 'political now' as a framework for locating how we talk about migration, both in the current conjuncture and as a historically situated site of knowledge. Specifically, the chapter explores the necessity of foregrounding colonial ties and imperial legacies in migration teaching. Failure to centre connections to the past in order to understand the present risks the reproduction of depoliticized and de-historicized migration knowledges in the classroom. The chapter also explores what this connection means for understanding how dominant narratives feed the immigrant imaginary and the ethical and political risks at stake in our complicity in the reproduction of normative assumptions about migration and knowledge practices.

Chapters 3 and 4 turn to the ethical and political implications and consequences of developing a critical pedagogy of migration in the 'political now'. Building on ideas introduced earlier in this chapter, Chapter 3 places teaching within the framework of discomfort, as generated through critical engagement with knowledges that challenge dominant narratives and the learning spaces we develop, and active empathy, as required to ensure we move from passive consumers of migration narratives to action for change. This chapter develops further the ethical imperative of 'doing good harm' as productive of disruption and transformation to unsettle dominant narratives and knowledge practices. Picking up on these themes, Chapter 4 explores the political dimensions of the critical classroom, knowledge production, where learning takes place and who gets access to it. The discussion turns to the politics of emotions in the classroom and explores some strategies we can develop through storytelling, counter-stories, witnessing and holding knowledge as ways to dismantle limited and reductive deficit-focused frames of understanding and centre personal testimony and expertise as serious knowledge.

In Chapter 5, I develop the concept of migration literacies. This conceptualization draws from and extends critical literacies, critical media literacies and racial literacy. It focuses on the need to develop a deeper critical understanding of the 'semantic institutionalization' (Piccoli et al 2023:2) of migration governance in migration knowledge production (both policy and scholarly), and it problematizes the colonial idioms that have come to dominate migration research and teaching, as well as ways of knowing and relating. The chapter (and book) argues for migration literacies because migration governance narratives not only prescribe migration as a problem but also offer technocratic solutions that come to be depoliticized and that, alongside colonial idioms of governance and control, function as tools of coloniality that sustain deep inequalities in seemingly unproblematic ways.

Chapter 6 considers the question of impact in the classroom and the role of the policy–research pipeline in driving research and teaching agendas, in shaping migration governance language, and in producing and privileging particular kinds of knowledge. Central to this discussion is the politics of refusal and practices of resistance that we undertake in the classroom and beyond that a critical pedagogy of migration can instil in us as a commitment to social justice education and transformative practice through alternative, radically imagined ways of doing and delivering impact. This chapter explores practices of resistance that interrupt what and how we learn along the way, suggesting pedagogical methods that push us towards thinking 'what if'.

Finally, Chapter 7 focuses on connections: the kinds we can build in a community-driven pedagogy and the care we need to take to do this in an ethically and politically sound way. The chapter demonstrates: what happens when we make that commitment to dismantling normative practices, centring the communities we serve as experts with serious knowledge; how we manage discomfort that does good harm; and how refusal as transformative resistance can tear down problematic practices. It explores the ethical and political consequences of forging meaningful connections with the communities we serve as they connect into the classroom and at different stages of curriculum design as we connect across borders to other communities of learners. The chapter ends by pulling the connecting threads of the book together.

Pedagogical features

This book hopes to ignite in its readers 'a concern with education as liberatory practice and with pedagogical strategies that may be not just for our students but for ourselves' (hooks, 1994: 134). With bell hooks' words in mind, pedagogical features like reflective tasks, problem-posing tasks, theory to practice teaching activities, teachable moments, topic-driven case studies, reflective case studies and talking points are woven throughout to provide space for reflection and discussion, as well as to facilitate the creation of critical classrooms. Through these various features, some of which have already been introduced in this chapter, the book offers the reader a practical toolbox to begin the work of building the critical classroom, such as how to embed participatory dialogue in learning, how to incorporate diverse voices and perspectives in the curriculum, and how to facilitate critical discussions that encourage students to question power structures and think critically about social issues. The pedagogical devices are intended as suggestions, prompts and ideas that can be adapted in several ways across disciplinary boundaries, including being integrated into forms of assessment. That is up to you.

A final word is warranted before we begin the journey of the book. *Developing a Critical Pedagogy of Migration* encourages its readers to think critically about their place in relation to the knowledge they bring and the knowledge they gain. It invites readers to examine their own relationships with, and understandings of, migration, ethics, politics and power. It promotes critical engagement with the materials we use, how we teach and the ways in which different aspects of our practice have the potential to be transformative and connect directly to the voices, experiences and needs of our students and communities we serve. In the end, the book is for you, teachers and students of migration, to develop the knowledge, skills and reflexive understandings you will need to think critically about what it means to learn about migration in the 'political now'.

2

The 'Political Now'

A teachable moment: Knowsley

In the early evening of 10 February 2023, a violent and racist anti-asylum riot took place in Knowsley, just outside of Liverpool in the north-west of England. A mob of several hundred far-right protestors stood outside a hotel where the Home Office had been housing people seeking asylum since January 2022. Videos circulating online showed rioters referring to the people in the hotel as 'nonces', some were filmed chanting 'get them out', carrying signs saying 'THIS IS OUR CITY'. Missiles were thrown and a police van was set on fire by far-right supporters. According to police statements, people had turned up with hammers and fireworks, with a clear intent on causing damage through intimidation. Anti-fascist supporters attending in counter-protest were outnumbered and encircled by the far-right protestors. Reports circulated on social media that the protest was organized by the British far-right group Patriotic Alternative, as was the apparent catalyst for the protest: a decontextualized video of a young girl of 15 seemingly being propositioned by a man asking to visit her home. A later police statement reported that a man in his 20s had been arrested but released with no further action.

Knowsley's Labour MP Sir George Howarth posted the following statement on Twitter (now X) the night of the protest:

> I have referred an alleged incident posted on social media, which has triggered a demonstration outside the Suites hotel, to Merseyside police and Knowsley council. Until the police have investigated the matter, it is too soon to jump to conclusions and the effort on the part of some to inflame the situation is emphatically wrong. If an offence has been committed, the police should deal with it appropriately through due process. In addition, the misinformation about refugees being feather-bedded is untrue and intended to paint a picture that does not at all represent the facts. The people of Knowsley are not bigots and

are welcoming to people escaping from some of the most dangerous places in the world in search of a place of safety. Those demonstrating against refugees at this protest tonight do not represent this community. We are not like that and overwhelmingly behave with sympathy and kindness to others regardless of where they come from. (10 February)

Merseyside's Assistant Chief Constable Paul White commented in a *Guardian* newspaper article on 10 February on the right to peaceful protest, saying: 'thankfully we have not had any serious injuries reported up to this point, but for officers and police vehicles to be damaged in the course of their duty protecting the public is disgraceful' (Taylor, 2019). On 11 February, Merseyside Police reported that 15 people, aged between 13 and 54, had been arrested on suspicion of violent disorder, a later statement that same day more widely condemned the organized violence. Home Secretary Suella Braverman tweeted on 11 February at 4.49 pm: 'I condemn the appalling disorder in Knowsley last night. The alleged behaviour of some asylum seekers is never an excuse for violence and intimidation. Thank you to @merseypolice officers for keeping everyone safe.' On 13 February, at 8.34 pm, Nigel Farage, former leader of UKIP and the Brexit Party, tweeted:

> The migrant hotel protest in Knowsley happened because many local parents are concerned for the safety of young schoolgirls. They are decent, honest people with genuine worry – and certainly not 'far right'. The Independent newspaper reported on 15 February 2023 that since the protest the people in the hotels had been put under a daytime curfew, as part of a 'range of intensified safety measures'.

There were many more anti-immigrant protests across the UK and in Ireland in the days and weeks that followed Knowsley. For every racist protest, there has been a counter-protest made up of anti-racist, anti-fascist and feminist groups and local people. On 18 February, there was a huge police presence on the outskirts of Rotherham at a far-right protest outside a Holiday Inn Express housing people seeking asylum, with protestors holding banners saying, 'invasions' and 'this is our city'. This was reported as being one of five such far-right events organized for that weekend. Far-right organizers posted on Facebook using racist slogans, such as 'England for the English, stop white genocide' and 'protect our women'. Patriotic Alternative and Britain First posted on Facebook about visiting protests and organizing groups. In Skegness on 26 February, Patriotic Alternative protestors held banners repeating white supremacy tropes: 'stop the invasion we will not be replaced' and 'you stay, migrants pay'. On 14 May 2023, Irish far-right group Real Message Eire claimed responsibility for setting fire to a makeshift tent camp of people seeking asylum on the streets of Dublin.

Just a few months before Knowsley, on 31 October 2022, Home Secretary Suella Braverman made the following statement in a speech to the House of Commons in response to the so-called crisis of 'small boat crossings' in the Channel:

> Let's be clear about what is really going on here: the British people deserve to know which party is serious about stopping the invasion on our southern coast and which party is not. Some 40,000 people have arrived on the south coast this year alone. Many of them facilitated by criminal gangs, some of them actual members of criminal gangs. So, let's stop pretending that they are all refugees in distress. The whole country knows that is not true. It's only the honourable members opposite who pretend otherwise. We need to be straight with the public. The system is broken. Illegal migration is out of control and too many people are interested in playing political parlour games, covering up the truth than solving the problem.

This statement was made the day after an immigration processing centre in Dover was fire-bombed in a terrorist attack, with Braverman having already earlier on that same day called people complaining about the abject conditions in the processing centre 'indulgent and ungrateful' (Hansard, 2022). Liz Fekete (2023) describes this kind of anti-immigrant rhetoric as governing through spectacle, which has been happening for decades, framing certain people as deserving of help, while writing others off as disposable. After Russia invaded Ukraine on 24 February 2022, media reporting described Ukrainian nationals as being deserving of refuge, emphasizing the similarities drawn between Ukrainians and Western populations through a Eurocentric lens (Fekete, 2023), and depicting war as something that can happen to anyone rather than being limited to impoverished or remote populations. There are many examples of an unapologetic racial and racist bias in Western media reporting on Ukraine, as well as in the development of differential and hierarchized resettlement policies, depending on where people are coming from and what they look like. On 26 February 2023, just two days after the first anniversary of the war in Ukraine, there was another terrible mass drowning off the Italian coast at Europe's deadly borders. At least 100 people, including 12 children, drowned in the Mediterranean after a boat carrying more than 200 people crashed in stormy weather. With no official search and rescue in place, there was little chance of survival; any who did survive were mainly from Afghanistan, some were from Iran and Pakistan, and a couple were from Somalia. There has been no outpouring of support for them or demands to provide safe passage.[1]

Understanding the 'political now'

> **Reflective task**
>
> Where and how do you incorporate discussions on the power and effects of migration discourse in your teaching? What might be the impact of dedicating a session to examining the politicization, depoliticization or repoliticization of migration on the foundational understandings that characterize your discipline?
>
> Initiating this conversation early on encourages each of us to seriously engage with and critically analyse our current and historical context. It prompts reflection on subject matter and ideological stances, as well as the learning process and the consequences of using neutralizing language in shaping our perspectives and conversations about migration.

Using Knowsley as our jumping-off point, this chapter introduces the idea of the 'political now'. The 'political now' refers to the current moment in which political events, actions and discussions unfold, often in easily accessible and fragmented forms through various media platforms. However, it is not limited to the contemporary moment because the 'political now' has important historical dimensions. It is influenced by contemporary and historical local, national and global factors, including the legacies of empire, colonialism and the slave trade. Making these connections between the past and the present is vital to challenge the tendency to separate issues into categories of 'here' and 'there', and 'then' and 'now', instead emphasizing the intertwined nature of political phenomena across space and time.

Several recent trends shape how we integrate the 'political now' into our research and teaching. First, the classroom is a space where students engage with the political moment, discussing current events and issues that have taken place recently. These may include the influence of movements like Black Lives Matter, decolonizing the university, the debate about slavery reparations, critical examinations of the geopolitics of knowledge production, and digital activism and resistance. Students are also increasingly holding teachers accountable for their teaching practices, demanding the decentring of certain epistemologies, positionalities and politics within the classroom. We need to locate ourselves in this moment, write ourselves into the stories and bring our positionalities and affective experiences to how we read the world, to knowing and relating. This raises important questions of care and harm in developing a critical consciousness, and requires deep awareness and engagement with an ethics and politics of learning.

Second, the COVID-19 pandemic has deeply impacted social relationships and structural inequalities, fundamentally altering the 'political now'. COVID-19 not only profoundly reduced the global movement of people but also deepened the immobility of immobile populations, from people seeking refuge trapped in camps and hotspots at the borders of Europe (Meer et al, 2021) to those resident in-country, trapped in the limbo of contemporary asylum processing, who faced an enforced decline in living conditions, including detention in hotels as a so-called public safety measure (Burns et al, 2022). These COVID-19 measures and the current post-COVID-19 crisis of increased hostility towards racialized migrants is a mirror reflection of long-established historical technologies of isolation, control, containment and surveillance of those same people. Many COVID-19 measures are an extension of existing racial bordering controls, such as immobilization, coercive housing and border closures; they replicate colonial governance and are central to the maintenance of the 'racial state' (Lentin, 2007). Reframing COVID-19 and post-COVID-19 measures applied to migrants in such ways forces us to contend with ethical, political and power-related questions regarding how migration is understood, discussed and taught at local, national and global levels.

Third, there is a growing trend in the social sciences generally, and in migration-related work specifically, for 'relevant' and 'impactful' research, demanding, rightly so, increasing accountability to others outside the academy. This will be explored in greater detail in Chapter 6, but here we can refer to a fundamental change in migration research in recent decades, as observed by Janine Dahinden in her work (Dahinden, 2016; Wyss and Dahinden, 2022) and by Maurice Stierl (2022). They observe that it has gained prominence and institutional recognition, with the establishment of specialized degree programmes, dedicated journals and careers built on this growth in the field, accompanied by significant demands for evidencing impact. Arguably, we lack an equivalent rich critical scholarship on the ethics of migration pedagogy as praxis.

Fourth is the head-spinning nature of legislative change and damaging racist and racism-fuelling anti-immigration rhetoric. This has become increasingly prevalent in the UK across parliamentary debates, public commentary and social media over the past few decades. Social media has created a platform where politicians and political commentators increasingly seem to be able to say what they feel in racialized terms with little or no accountability, creating what Nicholas Reed Langen (2023) observes as emblematic of today's 'reaction economy', where 'the age of social media means that governments, companies, and others in the public eye are not ruled by accountants assessing their bottom line or journalists scrutinising their actions, but by voters tapping onto their screens at home'. It would be disingenuous to suggest that this rhetoric comes from one side of the political spectrum; in the UK, for example, it has been a feature of Labour and Conservative governments for decades. One moment of legislative change that significantly moved the terms of debate was in 2012, when then Home Secretary Theresa May publicly used the term 'hostile environment' to describe a set of policies designed to make life as difficult as possible for anyone unable to prove their formal immigration permission to be in the UK. While there was no official white paper outlining the policies, Melanie Griffiths and Colin Yeo (2021) observe that the term's policy ambiguity obscures the true extent and impact of this approach, which, in reality, has been implemented over a number of decades through various immigration acts, rules and regulations, affecting multiple sectors and policy areas. It heralded a step-change expansion of everyday borders in the UK in its scale, scope and speed, and its meaning has evolved in academic, media and public discourse to encompass a broader stance of explicit animosity and nastiness towards racialized migrants.

Importantly, anti-immigrant hostility is neither administered nor felt equally. Nor is it new; its racialized underpinnings and punitive migration management policies can be traced back decades in the UK. For example, the Aliens Act 1905 was a significant milestone in British history, as it introduced immigration controls and registration (El-Enany, 2020). This was a watershed in British immigration legislation and marked the first time that the notion of an 'undesirable immigrant' was defined in British law, with restrictions primarily targeting Jewish and Eastern European immigrants. The so-called 'newness' of hostile environment rhetoric in current legislation has great appeal: it demonstrates the notion of responsiveness and 'something being done'. This rhetoric has also very effectively de-racialized and de-historicized migration management approaches, obscuring the historic racial discrimination, wrongful detention and deportation of thousands that have resulted from these decades-long policies. The hostility of the 'political now', when understood through the historical lens, reveals to us the remarkably unexceptional and very ordinary nature of contemporary racialized and colonial border logics that have the power to categorize, include and exclude in racially ordered terms.

Problem posing: the hostile environment

Begin with posing this problem: what do we understand by the hostile environment? The term 'hostile environment' is highly political, but it is also at risk of obscuring the deeply embedded and enduring hostility that is a key feature of UK immigration legislation. Using the search tool from the UK government webpages (see: www.legislation.gov.uk/), search for legislation related to 'asylum', 'immigration', 'aliens', 'borders' or select other search terms. Encourage students to reflect on how hostility comes to be represented in act titles and descriptive opening paragraphs. Who is the

> focus of restrictive measures? Can we map legislation change to political events? What might this raise about the framing of the movement of certain people as a 'problem' requiring solutions? Reflect on evolving racialization processes over time and what this makes us think about migration narratives and discourse in the current moment.

This chapter will explore two key features of the 'political now' in relation to migration teaching: (1) its location in historical context and its intersections with race; and (2) its contribution to the immigrant imaginary and migrantizing effects on forms of knowledge we have and use about migration.

The 'political now' at the intersections of race and history

The prominence given to people moving in search of a better life towards the 'Global North' as a contemporary problem requiring a solution has not emerged from a contextual vacuum, nor is it recent, despite rhetoric suggesting it is somehow new, current or unprecedented. As Gurminder Bhambra and John Holmwood (2021: ix) observe, 'in the course of colonial history, European populations moved in greater numbers and with greater effect on the populations they encountered than is the case in the course of migration to Europe'. The critical work of W.E.B. DuBois and Frantz Fanon, for example, reveals race as a system of domination that has historically relied on the management of mobility globally and hierarchies of human worth along racialized lines that have translated historically into racialized social relations, systems of labour and exploitation. These did not disappear with the end of colonialism. Coloniality (Quijano, 2000) describes this living legacy of colonialism in contemporary societies and the continued formal and informal practices of racial rule (Hesse and Sayyid, 2006), and it is coloniality that continues to map people onto racial categories through their relationship to colonial knowledge systems and progress. As Lucy Mayblin and Joe Turner (2021: 203) argue, 'colonialism continues to condition why, how and where people move, just as it shapes the forms of knowledge we have about what migration is in migration studies ... as well as the fact that colonialism produced the forms of racialized management that control "migration"'. In their carefully crafted analysis, Mayblin and Turner urge a rethink of migration studies through the lens of colonialism and its enduring legacies, exploring the silences in the field of migration studies and offering alternative approaches, including from postcolonial and decolonial scholarship and indigenous studies. They also argue that migration studies, as it has developed, reproduces coloniality and therefore racism in its methodological whiteness. Methodological whiteness relates to ways of reflecting on the world that fail to acknowledge the role played by race in the very structuring of that world and of the ways in which knowledge is constructed and legitimated within it (Bhambra, 2017). This silencing of racialized systems of power disconnects understanding of migration, and therefore teaching and learning about migration, from post-colonial analysis (Collins, 2022).

Disregarding racialized and colonial histories limits our understanding of the present, brackets contemporary migration management governance off from colonial governance and enables the denial of complicity with coloniality, thus suppressing efforts for social justice (Collins, 2022). This critique of the decoupling of race from migration studies stems from a notable division between US and European migration studies in terms of research and scholarship on race and migration (Mayblin and Turner, 2021). While the study of race and ethnicity in Europe has historically focused on imperial pasts, postcolonial presents and constructions of race across the continent, migration studies have primarily addressed questions related to the reasons for migration, migration processes, public attitudes towards migration and migration management by nation states. As mentioned earlier, there have been notable efforts by critical scholars, including Francis Collins, Alana Lentin, Nicola De Genova, Martina Tazzioli, Lucy Mayblin and Joe Turner, Umut Erel and Karim Murji who have made significant contributions to bridging the gap between these two fields, demonstrating the interconnectedness of contemporary and historic racism, state violence, and immigration policies, and they have made significant contributions in this regard. This critical work also emphasizes that overlooking the analytical lens of race in migration studies undermines our understanding of the challenges faced by racialized migrants and refugees. By connecting the historical context of colonial rule, violence and exploitation to contemporary discussions on migration, we can develop better migration literacies, as will be explored in Chapter 5. Such an approach challenges the division between 'here' and 'there' in geopolitical and spatial terms, highlights the interplay between the 'then' and now', and questions the distinctions between 'us' and 'them' by emphasizing the interconnectedness of social relations, positionalities and subjectivities across space and time. Making these connections can be unsettling and may evoke discomfort, as doing so challenges established narratives and exposes the structural injustices embedded in migration systems (Boler and Zembylas, 2003).

From theory to practice: making empire visible in the present

Migration studies faces heavy criticism for overlooking the spatial and temporal dimensions of migration, particularly its colonial and imperial aspects. Ipek Demir (2022) highlights this methodological amnesia, where colonial and imperial legacies are often erased, in part, due to a focus on French and British colonialism, neglecting the broader European colonial history of other nations. To bridge this gap and understand migration more comprehensively, we must acknowledge the enduring impacts of empire on our understanding of migration how it is framed politically, and its impacts on our cultural memory and built environments. Recognizing historical and contemporary Western interventions in other countries also helps contextualize migration within larger socio-political developments, offering insights into the entanglement of migration dynamics with historical and geopolitical contexts.

Activities

Listen to George Mpanga (George the Poet) talk about refusing his MBE on his podcast series in 2019 (available at: https://podcasts.apple.com/us/podcast/18-concurrent-affairs/id1436036246?i=1000461670508). He offers an alternative framing to dominant narratives of empire though the counter-story. Counter-stories are pedagogical and methodological frameworks which reveal that dominant stories are never neutral. They offer diverse perspectives and experiences that have been marginalized or silenced, spotlight systemic forms of oppression by exposing the structural injustices embedded in dominant narratives that are too often reductive or stereotypical, and emphasize spaces of mobilization and action towards dismantling oppressive structures. Questions for discussion may include:

- How does George the Poet's story of MBE refusal work to disrupt dominant narratives of empire, belonging and gratitude?
- How do we feel listening to this counter-story? What emotional work does it do?
- Draw up a list of place names, murals in cities or logos used in advertising in any West European country (you can begin with the resources listed below). Think about representations in our everyday physical and built environments (murals, monuments, statues, street names, neighbourhoods and so on). Envision alternatives. Consider how we can resist the invisibility of empire and colonialism in migration learning. What would this demand of us as learners in the classroom?

Talking points

- What does the word 'empire' mean to you?
- What are the legacies of empire today, and what do we think their relationship is to contemporary migration governance?
- How do we connect empire to how we talk about migration?
- What and where are the traces of colonialism in language, culture, institutions and the built environment?

Further resources for exploring the presence of empire in the everyday include:

- www.glasgowlive.co.uk/news/history/glasgow-history-slavery-street-names-18369259

- https://observers.france24.com/en/20190412-french-national-assembly-criticised-mural-depicting-racist-stereotypes
- https://newpublic.co/blog/decolonizing-banania-part-1
- https://storymaps.arcgis.com/stories/73b5882d346d4218b623902f87baebe5
- www.bbc.co.uk/news/world-europe-53017188
- www.thelocal.se/20200615/how-can-sweden-better-face-up-to-its-colonial-past
- www.bbc.co.uk/news/world-europe-43742676
- www.voanews.com/a/europe_france-street-names-carry-colonial-burden/6191228.html
- www.newyorker.com/magazine/2020/11/02/misremembering-the-british-empire

Another feature of the 'political now' that we can explore in our teaching is the often-overlooked connection between histories of colonialism and current migration governance. The dominant discourse on migration governance and management, as well as the subsequent policy agenda that emerged after the Cold War, often omits reference to the colonial roots that have shaped contemporary migration patterns (Mayblin, 2017; Collins, 2022). However, contemporary governance mirrors enduring colonial discourse 'created to orient a policy-minded audience to (racialized) migration as a problem that can be catalogued and then solved' (Pécoud, 2015: vii). The non-stop generation and churn of legislation and policy is a deliberate strategy of neoliberal, racialized migration governance. It comes to be codified by policy makers, think tanks and some academics in their research and teaching through reusing neutralized language, thus decontextualizing colonial histories and reproducing racialized differences (Hadj Abdou and Pettrachin, 2021). Moreover, in the West in the period since 2015, there has been an increasingly knotted entanglement of migration and security studies, where movements have been equated to 'invasions', 'threats' and 'crises' all requiring 'better management'. All of this matters because migration policies globally are not simply technocratic solutions. Indeed, this problem-solving logic is deeply shaped by racialized ordering and hierarchies along historical forms of oppression, causing deep devastation and extensive harms. These ideas will be explored in greater detail in Chapter 5. The de-racialization of migration knowledge that results from the decoupling of contemporary migration governance from colonial histories is just one aspect of the problem. Addressing social injustice requires a deeper reflection on how knowledge is produced and reproduced across disciplines. How do we acknowledge missing narratives and historical connections in our teaching of the contemporary moment? How do we respond in our teaching to the dominant international migration narratives and their effects? How do we avoid epistemic violence? Are we articulating and discussing these narratives and their implications in our classrooms? Do we consider how we teach and learn about the racialized hierarchization embedded in migration governance and the epistemic harm caused? How do we avoid doing the same harms in the classroom?

To bridge the gap between abstract theoretical concepts and practical application, case studies prove to be a valuable tool. They are versatile and effective for both group learning and individual study, using problem-based learning to help develop analytical skills while applying theoretical ideas to real-world scenarios. The following three mini-case studies provide illustrative examples of the intersections of the current moment decontextualized from its colonial histories, race/racism and migration, the productive nature of racialized difference, and the neutralizing language of migration governance narratives.

Case Study 2.1: Windrush

The 'Windrush Scandal' in the UK illustrates how contemporary borders perpetuate racial distinctions rooted in historical racialization and how past citizenship and immigration laws shape new racial identities (Grosfoguel et al, 2015). The scandal, which emerged in 2017 through investigative reports in *The Guardian* (Gentleman, 2019), refers to the post-Second World War restructuring of migration from British colonies encouraged by the UK government. At that time, individuals from the Commonwealth were legally entitled to enter the UK as British citizens, often without the need for specific documents. The 'Windrush Generation' refers to those who arrived from the Caribbean on their parents' passports, named after the ship HMT Empire Windrush that transported workers from Jamaica in 1948. Despite growing up in Britain and considering themselves British, many in the Windrush Generation never formalized their citizenship and lacked the necessary documents, despite residing and working in the UK for several decades. In 2018, *The Guardian* revealed numerous cases of Black British women and men who were misclassified as 'illegal immigrants' during passport applications. People were not only denied passports but sent to immigration detention centres; many faced deportation, legal threats and even statelessness. Others discovered their lack of documentation during routine checks in schools, workplaces, general practitioner (GP) surgeries and elsewhere due to the 'hostile environment' policies outlined in the Immigration Act 2016 (Griffiths and Yeo, 2021). The Windrush Scandal exposed long-standing racism and discrimination against not only the Windrush Generation but also individuals from the Commonwealth who came to the UK. Immigration legislation, highly intricate and rapidly changing, failed to consider the impact of successive tightening of legislation and policies to curb net migration on this earlier generation. The case of Windrush can only be analysed through its racial and racist dimensions, along with the historical debates surrounding migrants from the colonies and the Commonwealth, as well as the influence of legislative imperatives rooted in colonial histories.

Further reading and resources

- The National Archives, 'Voices of the Windrush Generation'. Available at: https://media.nationalarchives.gov.uk/index.php/voices-windrush-generation/
- Channel 4 News Special, 'Windrush Generation: the scandal that shook Britain explained and debated'. Available at: www.youtube.com/watch?v=izsLi-FB5Fg
- Windrush Compensation Scheme. Available at: https://hansard.parliament.uk/commons/2022-03-03/debates/5ACC58B3-8685-4AE1-9F2A-4E41D0341BBC/WindrushCompensationScheme
- BBC, 'Home Office "ignorant of race" over Windrush', 19 March 2020. Available at: www.bbc.co.uk/news/uk-politics-51961933
- Home Office, 'Windrush lessons learned review by Wendy Williams', 19 July 2018. Available at: www.gov.uk/government/publications/windrush-lessons-learned-review
- Colin Grant, ' "What comes across clearly is the emotional cost of migration": Windrush commemorated in books', *The Observer*, 11 June 2023. Available at: www.theguardian.com/books/2023/jun/11/what-comes-across-clearly-is-the-emotional-cost-of-migration-windrush-commemorated-in-books

Case Study 2.2: The *Gilets Noirs*

The *Gilets Noirs* represent a political movement in France comprising undocumented immigrant workers primarily from France's former African colonies, such as Côte d'Ivoire, Senegal, Mali, Burkina Faso, Benin and Niger. Their advocacy focuses on obtaining administrative documents for all immigrants, better housing and an end to deportations, police repression and state persecution of undocumented individuals (the *sans papiers*). They adopted the name '*Gilets Noirs*' to align their cause with the *Gilets Jaunes* ('yellow vest') movement, symbolizing their racialization and the legacy and enduring coloniality and racism in contemporary France. Their slogan, '*La Chappelle debout!*', is a call and response to the *sans papiers* movement in St Bernard de la Chappelle in Paris during the 1990s. The *Gilets Noirs* pursue an explicitly stated anti-racist human rights agenda, striving for equal social and political rights, freedom, and rights for all present in France and throughout Europe. They reject the idea that only state-recognized migrants should have access to residence rights, work rights and family reunification. The *Gilets Noirs* argue that France and Europe have historically relied on cheap labour and resources from their former colonies. In addition to community organizing, they have staged numerous large-scale occupations of symbolic locations and businesses that profit from exploiting undocumented workers or participate in the wider deportation machine, including Charles de Gaulle Airport and Elior, a global catering and cleaning business that employs undocumented migrants to work as cleaners and cooks in detention centres. Their imperial connection to France's former colonies adds significant power to their movement, challenging prevailing narratives that often marginalize immigrants in France and further complicating France's claims to 'colour-blind citizenship', notably marked by the removal of the term 'race' from its constitution in 2018. The primary goal of the *Gilets Noirs* is to dismantle the system that generates undocumented individuals, igniting a broader European debate on residency rights, the exploitation of undocumented people and, by extension, European Union (EU) citizenship rights (IRR, 2019).

Further reading and resources

- Luke Butterly, 'Black vests: who are the gilets noirs and what do they want?', *AlJazeera*, 13 August 2019. Available at: www.aljazeera.com/features/2019/8/13/black-vests-who-are-the-gilets-noirs-and-what-do-they-want
- Luke Butterly, 'The "Gilets Noirs": the undocumented migrant movement in France', 4 June 2019. Available at: www.versobooks.com/en-gb/blogs/news/4341-the-gilets-noirs-the-undocumented-migrant-movement-in-france
- Anya Edmond-Pettitt, '"I'm mad as hell and I'm not going to take it anymore!": a guide to the Gilets Noirs', Institute of Race Relations, 17 October 2019. Available at: https://irr.org.uk/article/im-mad-as-hell-and-im-not-going-to-take-it-anymore-a-guide-to-the-gilets-noirs-and-why-is-their-movement-is-growing-beyond-france/
- Camille Baker, 'A "Black Vests" movement emerges in France to protest treatment of undocumented migrants', *The Intercept*, 17 October 2019. Available at: https://theintercept.com/2019/10/27/france-black-vests-gilets-noirs/

- Staz, 'Who's afraid of the Black Vests? The Gilets Noirs and the struggle for migrant rights in France', *Freedom News*, 1 February 2020. Available at: https://freedomnews.org.uk/2020/02/01/whos-afraid-of-the-black-vests-the-gilets-noirs-and-the-struggle-for-migrant-rights-in-france/
- Gilet Noirs, 'Un appel des Gilets noirs: Autodéfense immigrée: seule la lutte donnera les papiers', Syndicat de la Médécine Générale, 2020. Available at: www.syndicat-smg.fr/un-appel-des-gilets-noirs-autodefense-immigree-seule-la-lutte-donnera-les

Case Study 2.3: 'Do not come'

In 2014, Australia launched Operation Sovereign Borders, intercepting and turning back boats with people seeking asylum, without processing their claims. Their controversial 'No Way' poster campaign signalled clearly and forcefully that boat arrivals would not be accepted. The campaign was accompanied by a warning video message from General Campbell, Commander of Operation Sovereign Borders, stating: 'it is the policy and practice of the Australian government to intercept any vessel that is seeking to illegally enter Australia and safely remove it beyond their waters ... The rules apply to everyone: families, children, unaccompanied children, educated and skilled. There are no exceptions.' (Video available at: www.theguardian.com/world/video/2014/apr/11/140411nowayfromgaus). The national sovereign message 'Do not come' has since become a global warning, discouraging refugees and migrants from seeking safety through boat and border crossings. However, as an approach, it reflects historical colonial attempts to control the movement of non-white individuals, akin to Australia's late 19th-century White Australia Policy. This rhetoric has been replicated in various contexts in recent years, including efforts to deter Guatemalans seeking entry to the US in 2021 and forming a central strategy in the UK's Illegal Immigration Act 2023, which has come to be known as the 'Stop the Boats' law. These campaigns present a dangerous but powerful entanglement of securitization and humanitarianism in border control, surveillance and migration management, presenting a strong deterrence message while emphasizing the saving of lives. They also share a focus on combatting smuggling and employing military responses, shifting responsibility for deaths resulting from irregular migration away from restrictive border security and migration governance (Little and Vaughn-Williams, 2017). Furthermore, they are connected to what Thom Davies and colleagues

(2021: 2312) call a 'colonial fantasy of "offshoring"', drawing upon colonial distinctions between valuable and disposable lives, often overlooking or erasing colonial histories and imperial ties, with militarized language portraying racialized migrants as a threatening, invading force requiring the harshest of military-led responses.

Further reading and resources

- Australian Times, '"No Way" asylum posters draw criticism', 21 October 2014. Available at: www.australiantimes.co.uk/news/no-way-asylum-posters-draw-criticism/
- Australian Customs, '"There is no way you will make Australia home" – video', *The Guardian*, 11 April 2014. Available at: www.theguardian.com/world/video/2014/apr/11/140411nowayfromgaus
- BBC News, 'Kamala Harris tells Guatemala migrants: "Do not come to US"', 8 June 2021. Available at: www.bbc.com/news/world-us-canada-57387350
- YouTube, 'Illegal immigrants "can't stay": Rishi Sunak launches "Stop the boats" campaign'. Available at: www.youtube.com/watch?v=siXOLZRfKvY
- Forensic Architecture, 'The left to die boat – investigative report'. Available at: https://forensic-architecture.org/investigation/the-left-to-die-boat

Talking points and teaching activities for understanding the racial dynamics of migration in the 'political now'

Case Studies 2.1–2.3 critically examine historical and contemporary racial dynamics in the context of migration. You can use them in various ways. Ask students to research each case study, using the provided resources as a starting point. Encourage them to explore the colonial histories in the UK, France and Australia that connect these contemporary issues to historical contexts. Students can examine how these case studies relate to local actions and community mobilization for migrant rights. Consider a multidisciplinary approach, inviting students to identify commonalities in legal questions, securitization narratives and rights-based activism, as well as transnational practices and responses. Encourage them to explore points of convergence and divergence, and to reflect on the insights that a multidisciplinary and cross-disciplinary lens can provide. What follows are some more directed activities and talking points to get discussions and reflections started that can be tailored to your specific academic focus.

- Have students select one of the case studies. In small groups, ask them to frame the issue in different ways, for example, a problem requiring a solution, a matter of social justice, an economic concern or a historical injustice. Encourage students to discuss the implications of different framings and how these influence the analysis. Now consider this either specifically in relation to your discipline or from a cross-disciplinary perspective. For example, how might a human rights disciplinary lens applied to the Gilets Noirs case benefit from insights about colonialism?

- Engage with additional materials for the case study, and invite students to consider how they explicitly discuss race or subtly reinforce racial stereotypes. Facilitate group discussions about the consequences of acknowledging or hiding race, considering perspectives from different disciplines. Consider how this connects to wider learning and aligns with practices in your disciplinary area. For example, what changes the securitization focus in the 'Do not come' case or the Forensic Architecture investigative report when we fold in racialization processes?
- Encourage students to research further, identifying readings or documentaries related to the colonial histories underpinning the case study in question, and analysing how colonialism shapes present-day issues in your field. Organize a class debate or discussion on the insights that a historical or postcolonial lens can offer to these case studies, allowing students to engage critically with the material and reflect on the value of multidisciplinary and cross-disciplinary perspectives.
- Provide students with the formal texts or speeches relating to the case study in question and consider how they have undergone de-racialization and depoliticization processes. Ask them to identify elements that contribute to de-racialization and how this affects the political dimensions of the knowledge produced, not only in these texts but also in your discipline.
- Consider how categorization and labelling play a role in each of these case studies and their migrantizing effects. Challenge students to examine how these categorizations affect perceptions, policies and societal responses. Discuss the implications for different disciplines, such as journalism studies, international relations and securitization studies, when informed by sociological understandings of migrantization and racialization processes.
- Encourage students to research and create counter-stories for each case that challenge dominant narratives within your field. Have them present these counter-stories through essays, presentations or creative mediums. Facilitate a discussion about how counter-stories can disrupt prevailing disciplinary norms and assumptions, potentially bringing about change to knowledge production.
- Ask students to keep reflective journals focusing on their experiences of (un)learning. Prompt them to document moments of (un)learning, personal and disciplinary biases or assumptions, and emotional impact, such as feelings of discomfort, empathy or frustration. Guide them to connect this to their personal and academic growth, emphasizing the value of critical reflection and unlearning as an integral part of their education. Students may also share their reflections and insights with the class. This also promotes a deeper connection between their academic learning and its real-world applications.

Feeding the immigrant imaginary in the 'political now'

We turn now to a second important feature of the 'political now' in migration teaching and knowledge production, namely, the construction of the problematic migrant. Often produced as impoverished, demanding, racialized, gendered and classed (Hadj Abou and Pettrachin, 2021), he (the problematic migrant other is often masculinized) does not simply exist or come to be. Rather, he is a product of policy discourse and debates, themselves shaped by enduring legacies of colonialism and empire, even though these are often masked by de-racialized language. Central to any understanding or analysis of 'the migrant' is recognition that the discourses created about the migrant figure, regardless of how they are presented in the contemporary moment and historically, are constructed in what Sivanandan (2009) calls 'the engine rooms of power' that create and inform popular racism, and influence government policy. Attentiveness to this very issue helps us build better migration literacies (as will be explored in Chapter 5) and avoid becoming 'implicated in the normalization of seemingly objective, value-neutral, and technocratic labels, and thus risk becoming complicit in the disciplining of migration' (Stierl, 2022: 8).

> **Problem posing: the language of migration and 'the migrant'**
>
> Begin with the following two questions: 'What does migration mean to you?'; and 'What are your questions about migration?' (you can substitute 'migration' with a number of key concepts from migration studies, for example, 'integration', 'host society', inclusion, social cohesion, borders and so on). Posing these questions encourages students to reflect on their knowledge in their own language and idioms (Shor, 1992). Invite students to write their questions and share with their peers. You can then pose further problems:
>
> - How do you define the migrant?
> - Do we need to define the migrant, and why might it matter?
> - Why and when do we use certain terms over others?
>
> Encourage students to write their responses and read them to each other before reporting back their discussion to the whole class. You can then pose further problems: ask students to reflect on where they see this language, who speak its and why that might matter to questions of legitimation of knowledge.

From theory to practice: problematizing labels

Consider together ways that the migrant is often reduced to a neutralized and depoliticized description of persons crossing international borders. This presents a nation-state-centred perspective, where the migrant from Nation State A moves to Nation State B. The focus on border crossing renders migrants as a concern (problem) for nation-state governments to control. Bridget Anderson (2019) reminds us that migration signifies problematic mobility. Stephan Scheel and Martina Tazzioli (2022: 3) suggest an alternative definition that also seeks to centre borders but instead focuses on border governance: 'A migrant is a person who, in order to move to or stay in a desired place, has to struggle against bordering practices and processes of boundary-making that are implicated by the national order of things.' They argue that it is at the border (physical, digital or imagined) that the figure of the migrant comes to be enacted. Moreover, it is through the process of border practices and boundary making that processes of migrantization and racialization emerge.[2]

Further reading and resources

- Anderson, B. and Blinder, S. (2015) 'Who counts as a migrant? Definitions and their consequences', Migration Observatory Briefing, University of Oxford, Centre on Migration, Policy and Society.
- De Genova, N. (2018) 'The "migrant crisis" as racial crisis: do Black Lives Matter in Europe?', *Ethnic and Racial Studies*, 41(10): 1765–82.
- Hadj Abdou, L. and Pettrachin, A. (2021) 'From "bogus" asylum seekers to "genuine" refugees; shifting discourses and attitudes towards Afghan migrants', University of Oxford, Centre on Migration, Policy and Society, 12 November. Available at: www.compas.ox.ac.uk/2021/from-bogus-asylum-seekers-to-genuine-refugees-shifting-discourses-and-attitudes-towards-afghan-migrants/
- Hadj Abdou, L., Pettrachin, A. and Crawley, H. (2022) 'Who is a refugee? Understanding Europe's diverse responses to the 2015 and the 2022 refugee arrivals', EURAC, 23 March. Available at: www.eurac.edu/en/blogs/mobile-people-and-diverse-societies/who-is-a-refugee-understanding-europe-s-diverse-responses-to-the-2015-and-the-202
- Scheel, S. and Tazzioli, M. (2022) 'Who is a migrant? Abandoning the nation-state point of view in the study of migration', *Migration Politics*, 1(1): Art 002.

Talking points

- What does Stephan Scheel and Martina Tazzioli's alternative definition offer to us that a nation-state-centred definition cannot?
- What do we think about the power of language, the kind of work that naming does and the effects it produces (for example, minorities become migrants, Muslims become migrants and so on), and does this differ across disciplines?
- Why have some labels (for example, 'illegal asylum seeker', 'economic migrant', 'genuine refugee' and so on) come to be politically loaded and conflated, and what purpose does this serve in political discourse? What others labels can you identify?
- What unlearning are we doing with problematizing the label, and what might this change about ways of knowing and relating inside and outside the classroom?

Salman Sayyid (2004, 2009) argues that how we talk about, understand, research and teach migration is shaped by the 'immigrant imaginary'. This imaginary means we uncritically reproduce the very tools by which the identity of 'immigrants' can be regulated and disciplined, and it has four key features. The first is the distinction between 'the host' and 'the migrant' (Sayyid, 2009: 89), which establishes differential senses of social positioning and social being, for example, 'host' populations have social networks, while migrants have kinship. Second, communities of colour are viewed as 'exotic' or 'banal' (Sayyid, 2009: 90). The exotic is represented through a superficial celebration of difference, such as ritual, dress and customs (Arun Kundnani, for example, described celebrations of multiculturalism as reduced to steel bands, samosas and saris). The banal is linked to ideas of colour- and power-blindness, with a reluctance to recognize the different, varied and textured historical trajectories of migrants (Sian, 2022). Immigrants are both exoticized through difference and banalized through indistinction. Importantly here, the norm or standard against which this homogenization is measured is what Sayyid calls the 'ethnically unmarked host'. Third is the idea that migrants will (and should) 'integrate' fully into the 'host culture' through a process of uncritical assimilation (Sayyid, 2009: 90). This assumes that the destiny of communities of colour is total assimilation into a so-called 'majority community'. The migrant is 'consumed' by the 'host' in this sense, absorbed into the 'host society' and the general population, and it is the migrant who is expected to adapt and change, leaving behind distinct practices while the 'host' remains the same. The final feature of the immigrant imaginary is centred upon the theme of generational progress. Here, each generation of migrants marks progress towards integration. However, the categories of 'first', 'second' or 'third generation' conveniently defer the moment when migrants can be considered full members of society. In this sense, the migrant will always represent being a newcomer and the process is never finished (Sayyid, 2009: 91). Generational progress also de-historicizes and depoliticizes because 'the differences between the "first" and "second" generation are narrated as being due to the differences in assimilation into the host society and not as changes in historical context' (Sayyid, 2009: 91).

The immigrant imaginary provides a cross-disciplinary way to think critically with dominant tropes and build better migration literacies (see Chapter 5), as it provides a valuable framework to critically engage with the kinds of narratives and discourse that dominate migration studies but that are also deeply embedded in colonial tropes of otherness, difference, exoticization and liminal identities. Working with such frameworks means that we will: first, be better equipped to recognize what Lorenzo Piccoli and colleagues (2023) call the semantic institutionalization of migration governance in policy and everyday language; and, second, be better equipped to catch our uncritical use of such highly mobile tropes that reproduce inequalities and social injustice in seemingly innocuous ways.

> **Reflective task**
>
> As you review your course reading lists and supplementary materials, consider the influence of the 'immigrant imaginary'. How does this concept shape our perceptions, conversations, observations and understanding of migration, including the perpetuation of common migrant narratives within our classrooms?
>
> In your engagement with scholarly work, think about how the ordinary and extraordinary aspects influence the prioritization or neglect of specific migrant experiences. This often leads to the de-historicization and depoliticization of their stories, with crucial elements being overlooked.
>
> Now explore how adopting the lens of the 'immigrant imaginary' might alter our interpretations of the case studies in this chapter. Revisit these with your students and reflect on how connecting to knowledge and perspectives beyond the classroom can offer opportunities for a critical examination and challenge to the 'immigrant imaginary'.

The immigrant imaginary is also constructed, fed and sustained through data. Statistics are often presented as objective and neutral but can perpetuate a depoliticized and de-historicized view of migration. Numbers become 'key actors in debates and policy about migration' (M'charek and Black, 2020: 87). Which people are counted, how and why are decisions driven by contemporary political agendas, shaped by historical frames of reference and rationales established under colonial administrations. As critical scholars have shown, border technologies have long monitored movement, permitting settler-colonial sites to formalize and institutionalize mobility and immigration laws. Contemporary migration governance mechanisms of containment, control and surveillance were crafted and sharpened in the colonial era (Mayblin, 2017; Maybin and Turner, 2021). Simone Browne's (2010) work on the 'epidermalization of race' powerfully illustrates how slavery operated as a system of immobility that shaped future projects of immigration, including slave logbooks, sorting enslaved people at ports, port inspections of passengers and branding as modes of documentation. Private companies and ships' captains were implicated in this monitoring of passengers. In the plantation economy, accounting spreadsheets would be used and slaves needed a pass to leave a master's property for a specified time and to delimited places. All of this preceded and shaped the invention of paper documentation and the passport (Torpey, 2018), which facilitated, contained and surveilled mobility, as well as access to public services, housing and employment, as the earlier Windrush case study highlights. The collection and uses of data highlight the importance of asking searching questions about why particular data are sought, by whom and for what purpose, and how they endure in the immigrant imaginary, in migration governance narratives (see Chapter 5) and in the policy–research pipeline (see Chapter 6).

The immigrant imaginary contributes directly to contemporary processes of migrantization (the act of making someone or a group of people into migrants) and racialization (the process of ascribing racial identities) in the 'political now'. In turn, these shape migration experiences. When the UK Home Office commissions research into 'integration' (it has released two versions of its 'indicators of integration' framework [in 2004 and 2019]), it reflects the kinds of problematic entanglements of a dominant empirical focus that reactivates, reinforces and normalizes the notion of racialized difference that continues to feed the immigrant imaginary, and this is an ideology established during colonialism. The questions for us as we teach and research migration and, for example, the idea of 'integration' (to be explored in Chapter 5) are: to what extent do we rely on a state apparatus and its normalized categorizations to understand phenomena? And, subsequently, to what extent do we reproduce the immigrant imaginary? Where do we position ourselves in our research and our teaching to avoid complicity in naturalizing and normalizing the state apparatus? Janine Dahinden (2016: 2212) asks whether 'a reflexive attitude could be pursued, one that involves a search for new ways to explore these topics, to position oneself outside the normalization discourse and disentangle research from the migration apparatus'. Can we challenge and disrupt research priorities that sustain the immigrant imaginary? One way to do so, she suggests, is to clearly distinguish between analytical and common-sense categories, an approach that speaks directly to critical pedagogy in the 'political now'. Chapter 5 delves deeper into the possibilities of better migration literacies to do some of this work.

Concluding comments

Let us return to Knowsley. Knowsley was a powder keg of explosive social media speculation, misinformation and rumour, set alight by anti-immigration policy and rhetoric that feeds into and off the immigrant imaginary in dangerous ways. It would also have been terrifying for the people in the hotel to experience and relive this moment through the rolling reportage online. The 'political now' is made up of many such cultural and political moments of violence, horror and harm that seep into our teaching encounters and pedagogical craft all the time (Zembylas, 2013b). Critical-pedagogical approaches should be attuned to challenging the kinds of dominant beliefs revealed in these moments that sustain social inequalities and reproduce the immigrant imaginary in the contemporary conjuncture. What we can do in response is emphasize the diversity of migrant experiences, centre structural inequalities and power dynamics, and question dominant narratives and stereotypes. However, just as important is constantly searching for ways to connect the present to the past, so that we emphasise coloniality, we foreground the legacies of colonialism and imperial ties in migration governance and in how the immigrant is imagined. This disrupts the limitations of teaching and learning about the 'political now' presented as in some way exceptional or unprecedented. There are implications and emotional consequences for the accompanying discomfort in how we deal with such moments, and the spaces needed to explore these emotions are often missing in the more hardened binaries of a Freirean model of critical pedagogy. Chapter 3 will delve into the questions surrounding the role of emotions, affect and pedagogies of discomfort in this context, and introduces the idea of productive discomfort through 'doing good harm'.

3

The Ethical Classroom

Introduction

Teaching about migration is hard work that brings forth a range of emotions and challenges. As Chapter 2 has shown, to understand the urgency and complexity of the current moment, its xenophobia and racist populism, the way that certain migrants are criminalized, the enduring impact of COVID-19, and the long-standing effects of deeply rooted social inequalities, we need to locate these issues within their historical context. Learning from history also means acknowledging that histories are ordered, some are obscured or systemically erased. However, when our default ways of knowing and relating are called into question, it can feel discomforting, revealing the need for an ethics of care as we confront a new way of seeing. Ethical engagement involves embracing discomfort as a catalyst for critical consciousness and empathy, which in turn prompts us to challenge biases, question dominant narratives and better understand complex social issues. In this chapter, we explore the ethical challenges that arise when teaching about migration and the pedagogical practices we use. A key question will be how we manage and justify discomfort in the learning process. Within this framework, the ideas of active empathy and 'doing good harm' are introduced: active empathy is what comes 'after empathy' (Boler, 1999) and is offered as an action-oriented device; and 'doing good harm' is offered as a pedagogical device to understand how discomfort stemming from tackling challenging topics is necessary for intellectual and ethical growth. The chapter opens with an exploration of what ethics has come to mean in HE and what this can mean when it translates to the classroom.

Ethics in research and teaching

> **Problem posing: ethics in learning**
>
> Pose the following problems with students: what does ethics mean in the teaching and learning context? Who and what does it relate to? When should ethics be a consideration in what and how we learn? Students can write down their understanding of ethics and how they apply this to knowledge production in the classroom. Encourage them to begin with individual reflection, followed by think–pair–share, then a whole-class discussion. Present students with a series of ethical dilemmas that could involve issues like citation bias, the inclusion of under-represented voices and the responsibility of teachers to critically engage with a discipline's colonial legacy. Share reflections and try to identify ethical approaches you might adopt. As a class, you can work together to define a set of ethical principles for knowledge production, anti-racist citation practices and decolonizing learning. Consider their significance and how these principles apply across various disciplines. Students could also write a personal ethical statement outlining their commitment to upholding these principles in their academic journey and within the broader community.

Ethics in the context of HE is considered crucial to protect the rights and well-being of research participants, and ethical guidelines and institutional review boards play an important role in ensuring that research is conducted in a responsible and ethical manner. University-based researchers cannot proceed to fieldwork without approval from an independent institutional ethics review board, and 'being ethical' in the field has come to be enshrined in codes of conduct, statements of good practice and institutionally recognized acceptable standards of behaviour. Perhaps the most widely referenced code of professional conduct is the Hippocratic Oath ('First of all, do no harm'): 'do no harm' is largely understood as an approach that avoids injury and physical harm, and respects fairness, justice and equality, and is a way to demonstrate a serious and committed engagement to avoiding harmful effects on others.

Many different professional associations, government agencies, universities and funding bodies have adopted ethical statements encompassing specific codes, rules and policies.[1] In the social sciences, discipline-specific guidance is deeply rooted in a doctrinaire system of rights and wrongs, used synonymously with a concern for 'morality', often relying on Western and Eurocentric concepts of ethics, emphasizing principles like the safety of, and respect for, research participants, and addressing issues like impartiality, neutrality, researcher bias and positionality. However, there are evolving perspectives on research ethics. First, there has been a shift in thinking towards an ethics-in-practice or a lifecycle approach, with ethics embedded in every stage of design rather than being a bureaucratic, box-ticking process limited to concerns in 'the field'. Linda Tuhiwai Smith's (2012) vital work on decolonizing methodologies urges academics to approach research with indigenous peoples as full partners driving project planning, design and delivery, and deciding on the framing and use of results. Second, more attention is being paid to including participants as active partners in the research process, from design to delivery, for example, through authentic collaboration and co-production committed to the politics of better research practice (Held, 2020; Lenette, 2022). Third, there is a growth in migration-specific ethics guidance; for example, in 2022, University College Dublin published a briefing paper about 'grounding a discussion of ethics in the direct experiences of people of a refugee background who have been involved in recent research in Ireland and Scotland' (Albtran et al, 2022: 4). The International Association for the Study of Forced Migration offers guidance specific to forced migration, as does the Canadian Council for Refugees. The Centre for Refugee Studies and Canadian Association for Refugee and Forced Migration Studies published *Ethical Guidelines for Research with People in Situations of Forced Migration* in (Clark-Kazak, 2017), and the *Forced Migration Review* published an ethics special issue in 2019.

We should also acknowledge that much ethical guidance is rooted in Western and Eurocentric perspectives shaped by colonial scientific practices (Haggerty, 2004). Carolyn Pedwell (2016) argues that such colonial science origins objectified, sorted and classified the 'other', questioning who is deemed capable of empathy and sympathy, and who is not. Additionally, Sarah Dyer and David Demeritt (2009) have observed the limitations of ethical review processes as often rooted in medical research governance models and that principles like 'do no harm' cannot be indiscriminately applied to the social sciences. Harm can also arise from assumptions of superiority or vulnerability when studying marginalized or disadvantaged groups, reinforcing power imbalances between researchers and participants. Taking these critiques seriously means challenging any limited view of ethics that neglects historical practices and imperatives, as well as diverse cultural and epistemological perspectives, and that overlooks complex and context-specific ethical considerations that may contradict conventional ethical norms (Lenette, 2022).

There is a growing movement advocating for the decolonization of ethical frameworks in HE institutions in the West, as well as in ethical review processes themselves (the work of Linda Tuhiwai-Smith and Caroline Lenette is groundbreaking in this regard). Writing about decolonizing and indigenizing ethics from a settler-Inuit perspective that is gaining ground in Canada, the US, New Zealand and Australia, Mirjam Held (2020) and Fern Brunger and colleagues (2020) emphasize that research ethics guidelines are neither apolitical nor value-free and that moves towards better understanding of 'risks' to 'communities' are also part of historical and political processes of the oppression of vulnerabilized people. Such processes and the ethics frameworks they shape remain directed by normative assumptions about what constitutes 'communities' as relations of power, how 'risk' and 'harm' are understood, and how refusal can be enacted.

> **Reflective task**
>
> When curating course materials for your classroom, do you consciously consider the ethical dimensions of your choices? Can you describe the ethical framework that informs your decision-making process? Are there conventional disciplinary standards that might unconsciously influence your selections? How do you ethically navigate the challenges of teaching about migration, especially within the current political climate? This includes addressing concerns tied to our own positionality, the potential for harm, the concepts of neutrality and objectivity, and the political implications of our choices. Additionally, how do we deal with any discomfort that may arise during these discussions? One perspective suggests that by not openly discussing our ethical positions, we inadvertently underscore their presence through their absence. Do you agree?

Knowledge production can be a deep source of harm, or what Giyatri Spivak (1992: 280) calls epistemic violence, 'the remotely orchestrated, far-flung, and heterogeneous project to constitute the colonial subject as Other'. Epistemic violence may stem from how knowledge is used and how it is produced (via classifications, objectification and so forth) (Colombo, 2020). It is also deeply rooted in the colonial condition of the present and sedimented in hierarchized orders of knowledge, and so can be in direct conflict with what is considered ethical in more collaborative approaches, as Caroline Lenette has written about. Let us take the example of anonymization practices. Anonymization is most often understood as necessary to safeguard privacy and comply with data protection laws, and there will be many cases where it will be considered essential. However, it is also crucial to critically examine its effect as continued oppression in the way in which it privileges some as knowledge producers over others as knowledge holders. As a practice, anonymization can diminish the recognition of individuals' experiences and expertise by reducing them to anonymous data points, undermining acknowledgement of their knowledge production, wisdom and insights (Adu-Gyamfi, 2015; Di Feliciantonio, 2021). Participants' voices may be silenced or marginalized, perpetuating a power imbalance between the researcher and the researched. This can reinforce the colonial division between both, where the researcher's position is privileged as the expert over the lived and live experiences of participants (Pedwell, 2016). Testimony is understood as 'raw data', only to be validated as 'knowledge' once it has been finessed and put through the analysis of the researcher's expertise. This taking of knowledge, or 'information and knowledge theft' (Tommasselli, 2014), from who Caroline Lenette (2019) calls 'knowledge holders' can be understood as counter to the principle of co-produced knowledge, if that is our aim (Wood, 2017). From these critical anti-oppressive, anti-racist and decolonizing perspectives, anonymization risks doing more harm than good.

Decolonizing and indigenizing methodologies urge us to question such normative assumptions and practices. Linda Tuhiwai Smith's (2012) work has been groundbreaking in showing how scientific racism has remained foundational to academic knowledge production, from extractive research to the marginalization of indigenous knowledges. Caroline Lenette's (2022) work explores these questions from the perspective of participatory action research methodologies, but the same questions can apply across a range of qualitative and quantitative research methods. By naming participants and engaging them in conversations as credible creators and holders of knowledge, we can, it is argued, challenge hierarchical dynamics and create space for systematically erased people to be seen and heard as people with experiences and ideas rather than interchangeable members of a target group, or as sorted into a designated 'community' that itself often draws from colonial systems of classification (Smith, 2012). This work may involve exploring alternative consent and data protection methods that respect individuals' privacy while acknowledging their active role in knowledge creation. While traditional perspectives have relied on anonymization to protect privacy, it is vital to critically examine its implications, especially in the context of decolonizing and participatory research. This underscores the ongoing importance of challenging normative ethical assumptions. Reassessing ethics entails recognizing how knowledge creation can perpetuate harm and epistemic violence, a concern applicable in educational settings where diverse knowledge, marginalized voices and knowledge-production processes should be prioritized and critically evaluated.

Critical pedagogy facilitates the development of an ethical imagination by encouraging a broader exploration of ethical questions and possibilities within teaching, as well as around our default perspectives. While classroom ethics may not follow the same formal structures as research ethics, they are foundational to critical-pedagogical praxis and our ways of knowing and relating. Ethical dispositions and ambitions are integral to the learning environment, encompassing thinking critically, being committed to social justice, addressing inequality, promoting anti-racism, fostering empathy, enhancing migration literacy and envisioning possibilities beyond the status quo as we move from 'what is' to 'what if'. Ethical considerations also extend to nurturing relationships, including radical openness to 'others' and connecting with the broader community (hooks, 1994). Critical, public pedagogy, as advocated by Giroux, entails embracing a 'politics of possibility', engaging with various forms of knowledge and transforming them into pedagogical practices. In the critical classroom, the goal is to deeply integrate these ethical dispositions into students' thinking and actions, so they 'don't merely "sit on the surface" but influence their ways of thinking in diverse ways' (Giroux, 2020: 76), encouraging critical reflection, dialogue and the exploration of different perspectives. This integration extends to practical application both within and beyond the classroom, encompassing community engagement, activism and real-world problem solving.

Case Study 3.1: The ethics of breaking free of the classroom

Alternative learning environments offer opportunities to break free of the confines of the traditional classroom. I would like to share here my efforts to do this with undergraduate and postgraduate students on a course exploring migration, settlement and belonging. The session involves taking students on a city walk to two adjacent neighbourhoods in the Southside of the city of Glasgow. Less than one mile apart, one is where I live and is home to Scotland's largest minority ethnic population, and the other, where I grew up, has a centuries-long history of being Scotland's most diverse neighbourhood and popular settlement area for people coming to Glasgow and Scotland. During the city walk session, I present students with problem-posing questions, such as: 'How do we see settlement and belonging?'; 'What does it look like?'; 'Where is it happening?'; 'How does it sound?'; and 'How does it feel?'. I encourage them to reflect on the spaces and geographies of everyday encounters and diversity, relating these to the course content, debates and ideas we have explored throughout the semester. Instead of assigning readings, I provide students with notes on ethnographic thinking. To support our learning, I set up a class-wide collaborative online discussion board (a Google doc would also work) and ask each student to: (1) post at least one reflection on their walk, either in real time or after the experience; and (2) comment on at least one other student's reflection. Their posts should focus on what they observe and feel as they navigate through diverse and everyday spaces of encounter. These comments and reflections serve as the foundation for our final session, during which we collectively reflect on our experiences and learning during the course. It is a popular activity: students always show up and actively engage in the task, sharing follow-up notes, photos and additional resources they discover. In my role as the course leader, I moderate the discussions and can contribute my own reflections and resources.

This departure from traditional learning spaces presents challenges. While the activity has generally been well received, it has sparked thought-provoking ethical discussions within the class. When I first introduced this walk, students asked about its ethical implications, particularly whether it resembled a 'poverty safari', contributing to racialized narratives of the migrant 'other'. We would be walking around and, potentially at least, taking photos of a neighbourhood that not only is the most ethnically diverse in the city but also where parts of it are ranked among the most deprived in the country, according to the Scottish Index of Multiple Deprivation. Overcrowding, poor housing and rogue landlords have all been identified as key local problems. They questioned whether this walk might be reinforcing a passive voyeurism of the 'migrant other' and the damage this framing does. The option of posting photos simply reinforced this for many. I had not fully considered that students living in or from this neighbourhood would also feel othered by this place-based focus or task. Nor had I considered how ethical questions about positionality, doing harm, neutrality, objectivity and the politics of representation feature within and outwith the classroom. These questions were at first discomforting to me – I was, after all, trying to be creative and innovative, and I was also deeply committed to unpacking problematic narratives – but I was at risk here of reproducing them. Over the years, I have realized how vital this space for dialogue is. Simply put, we do not always get it right. It is only through this conversation, placing an increasing focus on the centrality of ethics to our pedagogy, that we can together learn to disrupt our normative assumptions. Such discussions have become central to our pursuit of a socially just pedagogy.

Now, every year the course runs, during the first week when I introduce the walk, we talk and listen. We collectively address concerns and establish our ethical guidelines. In some cases, we decide to do the walk together as a group and then proceed independently, while in other instances, we explore any neighbourhood, provided there is a connection to our course content. We work with community resources from a local housing association that let students follow a local points-of-interest walking trail or choose to spend time in a cafe or library, as we have agreed that our actions are determined by us and build on the foundations already in place from our in-class learning. We also collaboratively set ethical standards for recording memories and taking photos. Finally, we arrange a visit with a community organization advocating for housing and migrant rights. This visit offers us an opportunity to learn from and with them, to 'connect in' to the neighbourhood, and to discuss how their work relates to our broader learning and personal experiences. We also explore potential avenues for involvement in their work, such as volunteering, advocacy and campaigning.

> **Talking points**
>
> - What other ethical issues might arise when breaking free of the classroom and establishing alternative learning spaces?
> - How might neglecting ethical pedagogy perpetuate particular issues?
> - How can you work with the discomfort produced from thinking ethically, and what might be the transformative impact of discomfort? Does that justify discomfort?

Problem posing around ethics does several things: it urges us to talk about and locate ethics in the classroom context, centre ethics in all aspects of learning and reflect on their consequences; it challenges us to do some of the work of unlearning that is required to develop a critical consciousness and praxis; it connects our emotions to how we engage with knowledge production; and it forces us to listen. This is directly linked to critical inquiry, recognizing that what we consider to be ethical practices of 'do no harm' may be inflicting harm through, for example, epistemic violence. The unlearning that follows can be an unsettling, discomforting experience because it challenges our preconceived ideas and ways of seeing the world, but it remains integral for disruption and transformation. The idea of a pedagogy of discomfort holds promise for understanding how this plays out.

Pedagogies of discomfort and pedagogies of empathy

Henry Giroux, bell hooks, Megan Boler, Michalinos Zembylas and others have all pointed out that any theory of pedagogy must be willing and prepared to develop within it a serious and sustained engagement with emotions. Emotions can be viewed from different perspectives, either as individual and innate or as socially constructed and influenced by broader social norms, values and power structures, which can reinforce or challenge oppressive structures (Boler, 1999). Such norms and structures are also cultural and political, informing what is permitted, expected or deemed as 'correct and proper', what is to be avoided, and who gets to express which emotions. Sarah Ahmed (2004) talks about feeling our way through social worlds, emphasizing the intricate connection between emotions, social norms and our lived experiences. Megan Boler's (1999) work *Feeling Power* underscores the importance of discomfort as an indicator that learners are grappling with challenging and unsettling ideas that disrupt their established beliefs and emotional investments. Boler suggests that a pedagogy of discomfort involves teachers and students critically examining their values, cherished beliefs and self-perceptions in relation to how we have learned to perceive others, and 'within this culture of inquiry and flexibility, a central focus is to recognize how emotions define how and what one chooses to see, and conversely, not see' (Boler, 1999: 177). Feeling power involves recognizing the avoidance of certain knowledge by using emotions as a kind of protective barrier. A pedagogy of discomfort allows for the use of emotions to disrupt ingrained assumptions and beliefs (Zembylas and Boler, 2002), and it is this possibility that distinguishes discomfort from critical media literacy through its focus on identifying complex, underlying emotions that support dominant ideologies within the cultural apparatus.

There are three ways in which a pedagogy of discomfort maps onto critical pedagogy. The first is that all forms of anti-oppressive pedagogy that seek to unsettle taken-for-granted views demand an unavoidable affective confrontation. When we move out of our comfort zones, we feel and experience a fear of the unknown. There may be possible resistance, defensive anger, apathy, sadness, upset and frustration, a sense of disorientation, and a fear of change and of losing our personal and cultural identities (Boler, 1999; Kumashiro, 2002; Boler and Zembylas, 2003; Davis and Steyn, 2012). Some students will emphatically resist and oppose course content that challenges long-held views. Others may angrily reject or withdraw from conversation. Feelings of indifference or impassiveness, as other forms of resistance, may also arise to avoid discomfort, fear, guilt or shame. Importantly, the aim is not to overcome hostility or resistance but to find ways to cope with conflict, both inner and interpersonal (hooks, 1994). Another aim is to engage with knowledge that allows for a disruption of dominant narratives and offers new windows onto the world. Harrowing accounts can be hard to listen to, even if they are necessary. Sometimes, it can be a simple question to students about how engaging with particular materials and stories makes them feel. There may also be feelings of empathy, solidarity and hope. The act of recognizing what one does not want to know, and why that is, aligns with the idea that discomfort can be transformative, and what is vital to understand here is that it provides a space of possibilities, that is, for new ways of collective thinking and new ways of seeing and being in the world.

Second, a pedagogy of discomfort also provides comfort, in the sense that we gain truth from an expanded openness that shapes our learning experience. This is liberatory, as it provides a way to move beyond fear as we confront what we see and what we choose not to see (Boler, 1999: 182). Moving out of our comfort zones comes with a realization that we are not separate to and from, but deeply implicated in, the stories that get to be told and those that are silenced. These are also profoundly ethical questions. For example, in the EU's migration governance language, we increasingly hear of the development of 'unified European solutions to migration problems', which very effectively depoliticizes state violence and harm. This not only neutralizes their violent effects but also, through seemingly benign management-speak, neutralizes affect. If we fail to attend to the relationship between effect and affect in the classroom by uncritically adopting and reproducing neutralizing language and idioms, and talking about 'migration problems', then our pedagogy lacks criticality. Another example is that seeing certain migrants in certain ways reflects our capacities to absorb and reproduce, or resist and push back against, the dehumanizing of the other. In both instances, we use emotions to make sense of our responses and to rationalize our retelling of stories.

The third feature is that any reflexivity that generates discomfort is not enough to bring about conscientization. On its own, it risks producing a passive empathy through modes of 'easy identification' and 'spectating' that fail to challenge social injustice, placing students in a 'no-win trap of guilt vs. innocence' (Boler, 1999: 159, 187). 'Spectating', Boler argues, involves learning from a distance, or putting oneself in the shoes of others without actively engaging or taking responsibility for change. Achieving empathy in a passive sense becomes a non-controversial endpoint without meaningful action. This passive stance of 'spectating' replicates the limitations of a politics of declaration, following Sarah Ahmed (2004), where an issue is flagged and discussed, and we then move on. The 'spectating' Boler describes is directly implicated in the kinds of claims to neutrality and objectivity critical pedagogy pushes against. As Henry Giroux (1979: 261) points out:

> knowledge, parading under the guise of objectivity, has for too long been used to legitimate belief and value systems that are at the core of bondage. 'Objective' knowledge not only mystifies, but it also turns people into spectators by removing the norms, values, and interests underlying it from public debate.

Passive empathy aligns with neoliberalism, where emotions and affective relations can be controlled, packaged and even measured, perpetuating hierarchical narratives and reinforcing multiple forms of oppression, pitting one recipient of empathy over another (Pedwell, 2016).

Case Study 3.2: Responding to emotions and safety in the classroom

When teaching immigration detention, I incorporate academic research and real-life stories from detainees and their families, taking the form of audio-clips and written narratives.[2] In one particular session, our class delved into several key discussions around: (1) students' awareness gaps regarding immigration detention; (2) the shocking realisation of the absence of a detention time limit in the UK; (3) bewilderment at the diverse reasons for detaining different 'kinds' of migrant; (4) the emotional impact of hearing these stories, including feelings of helplessness, confusion and empathy; and (5) our collective anger and desire to act against the immigration detention system's injustice. This moment highlighted two important things: acknowledging diverse emotional responses; and directing students towards meaningful actions. Ideas we came up with included supporting anti-detention campaigns, sharing this information, joining a student action group and writing to members of parliament (MPs). This approach helped us manage feelings of frustration and helplessness, turning us into active researchers and advocates as we found out more about which campaigning organizations work in this area and how we might 'connect in' to their work. As the teacher guiding the learning, I also recognized not only the value of creating time and space for processing difficult information but also that this must be followed up with possibilities for action. For future sessions, I now prepare students in advance, ensuring a more informed and action-oriented learning experience.

Talking points

- 'Safety', suggests bell hooks (1989), is a space of privilege, and we instead need to attend to complexity. How might we think about safety and complexity ethically in our classroom, and what ethical ambitions and dispositions do we want to develop in the shared learning space?
- Hannah Jones (2021) talks about violent ignorance as the act of looking away from painful knowledge. What might be the ethical consequences of this looking away when we talk about migration? How can we use this analytic framework to confront our biases, defaults and assumptions beyond a level of abstraction that makes any confrontation someone else's problem?

While cultivating passive empathetic experiences that detach individuals from structural relations is neither effective nor desirable, it is also important to be vigilant and recognize that emotions alone do not guarantee justice in the classroom or necessarily lead to activism or transformative change (Zembylas and McGlynn, 2012: 43). Such responses can be very effectively appropriated by neoliberal regimes, politicians and media pundits to uphold inequalities and undermine the value of empathetic connections, as we have already seen in Chapter 2. The case of Ukrainian/Afghan resettlement schemes in the UK highlights very effectively the dynamics of passive and neoliberal empathy, where notions of deserving and worthy refugees become intertwined with a politics of declaration and individual capacity, or responsibility, to empathize. This perspective also deeply disavows the racialization processes at play, which activate passive empathy for some while disregarding others.

Teachable moment: #Linekergate and the 'right kinds' of empathy

On 7 March 2023, in response to Suella Braverman's 'Stop the Boats' campaign, TV presenter and football pundit Gary Lineker tweeted that it was 'an immeasurably cruel policy directed at the most vulnerable people in language that is not dissimilar to that used by Germany in the 30s'. The tweet led to a huge backlash that came to be framed as #Linekergate. Lineker was accused of going beyond his remit as a sports presenter, of being in breach of the BBC's impartiality rules, of fuelling racism that was not there and of showing a kind of soft-core Holocaust denial (Winter, 2023). Refusing to apologize or retract his words, Lineker temporarily stepped down from his usual presenting slot, as did several other presenters in solidarity. On 12 March 2023, a fiery clash took place between John Barnes (a former footballer and TV pundit) and Andrew Castle (a former tennis player and TV and radio pundit) in a filmed radio interview in the wake of '#Linekergate'. John Barnes pointed out that refugees from other countries (Syria, Iraq, Yemen and Afghanistan) who do not have safe and legal routes were not being as welcomed as the Ukrainians. Andrew Castle, who then revealed that he had opened his home to Ukrainian refugees, took deep offence at, in his view, being negatively judged, and asked, 'Are you suggesting I'm biased or prejudiced for taking Ukrainian refugees into my home?', adding, 'I resent the idea of having a finger pointed at me for being biased at people with a white skin' (for the full interview, see: https://twitter.com/LBC/status/1634871740328296448?s=20).

This clash reveals ways in which individual experience can be framed as expert knowledge whilst also exposing the racialized and privileged positioning of certain knowledge holders. It provides an excellent example of a passive and neoliberal empathy, and its limitations, as well as how 'not racism' (as argued by Alana Lentin) works, its hierarchizing effects on who is deemed worthy of empathy and the discomfiting effects produced.

Activities

Start by showing the full interview between John Barnes and Andrew Castle. Divide the class into small groups and ask each to identify moments in the discussion where emotions are weaponized to advance specific perspectives. Encourage students to reflect on how these emotional tactics impact the polarization of migration debates.

Assign students the task of analysing the media's role in framing and amplifying emotional responses in migration debates. Ask them to identify instances where the media may contribute to polarization and emotional manipulation. Encourage students to discuss the responsibility of media outlets in facilitating polarizing debates.

Talking points

- What does the weaponization of emotions in such debates reveal about our emotional responses to such discussions, including 'both sides' presentations?
- How do we feel about this exchange? Do we acknowledge passive and active empathy in our responses, and how might this influence how we absorb, reproduce or resist certain knowledge, both inside and outside the classroom?

Discomfort should serve as a catalyst for action, and in contrast to spectating and passive empathy, 'witnessing', being 'a dynamic process of perceiving without the luxury of static truth or fixed certainty' (Felman, 1992: 5), offers an alternative pedagogical aim. 'Witnessing' encompasses historical responsibility and complexity, questioning the forces that contribute to a 'crisis' (Boler, 1999). Intertwined with all structures of oppression, witnessing involves recognizing moral relations as a perspectival difference, in the sense of 'we all see things differently', as well as that how we see or choose not to see has ethical implications and may even cause others to suffer (Boler, 1999: 194: Zembylas, 2015). Witnessing can lead to collective action, as learners move from a position of privileged passivity to one of accountability. Following Sivanandan, when we witness, we move beyond mere thinking or feeling for its own sake and instead we think and feel in order to act (Srilangarajah, 2018). Connecting knowledge to social action is a central goal of critical pedagogy, and collective action can be inspired in many ways: inviting community organizations and activists into the classroom to discuss how to talk about, and act on, specific problems; identifying together ways of supporting each other through, for example, voluntary work, support with advocacy and campaigning; exploring the City/University of Sanctuary movement as a potential site for engagement; inviting student activist groups to discuss their work; and asking students to talk about their own community involvement and activism. Such actions are practical ways of building resources for change, and learning through these resources and bringing the outside in can strengthen communities of resistance via raising the visibility of dissenting voices in students' lives, building alliances and making more meaningful connections with each other around shared issues. Connecting knowledge to social action also means making connections between the 'political now' and the past. This kind of action-oriented work might take place at the classroom level or extend beyond.

> **Problem posing: community action in the classroom**
>
> Pose the following problem: what does community action mean in the classroom? How does your discipline influence your stance on the relevance of community action in education? Prompt students to independently reflect, then discuss together using a think–pair–share model the relationship between community action and knowledge production. Encourage collective thinking about meaningful learning contexts, personal experiences, disciplinary norms, applied learning, institutional boundaries, the forms of learning considered valid and 'assessable', and the privileging of certain knowledge. Invite students to share their community action experiences where they feel comfortable doing so and connect them to class learning. Consider ways to make space for diverse knowledge and knowledge holders. The Asylum University case study in Chapter 4 and the collaborating ethically case studies in Chapter 7 can be used as primers for imagining socially just practice and as guidance for what it can involve.

Engaging with discomfort can be understood as productive, raising critical awareness and therefore as 'doing good harm'. Michalinos Zembylas extends Megan Boler's framework on discomfort, suggesting that discomfort can be connected to active empathy, that is, what comes 'after empathy' (Boler, 1999: 157). This involves self-reflexive understanding of our own and others' social positioning, the power inequities that shape our relationships, and our own implication in the social forces that create obstacles others confront (Zembylas, 2012, 2013a). The #Linekergate case study provides an example for exploring this idea further. Navigating the kinds of emotions that arise 'after empathy' will not necessarily be easy, but it is in these spaces of discomfort that transformative potential lies. Witnessing can be valuable but may have conceptual limitations for individuals traversing migration regimes, who may themselves be seeking to define their roles in knowledge production within the learning environment. In light of this, I propose a third perspective, distinct from spectating and witnessing, which I call 'holding knowledge'. This concept builds upon the anti-oppressive work of Caroline Lenette, as discussed earlier in this chapter, and consists of two key features. First, it involves acknowledging that individuals with lived and live experiences hold and produce valuable knowledge. Second, it entails engaging in a collaborative learning process with students who possess such experiences, shifting the focus from providing testimony and creating a space for a more nuanced understanding of these experiences as expert knowledge, which can encompass various positionalities directly affected and shaped by migration processes, including governance structures.

Case Study 3.3: Ethically creating space for knowledge holders

I teach undergraduate and postgraduate students about the asylum regime in the UK. I curate materials and case studies from the local and national context, which I share with students through our university's virtual learning environment. On one occasion, after getting to know my postgraduate students in their first week, I realized that one of them, Mariama (a chosen pseudonym), a campaigner and activist, was also featured in an online rights advocacy group's campaign for an end to no recourse to public funds, a standard condition attached to people claiming asylum who are unable to access state welfare. Her story was featured in our online repository. I promptly, and without checking first with her, removed her case study from our class resources because I did not want her to be objectified in the classroom, reducing her to a mere resource. However, Mariama openly shared her valuable experiential knowledge with us throughout the course, guiding us to academic content and potential actions. Upon reflection, I recognized that my decision to remove her online story stemmed from my discomfort with us being spectators of her life - this was a confrontation with what it means, ethically and politically, when we use peoples' lives as 'resources' – and a perhaps misplaced attempt at creating 'safety' for her. However, I might have done more harm by removing her agency about how she wanted to position herself. Her activism *was* her safety. This was an ethical blind spot on my part: she was proud of her role as an expert by experience and knowledge holder; and it was for her, not me, to decide how her story and advocacy work should be shared. To provide a different perspective, Mohammed (who chose not to use a pseudonym), a community development worker, rights activist and filmmaker from a migrant background, also brought his expert knowledge to our classroom discussions. He openly shared his stories and experiences, and grounded topical and academic themes in his everyday work and activism. Mohammed directed our focus of study, the difference being that his story was not already 'curated' for us in the same way.

Mariama and Mohammed played pivotal roles as knowledge holders, exemplifying what Ira Shor (1992) calls 'situated learning', rooted in students' experiences and language, which offers an alternative way to connect with both society and knowledge. By working with Mariama and Mohammed as producing knowledge for learning with and from, on their terms and at their pace, our class discussions became significantly richer, enabling us to critically assess theories and conceptual ideas and bridge academic knowledge through the generative experiences of students.

Talking points

- Discuss the ethical dilemma I faced when removing Mariama's case study from the class resources. This situation raises questions about how teachers might navigate the line between respect for a student's agency and their role as knowledge holders.
- Consider the broader implications of this reflective case study for community engagement in HE. How can the inclusion of community activists and campaigners like Mariama and Mohammed enhance the learning experience for all students? But what expectations, assumptions and pressures might this also place on them?

Across all three positionalities – spectator, witness and knowledge holder – there is a deep ethics at play about how discomfort is introduced, presented and engaged with, and what and whose purpose it serves. The pedagogical framework of discomfort is not without its critics. It has been likened to shock therapy (Ivits, 2009), with the suggestion of coercing students into adopting a particular world view, eliciting only responses or the 'right kind of emotions' that the teacher desires. However, we are reminded of the underlying premise of the critical classroom that sets the foundation for discord and productive discomfort: education is always political, that is, teachers and students come to the learning space with their own perspectives and backgrounds, and in building dialogue and learning, we all need to be prepared and ready to feel discomfort.

Doing good harm as productive of disruption and transformation

Doing good harm through challenging belief systems and frameworks of understanding, and critically examining how we interpret the world, requires careful handling and preparation. Many critical scholars note the relationship between knowledge and discomfort, and the care required in their undoing and rebuilding. Avi Mintz (2013) has argued that to confront and dismantle inequalities, suffering and harm, we must learn about suffering and harm, and this learning about can also result in some suffering and harm. Gargi Bhattacharyya (2013: 1426) suggests that part of our role in HE is to try to explain why 'knowledge is painful but necessary'. Remi Joseph-Salisbury and Laura Connelly (2021: 200) talk about the productivity of discomfort as an 'unfinished and open-ended project', acted upon 'in the service of communities of resistance'. By creating feelings of discomfort, the foundation is laid for doing good harm, which involves intentionally disrupting the established ideas, dominant ideologies, narratives, vocabularies of our disciplines, teaching approaches and the search for so-called 'objective' facts and truths, all of which contribute to perpetuating forms of oppression. Doing good harm creates ruptures and offers opportunities to do critical, impactful work otherwise.

Doing good harm in a productive way can take different forms. It results from an epistemic intervention to counter the harm of epistemic violence caused by migration policies and migration governance that has crept into migration studies (Piccoli et al, 2023). Exposing students to dominant processes of knowledge production as a political and ethical imperative, and naming this as such, provides us with new vocabularies to analyse such processes, as well as to consider our affective responses to this new knowledge about epistemic injustice. Such an intervention can involve working with counter-empirics in the classroom (Stierl, 2022); for example, the counter-monitoring of border enforcement reveals the kinds of deadly migration management policies and regimes that can go under the radar. The following case study provides two examples that are helpful to illustrate how we might do this.

Case Study 3.4: Working with empirics/ counter-empirics

The Missing Migrants project was established by the International Organization for Migration (IOM) in 2013 to document and track deaths and disappearances along migratory routes worldwide.[3] It serves as an open-access database that provides data analysis, reports, briefings and infographics. It does not include deaths that occur in immigration detention facilities, after deportation or resulting from labour exploitation. The 'List of deaths' is published every 20 June on World Refugee Day and is an anti-racist, no borders database curated by UNITED for Intercultural Action, listing deaths related to Fortress Europe since 1993.[4] Both data sets underline the human tragedy facing certain racialized people on the move, though with clearly different political imperatives, with one used to bolster border management and the other for border abolition. Counting and accounting can be seen as both a bureaucratic procedure and a relation of care (M'charek and Black, 2020), and they work as pedagogical devices that disrupt the 'spectacle of statistics' used to instil the dominant narrative of 'crisis' regarding contemporary movements of people into and around Europe (Stierl et al, 2022). These data sets can be used individually to explore stories behind statistics, as well as comparatively to look at the kinds of information collected and documented by different actors with varying ethical and political imperatives, and how this impacts the narrative around a particular issue.

Further reading and resources

- Stierl, M., Heller, C. and De Genova, N. (2022) 'Numbers (or, the spectacle of statistics in the production of "crisis") Europe/crisis: new keywords of "the crisis" in and of "Europe" ', New Keywords Collective. Available at: https://nearfuturesonline.org/europecrisis-new-keywords-of-crisis-in-and-of-europe-part-4/
- Sigona, N. (2022) [Twitter] 3 March. Available at: https://twitter.com/nandosigona/status/1499367685624377348
- Sigona, N. (2015) 'Seeing double? How the EU miscounts migrants arriving at its borders', *The Conversation*. Available at: www./theconversation.com/seeing-double-how-the-eu-miscounts-migrants-arriving-at-its-borders-49242

Talking points

- Foreground your discussion with the following questions: Who is producing these statistics? What are their methods? For whom? And to what end?
- Define and discuss the concept of data bias. How can bias manifest in data, and what are its effects?
- Explore practices such as statistical gaming, double counting or omitting numbers. How might these practices contribute to misleading data? Discuss the potential impact of misleading data on reinforcing racist ideological arguments and rhetoric.
- Encourage students to consider the ethical implications of data collection. How do both data sets address issues such as informed consent, especially when dealing with sensitive topics like deaths and disappearances?

Listening and working with stories, produced through counter-empirics and in narrative form, can also be productive of a discomfort that does 'good harm'. All narratives require a disposition to listen, and in the fight for social justice, we must create conditions to listen to pain and respond to pain. In her work on suffering in justice-oriented education,

Sharon Todd (2003) has suggested that listening itself is an ethical response. The earlier example of George the Poet is a case in point. Part of exploring epistemic (in)justice is to consider who the narrators of knowledge are, when their knowledge is presented as testimony and when it is expertise. In the pedagogical context, these too are ethical decisions. We might read personal accounts of border crossings, watch video testimony of survivors and use images that capture terrifying moments of rescue at sea, all of which 'provide testimony'. However, if our engagement with such material is limited to spectating and the testimonial (Zembylas, 2023b), and only done in a passive way, where we absorb information absent of understanding the affective responses to this knowing and relating, or fail to ask what can be done and to identify collectively possible forms of action, then this kind of approach fails to be anti-oppressive. Moreover, the expected availability of migrant stories reflects deeply entrenched structural inequalities and power relations that influence which experiences are recognized and how that knowledge is constructed. Avi Mintz (2013: 223), writing about helping by hurting, asks two deeply important ethical questions that connect counter-stories to a pedagogy of discomfort that we should consider: first, why should the victims of injustice become the mere means through which students are encouraged to reflect on the injustice and the imbalances of power in the students' lives? This points to another means of consuming the oppressed: rather than experience a catharsis of their own guilt or shame, teachers and students consume the victims for the purpose of reflecting on contemporary injustices. The second question that one might also reasonably ask is: should not the victim of injustice, or the memory of that victim, be allowed to stand on its own, for all witnesses to behold in horror, rather than as mere curricular fodder?' The earlier reflection about Mariama and Mohammed speaks directly to these issues. Mintz points to the need to move from a position of experience as testimonial to one of experience as knowledge production that can be acknowledged, recognized and accredited as expertise.

Counter-stories, stories told from, or that appropriately amplify, racialized minority viewpoints (Schulz et al, 2023), offer a valuable perspective and pedagogical tool for decentring knowledge production and for understanding how racism is (re)produced (Blaisdell, 2021). Counter-stories are a pedagogical and methodological framework that have emerged from critical race theory in response to 'majoritarian narratives that deny the ongoing salience of race as a factor in people's lives' (Schulz et al, 2023). They involve people telling their stories rather than the dominant stories being told about them and, in this way, reveal that dominant stories are never neutral.

Teachable moment: *le Spiderman de Mali*

On 28 May 2018, Mamoudou Gassama, a Malian *sans papier*, heroically scaled a four-storey building in Paris to save a child who was dangling from a balcony. He was internationally fêted as a superhuman hero (nicknamed '*le Spiderman*'), was promised and fast-tracked French citizenship, met with President Macron, and even embarked on an internship with the French fire brigade. The story told about him was firmly located in the 'good immigrant' narrative: the hero selflessly doing good for others. However, it was also a story of the 'more than human' narrative, that is, of the exceptional achievement often demanded of migrants to prove they are 'deserving' and worthy. After the media coverage subsided, though, life away from the spotlight proved challenging. According to a blog about Mamoudou in August 2021 on French news site Mediàpart, entitled the 'La Chute de Mamoudou Gassama' ('The fall of Mamoudou Gassama'), he could not fulfil his aspirations to pursue a career with the Fire Brigade because he had not completed his Secondary School Leaving Certificate (*brevet scolaire*). To do so, in fact, would have been impossible for Mamoudou, who had left his family home in Mali (a former French colony) aged 15 to work on construction sites in Bamako, saving money to eventually make the perilous journey to Europe via Libya. Despite his heroic act and the initial attention he received, the challenges and barriers he faced in accessing education and stable employment highlight the systemic difficulties that many migrants encounter. In this sense, his life was far from extraordinary. Although lauded as an actual 'superhuman', when trying to forge his life on his own terms and in his own words as a 'contributing migrant', he was confronted with the colonial ties of history that shaped all his possibilities for building a new life in the metropole.

Further reading and resources

- Rachid Barbouch, 'Mamoudou Gassama déchu', *Mediàpart*, 15 August 2021. Available at: https://blogs.mediapart.fr/rachid-barbouch/blog/150821/mamoudou-gassama-dechu
- BBC News, 'The Spiderman of Paris: what happened next?', 24 December 2018. Available at: www.bbc.com/news/world-europe-46538253
- BBC News, 'Mamoudou Gassama: travelling is a rite of passage for many Malians', 28 May 2018. Available at: www.bbc.co.uk/news/world-africa-44279504
- Kim Willsher, ' "Spider-Man" of Paris to get French citizenship after child rescue', *The Guardian*, 29 May 2018. Available at: www.theguardian.com/world/2018/may/28/spider-man-of-paris-to-get-french-citizenship-after-rescuing-child

Talking points

- What does Mamoudou's story, its role in the 'good immigrant' narrative and the use of voice in storytelling reveal about the silencing of historical continuities in this retelling?

- Reading this alongside the *Gilets Noirs* case study (see Chapter 2), what do both stories reveal about the value of analysing the 'political now' through the historical lens and the enduring coloniality that racialized migrants face?

It is only in connecting the palatable, public version of Mamoudou's story to his counter-story of violent colonial histories and dangerous border governance that we disrupt the dominant celebratory narrative of the good immigrant, and reveal some of the multiple systemic and structural barriers in the way of many racialized migrants from former colonies to the European metropoles. Moving towards personal stories and seeing people as holders and keepers of knowledge in their biographies and histories – knowledge that is often placed to one side – provides a way to think ethically about productive discomfort so we avoid becoming what Ruben Andersson called 'migrant eaters': uncritical and unthinking greedy consumers of stories. We can also use the case studies from Chapter 2 as counter-stories that can be pedagogically disruptive. Some questions we might ask there are: what do each of these stories evoke? Whose stories are told? If stories and images contribute to the border spectacle, how do we also reproduce this spectacle in our teaching? What ethical standards do we apply to our use of stories in our teaching? How do we ethically and critically work with narrative, and how can it be used in different ways in the social justice classroom? As Natalie Avalos (2021: 27) observes, if we are interested in doing any critical, decolonial pedagogy, centring the voices of those we are discussing and learning about is key, where those same people are considered experts of their own experiences. There is also a politics involved here, as will be explored in Chapter 4.

Doing harm is necessary, but we must again be vigilant. First, in the diverse classroom, it remains important to consider the value of challenging and discomforting students, particularly those who identify with marginalized or oppressed groups. Avi Mintz's (2013: 225) concept of 'empowering suffering' draws on the ideas of Frederick Douglass and W.E.B. Du Bois, emphasizing how education can reveal injustices and lead to moments of awakening and reckoning. While it is reasonable for students to identify with the suffering of marginalized groups, it is essential to recognize that suffering, oppression and harm are not experienced uniformly within a particular group. Mintz's framework acknowledges the diverse forms of suffering and their associated risks and effects on learning, highlighting the importance of fostering transformative change. Second, counter-stories can serve various purposes, depending on the context and the audience involved. They can be powerful tools for activists, campaigners and civil society organizations to reshape discourse around deserving and undeserving migrants. In these cases, testimony is often described as having 'forensic power' (Saltsman and

Majidi, 2021), contributing to changing perspectives. However, counter-stories can also be co-opted by governments, aid and development agencies, and the academic community to advance their own agendas. It is crucial to approach the use of counter-stories with ethical and critical considerations, and to avoid making claims of 'empowerment' or 'giving voice'. Such claims can oversimplify the complex dynamics of power, often barely scratching the surface, and may inadvertently reinforce the notion that people are voiceless or powerless without external validation from researchers or spokespersons in the third sector.

A third way of doing good harm productively could be adopting an action-oriented approach that blurs the boundary between what we teach in the classroom and what goes on outside it. This approach involves fostering communities of resistance and working with counter-stories and counter-empirics as sources of knowledge to encourage new perspectives and thinking.

From theory to practice: learning *from* and *with* communities

These activities suggest opportunities to engage with communities mobilizing for migrant rights, ethically exploring how we value of community knowledge in activism. Identify and build multimedia resources (videos, documentaries, interviews and so on) about local campaigns. To get started, look at the campaign work of the Maryhill Integration Network (MiN) in Scotland. MiN is a user-led community organization supporting and bringing together people in the asylum system, refugees, migrants and Scottish people (see: http://maryhillintegration.org.uk/campaigns-research/).

Begin with a discussion on common stereotypes and narratives associated with refugees, people in the asylum system and migrants. Explore together articles, videos or personal testimonies (available on MiN's website but you can also research elsewhere) that challenge these stereotypes and emphasize resistance and organizing. Problem-pose how community groups challenge dominant narratives, and ask: what can we learn from this work? How does this knowledge contribute to our engagement with community knowledge, and how do we evaluate it as serious knowledge? Encourage students to reflect on the value of learning with community campaigns and activists in challenging dominant narratives, and undertake a critical analysis and discussion on the transformative power of community-driven initiatives.

Invite students to generate ideas and design student-led strategies and concrete next steps for supporting and collaborating with community organizations, as well as contributing to migrant rights advocacy. Encourage those who are already engaged in activism and communities to share their knowledge and practices, helping map out potential actions. If you are able, consider inviting a guest speaker or a representative from a community organization actively involved in rights advocacy to the classroom to share their expertise, the challenges faced and their mobilization practice as a pedagogic intervention.

Integrating diverse ways of knowing with habits of being is challenging and uncomfortable, but sharing this experience can create a closer community that recognizes interconnected oppressions. Collaboration is essential, and it requires clear communication of pedagogical goals and willingness from everyone involved. This includes preparing students to engage with course materials with care and promoting collective responsibility. Rather than avoiding conflict, it is important to think about how we cope with conflict in the pursuit of educated hope and the possibility that comes from doing good harm. Explaining to students that discomfort may arise helps manage expectations and aligns with the aim of promoting unlearning and critical thinking, fostering a collaborative learning space with mutual responsibility.

Doing good harm and ethically managing 'safety'

Discomfort and doing good harm do not necessarily equate to an absence of safety, and nor do safety or harm avoidance equate to the presence of comfort; for many critical pedagogues and social-justice-oriented thinkers, the issue of 'safety' is normative and as such ethical and political. In her article critiquing the notion of empowerment, Elizabeth Ellsworth (1989) urges us to ask whether a level playing field is even possible within the educational context. Such an assumption assumes that everyone in the classroom carries 'equal legitimacy, safety, and power' (Ellsworth, 1989: 317). It also overlooks the realities of power dynamics and the historical and embodied nature of the HE environment, as well as the intersecting and interlocking oppressions that exist beyond the classroom and enter with its participants. Safety, in this sense, is illusory. Michalinos Zembylas (2015) highlights the potential conflict between marginalized students' (and we can add teachers') need for safety (not being dominated) and privileged students' (and teachers') desire to avoid having their values and beliefs challenged; safety, in this context, may imply protecting privileged students from having their perspectives questioned. Kyoko Kishimoto and Mumbi Mwangi (2009: 95) further emphasize the necessity of an unsafe space in feminist pedagogy, challenging Eurocentric notions of teaching practices in which 'difference' in the predominantly white institution already means being seen as deviant and therefore threatening, and where safety is never in place. Considering the inherent institutional power that shapes classroom dynamics and the relations between teachers and students, Lauren Lichty and Eylin Palamaro-Munsell (2017) question if it is even ethical to ask that these be dismantled; the deeply embedded nature of these dynamics prompts the question of whether a classroom can truly claim to be liberatory, whether power can be shared and whether the concept of safe speaking, which assumes equal power and participation, can withstand scrutiny.

The confines and demands of HE present challenges, but we can create space within it. Collaborative practices between teachers and students in the classroom create a middle ground that can better challenge traditional power dynamics. Instead of seeking seamless harmony, our focus should be on equipping students with the skills for meaningful critical dialogue, even though it is a challenging task. Disagreement, critical exchange and thoughtful debate are valuable preparation for our everyday lives within and outwith academia. While these dialogues and spaces may feel uncomfortable at times, they are not necessarily dangerous. As teachers, we should recognize that the process of unlearning and discomfort can impact us personally as well. As illustrated earlier, it is important to acknowledge and address our own unsettling feelings as we navigate these conversations. The Worlding Classroom case study in Chapter 7 offers a deeper dive into many issues around how to involve communities in the development of curricula and how to navigate discomfort.

In much thinking about how to create inclusive, thought-provoking and transformative learning environments, one commonly used approach has tended to be the establishment of 'ground rules'. This approach usually involves setting out agreed-upon guidelines and expectations that govern the behaviour and interactions of students and teachers within the learning environment. Typically established collaboratively at the beginning of a course or class to foster a particular kind of learning environment, such rules are based on such notions as shared responsibility, respectful communication, attendance and punctuality, participation, appropriate use of technology, respect for diversity, collaboration, and teamwork. However, we can and should think beyond the kinds of 'rules' that fail to attend to normative assumptions that ignore interlocking oppressions within the classroom. Cynthia Hogue and colleagues (1998) suggest establishing ground rules and guiding principles for respectful listening and communication in the classroom, which acknowledge the existence of oppression in multiple forms and how the education system can sustain oppression through privilege, omission and the distortion of information. Brian Arao and Kristi Clemens (2013) propose the concept of 'brave spaces' as an alternative to traditional 'safe spaces'. Brave spaces require teachers to create conditions for students to confidently confront behaviours that perpetuate social injustice and inequalities. This approach encourages controversy with civility, reflection on the intentions and impact of words and views, challenging by choice, respect, and fostering clarifying conversations.

While these adaptations to the 'ground rules' approach are helpful, they do not provide all the answers. The notion of creating brave spaces may still maintain a focus on ensuring some level of comfort and preserving the status quo, as privilege and power are always present and active in the classroom. Lynn Verduzco-Barker (2018) raises important questions about whose bravery is privileged and recognized, and who is being asked, or is expected, to be brave. If not carefully cared for, the concept of brave spaces can become a source of misery for those expected to relive and/or speak to trauma. However, the idea of brave spaces does offer an effective starting point for productively engaging with discomfort, especially when navigating differing politics or perspectives on inequality and injustice. Verduzco-Barker suggests 'calling in' instead of 'calling out', building on activist Ngọc Loan Trần's (2016: 59) approach of 'calling in as a practice of loving each other enough to allow each other to make mistakes, a practice of loving ourselves enough to know that what we're trying to do here is a radical unlearning of everything we have been configured to believe is normal'. This involves several steps, including: repeating and restating a problematic comment; understanding the roots of a misconception, both historically and in contemporary culture; describing the harm caused; and exploring flawed assumptions underlying problematic comments (Verduzco-Baker, 2018: 589). This approach promotes a more constructive and compassionate engagement with differing viewpoints. Many activist organizations, students and scholars are doing invaluable work on building guidance for the creation of safer spaces that are critically aware of interlocking oppressions, for example, Abolitionist Futures, Sisters Uncut, the Anti-Racist Forum and the Safer Spaces Poster Project.[5] Their approaches remind us of bell hooks' advice that community cannot be built upon conflict avoidance, and that while we will not always get it right, as a collective of learners, we should keep striving for change. This means that we may sometimes fail, and there are examples of this across the book. However, failure, as much as it is part of struggle, is also part of our pedagogical practice in the classroom and beyond.

Concluding comments

This chapter has explored how we navigate the ethical landscape of teaching. It has emphasized the transformative power of discomfort and the importance of fostering critical consciousness through active empathy, which urges us to move away from passive observance and a politics of declaration towards action-oriented responses. Pedagogies of discomfort are a helpful framework for approaching the work that needs to be done. Discomfort can be a catalyst for developing critical awareness and active empathy, urging us to challenge biases, question prevailing narratives and gain a more profound comprehension of complex societal issues. Managing discomfort is an ethical concern, and the concept of doing good harm suggests that experiencing discomfort while grappling with challenging topics is necessary for disruption and transformation. Doing good harm involves engaging students in critical reflection and equipping them with the tools to become active agents of change in their communities. It does not necessarily equate to an absence of safety and is an invaluable reminder that safety does not necessarily equate to the presence of comfort. Whichever way we do good harm, it is essential to approach this with care and sensitivity, alongside our sustained commitment to social justice. Suggested teaching strategies include building brave spaces and calling in to help us do some of the work of building socially just learning spaces and communities. However, we must again be vigilant to normative assumptions, goals and pedagogical practices that claim safety, empowerment, voice and even dialogue so that they do not reproduce the 'repressive myths that perpetuate relations of domination' (Ellsworth, 1989: 298). Chapter 4 delves into the politics that also shapes the contours of this uneven and sometimes bumpy ethical terrain.

4

The Political Classroom

Introduction

Critical pedagogy foregrounds the political nature of education. Chapter 3's exploration of the ethical dimensions of discomfort in the classroom highlighted its productive role in fostering disruption and transformation, aligning with the idea of doing good harm. These ethical considerations are intertwined with political concerns, because the constant presence and messiness of politics in the world outside the classroom urges us to think critically and ethically about being political and how we engage with and practise politics within the learning setting. Today's context of increasing inequalities and cultural divisions means that we cannot afford to ignore or dismiss the place of politics in the classroom, necessitating open and searching conversations among teachers and students. Moreover, failure to do so can lead to intellectual and affective harm, as well as perpetuate epistemic injustices. Recognizing that we are not impervious to the political realities that shape our lives, world views and perspectives, it becomes clear that politics acts as a filter through which we learn and understand the world. At the same time, the current teaching context is subject to varying degrees of scrutiny and critique when it comes to the place of politics. There is an increasingly expressed sentiment in current debates that the classroom should not be a space for political discussions, most recently evidenced in the anti-critical race theory movement in US educational institutions, where syllabi and, subsequently, the academics teaching them have come under fire. This poses real challenges for teachers as they grapple with the ethical dilemma of determining the place of politics, either their own or that of their students, within the classroom. It is to these challenges that the discussion in this chapter now turns.

'Culture wars' and navigating politics beyond and within the classroom

Sivanandan (1990) reminds us that the personal is political, but the political is also personal. Politics shapes all aspects of research, teaching and learning within academia. It plays a significant role in determining the direction of research, the choice of topics to explore and even the language used to describe social phenomena. Funding bodies increasingly align their priorities with the needs of governments and businesses, directly influencing the types of research projects that receive financial support. It is worth noting here that researchers may choose to engage in unfunded research as a political decision, that is, as a form of resistance to the marketization of academia and extractive research practices (these and other questions will be explored further in Chapter 6). Politics extends into the classroom, shaping our decisions in teaching and learning, including deciding which knowledge we privilege, curriculum and content design, how we frame debates, and deciding on our limits of accommodation of, and/or resistance to, certain ideas (Macrine, 2009: 122). The politics of knowledge production also shapes whose knowledge is recognized and valued, whose perspectives and experiences are deemed authoritative, and in which situations they are allowed to be acknowledged and count. In practice, we need uncomfortable classrooms, where we are exposed to the politics of our knowledge claims and the politics of their positionalities, and where we are forced to reflect on our political agency beyond the classroom.

> **Problem posing: being political**
>
> Ask students to consider their classroom environment and pose the following problem: how do you define and interpret the concepts of 'politics' and 'being political' within this space? Encourage them to consider how these concepts relate to discussions on migration. Invite them to share their perspectives and experiences. They can do this through open dialogue, written reflections or other creative means, such as art, poetry or short narratives. How does this idea of being political resonate with personal experiences or the experiences of those you know? Encourage students to then consider how they might apply the understanding that 'the political is personal' to their participation in migration-related discussions and their interactions with others in the classroom.

Recognizing differing opinions, ideologies and experiences can be discomforting and unsettling but is vital for disruption and transformation. We must work out how we cope with conflict, especially when classroom discussions turn to increasingly prevalent claims for the legitimacy of 'all views' and when claims for 'both sides' arguments appear. Chapter 3 offered some suggestions for managing discomfort and coping with conflict without inherently accommodating views that uphold social injustices. However, it is fair to say that the rhetorical device of 'balance' and 'fairness' has become a widely used feature in many polarizing debates around 'culture wars' in political responses and in media reporting on migration matters. Increasingly in the UK, we hear about anti-immigrant views and violence as being the 'legitimate fears' of 'just ordinary people'. For example, following the racist violence in Knowsley (see Chapter 2), journalist Lewis Goodall tweeted the following on 23 February 2023 in his reporting on a racist anti-asylum protest in Rotherham: 'This isn't complicated. Are there local people with legitimate concerns about the hotel policy? Yes. Worth bearing in mind the asylum seekers don't want to be in the hotels either, but the system is backlogged. Are the far right using those concerns and spreading fear? Also, yes.' In addition, on 3 March, Conservative MP Lee Anderson said in a BBC podcast (Robinson 2023):

> When I heard that protestors, and these aren't far right extremists, they are just normal family people from some of these towns and villages and they are upset that overnight that 200 or 300 young men have arrived and they are saying things to young girls and there have been a few attacks and horrible incidents, of course people are going to be concerned, that's just human nature. At the end of the day, when you live in a community you expect to be safe, and you don't like sudden change and that's how humans behave.

So, what do we do when, for example, anti-asylum violence or the systemic racism in migration governance are considered things that *can* be debated, argued and even rationalized?

The term 'culture war' goes beyond mere disagreements and signifies a deeper conflict and struggle for dominance between seemingly irreconcilable orthodox and progressive world views. According to James Davison Hunter (1991), it describes the intense, existentially framed, binary conflict between two value systems and revolves around fundamental questions of what is considered right and wrong in our society, producing a subsequent sense of societal fragmentation. In the US, since the 1960s, 'culture wars' have often evolved around clashes between traditionalist positions seeking conservative restoration and right-wing ascendency (Macrine, 2009), and marginalized groups striving for recognition and social change. Grass-roots movements for civil rights, Black Lives Matter, feminism, abortion rights, LGBTQ+ rights and gun control have all been part of this struggle for social justice and equal rights. Huw Davies and Sheena Macrae (2023: 3) have described the British 'war on woke' as an 'intensive ideological campaign against social justice movements that is mobilising far-right tropes and conspiracy theories within mainstream British political discourse'. In the UK, the language of 'culture wars' has been used to encompass a wide range of issues since the Brexit referendum in 2016 (Benson et al, 2021: 3), and topics like lockdown measures, the removal of statues, expressions of national identity, the wearing of poppies and dietary choices have all been framed as fault lines in the 'culture wars'. The term itself often appears as a resistance to what is perceived as 'political correctness', expressed through divisive yet profoundly ideological terms, such as 'cultural Marxism', 'social justice warriors', 'woke/the wokerati', 'bleeding-heart liberals' and 'lefty do-gooders', among others, used to undermine progressive movements and dismiss concerns about social injustice. Language is very powerful here. The term 'woke', originally rooted the civil rights movement in African American responses to persecution and segregation, has been widely trivialized and misused in popular discourse, its memefication (Davies and MacRae, 2023) making it incredibly popular, if poorly understood. However, if we are to think that this is just about faddish language in the cultural apparatus, or that 'culture wars' may be easily dismissed, we need to think again. Mark Davis (2018) observes that they are a media product designed to sharpen social divides for electoral gain, and 'culture wars' discourse has become an enduring aspect of public discourse in Western societies, symbolically making what seem to be intractable differences real. Moreover, the idea of 'culture wars' often distracts from broader issues of power and economic inequality and fundamental shifts in income and wealth distribution; in the UK, government ministers regularly dismiss calls for progressive reform in key policy areas, often race and immigration related, as 'woke' to stifle debate.

Universities have always been places of ideas and debate, and the 'culture wars' play out in the sector in different ways: accusations of the dumbing down of education as a result of pedagogical perspectives that challenge traditional pedagogical approaches (West et al, 2011); scrutiny over what is taught, the materials used and the knowledges privileged and excluded; the framing of decolonization as rewriting history to fit progressive liberal agendas; and 'no-platforming' as a form of radical boycott preventing invited speakers whose views staff and/or students believe to be unacceptable or offensive. bell hooks (2003: 111) warned against the false portrayal of progressive professors 'as the culprits [who are] shutting down debate on university campuses and in school districts, and not the forces of the Right closing the door to all ways of thinking that offer an alternative to dominator culture'. Against such a backdrop, she also reminds us that as teachers we should remain the 'keepers of hope' (hooks, 1994). There are of course academics with significant public platforms who have co-opted the language of 'culture wars' to extend political ideologies and use it very effectively as evidence of education and academic freedom under threat. Davies and MacRae (2023: 3), for example, offer a forensic analysis of UK-based academics like Matthew Goodwin and Eric Kaufman, also regularly invited political and cultural commentators on various media platforms, who 'have framed wokeness as a "pseudo-religion" and placed themselves firmly as members of the "anti-woke community"'.

Teachable moment: is rising ethnic diversity a threat to the West?

In October 2018, a December panel event was announced in London under the title, 'Is rising ethnic diversity a threat to the West?'. Named panellists included writer David Aaronovitch, broadcaster Trevor Phillips, writer Claire Fox and academics Eric Kaufmann and Matthew Goodwin. The event was sponsored by UnHerd[1] (describing itself as a platform for 'bold thinking on otherwise unheard ideas') and the Academy of Ideas[2] (founded and run by Claire Fox; its website states 'we are not associated with any particular political party, but we are passionately interested in politics and taking a robust stance on contentious issues'). There was significant backlash, condemning the racist framing of the debate as mainstreaming far-right tropes and rehashing latent white supremacy ideology. A few days after the event was announced, Matthew Goodwin tweeted: 'After consideration, the title of the Dec 6 debate has been revised: "Immigration & Diversity Politics: A Challenge to Liberal Democracy?" Thanks for thoughts.' An open letter on openDemocracy was also published a few days later, signed by 230 academics, challenging the racist provocations in the original and revised title and the ideologically homogeneous composition of the panel, and expressing concern about the normalizing of far-right ideas. After the event, Koffman and Goodwin authored an article on Quillette, an alt-right website, where they claimed the name change was made as a compromise. In their article, they reiterated that the debate's title was not racist and argued that the change in title had minimal impact because the original title's logic still prevailed in the debate. They presented their case as a rational argument and criticized the effort to rename it as a damaging smear campaign, cautioning against the rise of 'anti-intellectualism' in universities.

Further reading and resources

- Victoria Sanusi, 'People are upset over an upcoming debate asking if ethnic diversity is a threat', *i*, 22 October 2018. Available at: https://inews.co.uk/news/uk/is-rising-ethnic-diversity-threat-west-debate-reaction-212005#:~:text=The%20debate%20was%20titled%20%E2%80%9CIs%20rising%20ethnic%20diversity
- Academics for Meaningful Debate, 'Framing ethnic diversity as a "threat" will normalise far-right hate, say academics', openDemocracy, 23 October 2018. Available at: www.opendemocracy.net/en/opendemocracyuk/framing-ethnic-diversity-debate-as-about-threat-legitimises-hat-0/

- Matthew Goodwin and Eric Kaufman, 'What happened when we tried to debate immigration', *Quillette*, 8 December 2018. Available at: https://quillette.com/2018/12/08/what-happened-when-we-tried-to-debate-immigration/

Activities

- Discuss together the ethical considerations surrounding the framing of academic debates. This provides an opportunity to delve into questions about the responsibility of academics, institutions and organizers in framing discussions on contentious issues, and to consider the potential implications of framing debates in ways that may perpetuate harmful stereotypes or normalize far-right ideologies.
- Critically analyse the tension between freedom of expression and the potential harm caused by certain forms of discourse. Is there a line to be drawn between academic freedom and the potential consequences of allowing harmful or racially biased discussions?
- Explore how the case study highlights the intersection of academic debate and media and public discourse. Encourage students to reflect on the tension around the politics of knowledge production in the 'political now'.

As evidenced earlier, there is a strong connection between the contemporary 'culture wars' of the 2020s and polarizing debates around immigration, borders, boundaries and belonging (Sobolewska and Ford, 2019, 2020). These issues contribute to a divisive 'us versus them' context that is pervasive not only in UK society, media and politics but also beyond. While some may argue that 'culture wars' are exaggerated or manufactured, it is worth remembering that polarized politics have always existed, though they may feel in many ways more pronounced in our contemporary moment, fuelled as they are by high-profile politicians.[3] Undoubtedly, the current 'war on woke' rhetoric feels more permissible, corrosive, destructive, increasingly prevalent and powerful, extending its reach into many aspects of society.

Giroux's (1997, 2000) concept of public pedagogy (see Chapter 1) provides an effective framework for critically engaging with 'culture wars' in several ways. First, if we recall, public pedagogy emphasizes not only the role of education and learning beyond formal educational institutions, recognizing multiple sites of literacies, but also that knowledge is produced, disseminated and contested in various public spheres, as well as the politics involved in this. Public pedagogy encompasses analysing the media, popular culture and public discourses that contribute to the construction of narratives and ideologies in 'culture wars', and it is in critically engaging with these texts and sites of knowledge that underlying power relations, dominant discourses and the ways in which 'culture wars' are framed come to be revealed. Second, the public pedagogy framework allows us to connect 'culture wars' to broader social issues by connecting cultural struggles to larger social, economic and political contexts. It can help us understand how 'culture wars' intersect with such issues as power, inequality, identity, social justice and democracy. Third, a public pedagogy encourages a critical consciousness that urges reflection on our own positions, biases and privileges while also examining the broader contemporary and historical societal and structural factors that shape 'culture wars'. Fourth, in the context of 'culture wars', public pedagogy prompts students to question whose knowledge is privileged, who gets to shape the narratives and whose voices are marginalized. Finally, a public pedagogy encourages active civic engagement as a means of challenging dominant narratives and participating in cultural and political debates. Participating in public forums, protests, community initiatives and social media activism is an important way to voice alternative perspectives and contest narratives perpetuated in 'culture wars'.

From theory to practice: calling out 'culture wars'

- Analyse media depictions: examine how migration and 'culture wars' are portrayed in various media, including news articles, opinion pieces, social media and documentaries. Identify the central messages and narratives, and discuss their influence on public opinion and policy debates.
- Work with language: list and analyse metaphors and language used in 'culture wars', as well as their impact on public perception and policy discussions regarding migration matters. Work together to deconstruct these representations, identifying rhetorical strategies, stereotypes and biases, and discussing their potential impact on public opinion.
- Incorporate personal narratives: include case studies and personal stories that shed light on individuals affected by or central to 'culture wars'. Research and share video clips, written accounts or interviews that offer first-hand experiences and emotional insights. Encourage critical thinking through open-ended questions about power dynamics, stereotypes and biases.
- Engage with primary sources: work with primary sources like policy documents, political speeches and interviews, historical texts, and legal frameworks related to migration and 'culture wars'. Analyse these sources critically, discussing the underlying values, power dynamics and policy implications they reflect, and how they are challenged.
- Foster critical media literacy: develop students' skills in critically analysing media messages and recognizing the influence of media on public discourse and its role in shaping public opinion on migration. Our biggest first step might be calling out problematic rhetorical framing in material we engage with and refusing to reproduce these in our teaching and learning.

- Encourage research and critical inquiry: assign mini-research projects that delve into 'culture wars' and migration. Students can collaboratively explore topics related to identity, belonging and national identity within the context of 'culture wars', using statistics, counter-empirics and counter-narratives to provide a comprehensive understanding.
- Connect to real-world issues: encourage students to explore the connections between 'culture wars', migration and contemporary social and political issues. Explore together how these debates intersect with other macro-, meso- and micro-level topics, such as nationalism, human rights, social justice, social inequalities, immigration legislation, health, housing, education, employment, identities, belonging, community, everyday life and experiences.
- Reflect on personal biases and values: facilitate reflective exercises, for example, thinking about where do we know from, that prompt students to examine their own biases, values and preconceptions regarding migration and 'culture wars'. Identify together ways of taking learning beyond the classroom, for example, by participating in community projects or advocacy campaigns to challenge misinformation and foster active empathy, dialogue and critical thinking in addressing these complex issues.
- Develop an ethical learning manifesto that addresses the intersection of ethics, social justice, human rights and inclusion within the 'culture wars' context: explore strategies for countering divisive narratives both inside and outwith the classroom, including how to share this manifesto (see Chapter 6).

Acknowledging the existence of 'culture wars' and their impact on the classroom allows teachers and students to critically examine power dynamics and create space for marginalized voices and perspectives. These questions and strategies offer some steps towards developing power awareness, which involves recognizing contending forces and interests, discovering how power and policymaking interact in society to produce particular narratives, identifying which groups are holding dominant control, and finally together working out scope for challenging dominant narratives.

The politics of knowledge production

The commitment to social justice in education requires confronting the politics of knowledge production and traditional hierarchies of expertise. It involves us trying harder to move away from 'knowing *from* others' towards 'knowing *with* others' and ethically producing mutually valued, relational, inter-epistemic knowledge. The discussion on anonymization in Chapter 3 is one example of how we can approach building better, socially just and politically engaged knowledge production. Remi Joseph-Salisbury and Louise Connelly's work on anti-racist scholar activism is immensely insightful to this knotty question of the politics of knowledge production. Following Sivanandan and Stuart Hall, they urge academics to work in service to social justice by 'working in service' to our communities, prioritizing their perspectives and needs, determining how research can best serve their interests, and putting research, teaching and learning to use with marginalized communities and groups as part of wider liberatory struggles (Joseph-Salisbury and Connelly, 2021: 57–9). There are clear parallels here with the indigenizing and decolonizing methodologies and pedagogies that are the focus of scholars like Caroline Lenette, Linda Tuhiwai Smith and Natalie Avalos, among others. Doing this from within the HE institution is challenging, and struggling where we are means being pragmatic, doing what is achievable, being part of a bigger movement and drawing on and repurposing the resources and capital we can access to help us enact being in, but not of, the university (Joseph-Salisbury and Connelly, 2021).

Knowledge production is a significant site of power and reproduction of inequalities, and academic standards and norms in knowledge production, including what gets published and who is cited, can perpetuate inequalities by privileging certain voices and perspectives while excluding others. The parameters of knowledge production, including who determines them (governments, policy makers, funding bodies, institutions and so on) and how positions are presented, have significant implications for both research and teaching practice. Therefore, it is crucial to critically examine where knowledge comes from (not always immediately evident in citational practice) and how knowledge can be transformed or obscured to hide its sources. These considerations should also prompt us to question the dominant forms of knowledge dissemination, such as journal articles behind paywalls, and to explore alternative platforms and creative interventions that make knowledge more accessible while maintaining rigour, clarity and precision, as this too is part of the work of struggling where we are and working in service to communities. Importantly, the knowledge generated through theoretical, empirical and methodological learning is not detached from other forms of knowledge, despite the routine tendency to create false dichotomies between academic and non-academic knowledge along false binaries of academic knowledge and 'lived experience' outside academia (Joseph-Salisbury and Connelly, 2021). These discussions align with broader debates around the exclusionary nature of academic peer-reviewed knowledge, the need to decolonize knowledge production and the questioning of what is considered 'serious knowledge'. This is often reflected in migration scholarship, where the questions of who speaks, whose voice is valued and who provides expertise come into play.

There is a last point to consider here, and it relates to the politics of access to learning spaces. It is crucial to critically examine whose politics are privileged and enacted within educational spaces, as well as who benefits from these dynamics. We work within tightly defined and deeply embedded institutional power structures and controls that place considerable constraints on how knowledge is produced. They also limit how the classroom is shaped, the scope for it to be reshaped and how we, all of us who find ourselves there, interact in those spaces and make space for others to join. Just as the 'political now' reaches back to the past, the broader societal inequalities and systemic barriers beyond the classroom reach in, shaping who can enter the classroom in the first place. Working in service to communities involves questioning those institutional power structures and barriers, and exploring where and how they may be challenged. These are inherently political concerns. How do we create a healthy, aware, critical, resourced and politically sensitive classroom environment that can be enabling, facilitating and progressive without the shackles of convention and hierarchy? Who will be in that classroom? Demanding the impossible should not stop us from dreaming the impossible (Joseph-Salisbury and Connelly, 2021). So, thinking with the 'what if', how could we go about creating 'a space of exchange where academic debates can join other ideas about what people want and how these things might be achieved' (Bhattacharyya, 2013: 1419)? And who gets to enter such spaces?

Case Study 4.1: The Asylum University

The Asylum University (AU), conceptualized by critical border studies scholars Kolar Aparna and Olivier Kramsch (2018), challenges the traditional understanding of the classroom and explores the idea of boundaries and transgressions within educational spaces. This project from the Netherlands (Radboud University) began experimentally in 2015, evolving into a ground-breaking radical liberatory initiative exploring the transformative potential of cross-border learning. The AU sought to provide opportunities for learning and dialogue with some of the 3,000 refugees residing in a refugee camp on the borders of its campus by opening its doors to them. As Aparna and Kramsch (2018: 99) explain, 'AU's modest aim is to try to keep classroom doors open, while building informal bridges between asylum centres and refugee-support organizations, alongside keeping an eye open for an opportunity to make connections with new people interested in enabling the same.' Challenging the hierarchical power dynamics often present in traditional educational institutions, it raised critical questions about the concept of borders and who has the authority to transgress them, challenging the notion of where the 'real work' of learning takes place. Based on an action-research design, the AU was an informal learning platform that brought together academics, students, volunteers, citizens, refugees and migrants, inviting refugees invited into geography lectures, thus transforming everyday processes of learning, and emphasizing the importance of dialogue and the exchange of ideas.

The AU disrupted the notion that education is limited to traditional classroom settings and that only certain individuals have the right to access knowledge. Opening the classroom and creating a patchwork of on- and off-campus spaces for learning in different ways allowed individuals to engage as thinking beings and foster new connections of sociality and solidarity, and for everyone involved to challenge the notion that certain spaces are exclusively designated for education and others for the study of marginalized groups. By sharing the learning space, students and staff become peer learners, disrupting power dynamics within the classroom and offering to everyone involved an opportunity to 'do academic work otherwise' (Aparna and Kramsch, 2018: 101). One significant aspect of the AU was the provision of certificates for course completion, endorsed by the home HE institution. These certificates held their own value, serving as oft-demanded evidence of so-called 'integration' by 'good refugees'. By offering formal recognition, the AU challenged the prevailing narratives surrounding waiting, learning and who is considered eligible to learn. The sociality and solidarity that emerged within the AU's learning spaces were not coincidental or serendipitous but the result of long-standing community and student solidarity and activism focused on challenging the marketization of universities and advocating for the rights of newly arriving refugees at the Dutch–German border (Aparna and Kramsch, 2018: 93). The AU also connected into informal networks of volunteers, activists, academics and advocacy groups who were dreaming the impossible and reimagining learning differently. By problematizing the academic–activist binary, the AU also challenged the idea that these roles are mutually exclusive.

Opening the classroom doors to refugees brought numerous challenges, including navigating surveillance controls within the institution, addressing language barriers and striving for equality of participation without weighing down individuals with constant testimonial burden. Creative solutions were found to address some of these, for instance, whisper corners were set up in classrooms for simultaneous translation and digital resources were informally circulated, reflecting the idea of reparative theft advocated by Joseph-Salisbury and Connelly (2021) in their anti-racist scholar-activist manifesto. Like decolonization and indigenization movements, reimagining the politics of the classroom not only presents possibilities but also requires individuals to both grapple with anxieties and uncertainties and confront the unsettling of core beliefs and values. The university institution often closes itself off to non-Eurocentric models of knowledge and practice, and the AU revealed that the line between campus and community can be a very thin one indeed. Questions remained about access and voice. There was some resistance from colleagues reluctant to participate in learning spaces beyond the confines of the institution; some refused to attend meetings in a city centre, as only institutional spaces were valued as appropriate sites of learning (Aparna and Kramsch, 2018). The AU produced discomfort; all participants were confronted with the structural inequalities and uneven funding contexts that shape neoliberal universities, with the segregation and othering of violent border regimes, and with the inherent instability and uncertainty faced by refugees. The experience of engaging with the AU also involved a constant state of not knowing what to expect. However, it was a process rather than an endpoint, offering an opportunity to reset and rethink how to do academic work otherwise and how to exist within the university while simultaneously challenging its limitations. The AU ultimately offered a more relational approach to politics and being political, emphasizing the importance of a full ethics of care and a commitment to social justice. It highlighted the significance of intertwining political engagement with a genuine ethical concern for well-being through the co-creation of shared learning spaces rather than simply reproducing more opportunities for the study of the migrant other.

Further reading about the Asylum University

- Paul van den Broek, 'Interview with Kolar Aparna', *Vox: Independent Magazine of Radboud University*, 17 September 2015, www.voxweb.nl/nieuws/radboud-als-echte-welcome-university

Talking points

- What does the AU reveal about how individuals are categorized in the classroom and what labels, such as 'international student', 'immigrant' or 'migrant', reveal about power dynamics? What impact do these categorizations have on educational access, opportunities and experiences?
- Who has, or should have, the authority to decide who can be present and engaged in the classroom? How do factors like social status, citizenship or institutional policies influence this determination? How do power dynamics affect the distribution and exercise of this right?

- What does the AU show about ways that structural constraints, policies and legislation contribute to excluding certain individuals from the classroom? What are the wider social, economic and political consequences of these exclusions, and how do they relate to the under-representation of specific groups?
- What does 'inclusion' mean in the AU learning context, and, more generally, how might it perpetuate hierarchies of deservedness and worth? Are there limits to inclusion within your current institutional framework, and how can it be reimagined to address systemic inequalities?
- Discuss the potential of the AU to challenge Eurocentric knowledge systems, power structures and institutional norms. What can we learn from this activism to disrupt dominant narratives and create space for a wider range of learners?
- Explore together strategies to make learning environments more inclusive and accessible. Identify obstacles to opening the classroom and the underlying reasons for these barriers. Consider the politics of breaking free of the classroom.
- Reflect on what aspects of the AU can be replicated or adapted in the classroom, considering challenges like institutional resistance, resource allocation and societal expectations. How can the classroom better serve communities, and what alternative approaches to academic work can be explored?
- Compare the radical nature of the AU to the more formally instituted 2022 initiative Radboud Welcomes Newcomers (see: www.ru.nl/english/education/exchange-phd-other/education-refugee-students-0/). In light of the previous points, how do both compare?

The emotional politics of storytelling, spectating, witnessing and holding knowledge

As explored in Chapter 3, understanding emotions as productive of social relations and hierarchies, as well as sites of power and resistance, provides a valuable framework for examining their role in the study of migration. Feelings and emotions have a substantive role in how knowledge is acquired and valued, and they can protect and reinforce entrenched ways of seeing, knowing, relating and thinking. Moreover, learning about migration in the 'political now' means that we are faced with the deeply racist and dehumanizing politics directed towards racialized migrants and refugees. These politics can evoke a range of emotions within the classroom, including anger, fury, shame and rage, as well as indifference and complacency. Drawing from Sarah Ahmed's (2014) work, the focus should be not only on defining what emotions are but also on examining what they do. By doing so, we can explore how emotions can be utilized and be politically disruptive and transformative. This is particularly evident in policy discussions surrounding migration, where there is often a stated preference for 'less hearts and more minds' in debates that seek to prioritize rational, technocratic and solution-focused rhetoric over rights-based approaches, and where emotionless narratives are privileged because they seemingly avoid discomfort and controversy in a 'this is simply about solutions' way.

Teachable moment: mass deaths as depoliticized tragedy

On 23 October 2019, 39 Vietnamese men and women were tragically discovered suffocated in a refrigerated lorry in Essex, UK. The lorry had arrived from Zeebrugge, Belgium. This devastating incident drew significant media attention and led then UK Prime Minister Boris Johnson to express, 'the whole nation and indeed the world has been shocked by this tragedy and the cruelty of the fate that has been suffered by innocent people who were hoping for a better life in this country' (Reuters 2019). Condemnation quickly turned to calls for stricter measures against the 'immoral' and 'inherently evil' people-smuggling business model to prevent future incidents, and the incident was used as a rationale for increased controls, monitoring and surveillance.

On 14 June 2023, a boat carrying approximately 750 people sank off the coast of Greece, resulting in 78 confirmed drowned at the time of writing, but clearly from images of the overcrowded boat taken by the Hellenic coast guard circulated online, many hundreds likely also drowned. According to Alarm Phone, a self-organized hotline for refugees in distress in the Mediterranean Sea, the boat was reported to authorities on 13 June, and Frontex spotted the boat the day before it sank. Nine survivors of the sinking were arrested on suspicion of people smuggling, and attention turned to the Greek Coast Guard's failure to intervene. Ylva Johannson, EU Commissioner for Home Affairs, tweeted that same day:

> Deeply affected by this deadly tragedy off the Greek coast. We have a collective moral duty to dismantle the criminal networks. The best way to ensure safety of migrants is to prevent these catastrophic journeys and invest in legal pathways. With member states and third countries, we must redouble efforts to fight these morally bankrupt smugglers.

Further reading and resources

- Imogen Dobie, 'The Essex lorry deaths are not just "tragic". They're political', *The Guardian*, 8 November 2019. Available at: www.theguardian.com/commentisfree/2019/nov/08/essex-lorry-deaths-tragic-political
- Robina Qureshi, 'Comment: Essex lorry deaths', *Positive Action in Housing*, 24 October 2019. Available at: www.paih.org/comment-essex-lorry-deaths
- Gabriella Sanchez, 'What the Essex case tells us about the current state of migrant smuggling from Europe into the UK', MPC Blog, 4 November 2019. Available at: https://blogs.eui.eu/migrationpolicycentre/essex-case-tells-us-current-state-migrant-smuggling-europe-uk/

- Alarm Phone, 'Europe's "shield": hundreds presumed to have drowned off Greece', 14 June 2023. Available at: https://alarmphone.org/en/2023/06/14/europes-shield/

Activities

Invite students to research both moments. Provide them with a blank piece of paper; ask them to map out or chart their emotional responses at corresponding moments in the stories and their politicized responses, and articulate the emotion triggered. Afterwards, invite students to discuss the factors that influenced their emotional responses and how these emotions shaped their understanding of the how mass death has come to be depoliticized through the language of securitization and international migration narratives. Consider where emotional politics go in these cases and, if absent, how we might bring them back in.

Talking points

- To what extent does framing events as 'emotional tragedies' disassociate them from the deadly politics of border governance?
- What are the politics and ethics of using emotions, particularly invoking humanitarian shock?
- What does Hannah Jones' (2021) concept of 'violent ignorance' help us understand better about power- and race-blindness in political responses to ongoing mass casualties?

Emotions are vital precisely because they help us engage in critical thought by connecting personal experiences to what we are learning. They also prompt students to critically reflect on their deeply ingrained assumptions, values, ethics and beliefs within a socio-historical context (Boler and Zembylas, 2016). Boler's concept of feeling power (see Chapter 3) not only shows us how emotions intersect with power relations but also reminds us of how emotions can be an expression of courage and resistance against oppression and subjugation. This resistance takes various forms and can be instrumental in challenging and transforming oppressive systems, with their power to motivate and mobilize us towards disruption and transformation. Resistance and refusal will be explored in different ways in Chapters 5, 6 and 7.

The practice of confessional narratives (hooks, 1994; see also Chapter 1) offers a valuable teaching approach for navigating the politics of emotions and feeling power in the classroom. This approach integrates personal stories with curriculum content, bridging the personal and the pedagogical, promoting critical and ethical thinking, connecting abstract ideas to everyday life, and teaching us to value the 'passion of experience and of remembrance' (hooks, 1994: 90). Confessional narratives foster empathy, challenge preconceptions and create a supportive learning environment where the personal is pedagogical and the pedagogical is personal. Sharing experiences through confessional narratives is a political act; it enables us to think critically about the dominant culture's values and our own affective investments. Sharing and listening to experiences can evoke a range of emotions, such as frustration, defensive anger, fear, disappointment, joy and compassion, and can lead to passionate and heated debates, revealing personal suffering and pain. Importantly, such experiences offer multiple ways of knowing that can transform pedagogical practices, and our responses really do matter. Alisha Mernick (2021) illustrates how students tap into their deep emotions to construct counter-narratives using multimedia, effectively reimagining their parents' migration stories within her high-school visual-arts classroom. Shane McCoy (2020) explores how students engage with their emotions while learning about writing composition, focusing on a specific event – the racist murder of Michael Brown in Ferguson, USA, in 2018. This emotional connection is instrumental in bringing the curriculum to life through teaching artefacts. Both examples underscore the vital role emotions play in both learning and the production of knowledge. A defining feature of any learning environment where this emotional engagement can thrive safely is the teacher's commitment to a socially just pedagogy.

If we default to closing off debate or relying solely on published stories that have gone through the filter of the researcher retelling them to turn them into 'serious knowledge', then we run the risk of erasing, silencing or obscuring personal experiences. Therefore, our aim should be to listen with awareness (Todd, 2003; Back, 2007). Confessional narratives, while upsetting established politics of knowing, can be emotionally overwhelming and produce helplessness in the face of relentless brutal immigration regimes and right-wing politics. This is a significant feature of the migration-focused classroom. Moreover, it is valuable to explore the implications of such affective investments in relation to migration teaching, and some questions that we can consider as helping us do that might be: what are the emotional experiences involved in studying the trauma of migration stories and narratives? How do our own migration stories, if we have them, impact our emotional response to studying these topics? What is the significance of the classroom in navigating these emotional experiences?

Working with alternative ways of knowing and relating is another approach to thinking about building the political classroom. Migrants are often cast in ways that not only frame them as a burden and threat to public order but also produce and reproduce dichotomies of good and bad migrants, the hierarchies that were central to the colonizing order (Gutiérrez Rodríguez, 2018), and the logics that make them consistently and continuously effective (Collins, 2022). The use of stories as testimony and of images can not only reproduce but also challenge these dominant frames. Taking again the example of Mamoudou Gassama (see Chapter 3), his counter-story was a confrontation with the national French story of *liberté, fraternité, egalité*. And as we saw with Mariama and Mohammed (also Chapter 3), counter-stories and narratives are not only testimony but also knowledge, and if we move towards this framing of personal stories, it provides a way to think about beginning to redress the politics of knowledge production. Migrant stories are about those who have been displaced, misplaced, replaced and strangely placed (Dhar, 2021). They help us highlight complexity, link the 'political now' to the past and provide a way to also politically work with the cognitive and emotional labour involved in understanding migration. The disruptive pedagogy of storytelling means that we can position lived, and live, experiences of oppression as valuable to interrupting the learning process and helps us build better migration literacies (see Chapter 5). It is also part of the broader repertoire of creative methodologies and decolonizing principles that confront the politics of learning (Moses, 2022; Ochoa, 2022). This is about resistance, reclaiming stories as a political act and pedagogical device. Working with counter-stories and first-hand accounts helps us avoid over-abstraction and provokes us to rethink the tension and relationship between narrative as testimony and serious knowledge. We are also challenged in not just what we listen to but how deeply and carefully, and with how much attention we do this listening and retelling (Todd, 2003; Back, 2007). For many teachers and students, testimony as knowledge will be a novel way to frame ways of knowing and relating that can have a transformative power for students.

From theory to practice: working with stories

A central aim of this exercise is for the students to try to critically engage with multidirectional and interlocking processes of migrantization, racialization, identification and categorization through stories people tell themselves about their lived and live experiences. A suggested entry point is Chimamanda Ngozi Adichie's 2009 TedX talk, 'The danger of the single story', where she explores how her own ideas shape her world view, potentially limiting her understanding of herself and others (see: www.ted.com/talks/chimamanda_adichie_the_danger_of_a_single_story?language=en). Ask students to consider:

- What does Chimamanda Ngozi Adichie mean by the single story?
- Can we relate to what she has to say?
- Why do certain stories have traction?
- Do you think 'the single story' contributes to the perpetuation of inequalities in society? In what ways?

Turning now to migration, work with a wider range of multifaceted migrant stories in various formats that offer alternative narratives. What follows are some examples to get started:

- Migrant stories available at: www.globalcitizen.org/en/content/migrant-first-person-stories-undp/
- Further migrant stories available at: www.theguardian.com/uk-news/2014/jul/09/six-real-life-stories-of-migration
- A documentary series available at: www.bbc.co.uk/programmes/p07bm41g
- A documentary on African migration from Europe to China titled 'Zwart Geld – black money'. Available at: www.youtube.com/watch?v=fsnY1EUbO8M&t=146s
- An exhibition titled 'Migrant workers: the raspberry planter'. Available at: https://merl.reading.ac.uk/explore/online-exhibitions/migrant-workers-the-raspberry-planter/
- An exhibition titled 'Summer on a strawberry farm'. Available at: https://merl.reading.ac.uk/explore/online-exhibitions/migrant-workers-summer-on-a-strawberry-farm/
- The Joint Council for the Welfare of Immigrants and Movement Against Xenophobia's 2015 poster campaign titled 'I am an immigrant', which aimed to confront prevailing narratives and recast immigration as a reflection of immigrants' contributions to society. Available at: https://newsframes.globalvoices.org/2018/03/30/brexit-and-bias-the-framing-of-immigrants-in-the-media/
- Maryhill Integration Network, a community organization supporting people seeking asylum and refugees with settlement and advocacy work on rights-based issues, has a range of resources available at: https://maryhillintegration.org.uk/films/
- Al Jazeera's mini-film on anti-black racism in Tunisia titled 'Are Black people welcome in Tunisia?', in particular, Khawla Ksiksi, Tunisian activist, lawyer and co-founder of Black Tunisian Women, discussing the lived and live experience of anti-black racism from an intersectional perspective. Available at: www.youtube.com/watch?v=QvfLWj9sH9g&t=62s
- Poet, writer and activist Suhaiymah Manzoor-Khan's 'This is not a humanising poem' (which could also be watched alongside the story of Mamoudou Gassama, see Chapter 3). Available at: https://youtu.be/SbLBJPdKkYk

Suggested activities

- Divide students into small groups and provide them with examples of narratives about migrants from various sources (for example, from media, literature, documentaries and so on). Ask each group to identify and deconstruct the single story narratives present in these sources. Discuss how these narratives are perpetuated and the potential consequences.
- Where students feel comfortable, invite them to share their own migration stories or those of their family members, considering how these stories relate to dominant narratives. Have a reflective discussion on how personal stories can challenge or reinforce prevailing narratives about migrants.
- Create a digital platform or classroom session where students can share diverse migrant experiences, whether their own or those they have encountered. Discuss the importance of such platforms for sharing and hearing these experiences.

- In pairs, invite students to take turns sharing personal stories related to migration. Consider together the affective impact of this dialogue, why emotions matter and what work they do. This exercise can serve as an act of epistemic justice and political engagement by allowing students to speak and be listened to.
- Engage in group discussions where students reflect on what they are unlearning through the process of exploring these narratives. Encourage them to identify biases, stereotypes or preconceived notions that have been challenged, including where we too fall into the trap of reproducing one-dimensional stories.

Narratives take many forms, and music offers novel ways to engage with the 'political now' as located firmly in the past. An excellent case example is the 2021 Hamilton Mix Tape.

Case Study 4.2: 'Immigrants, we get the job done'

Performed by rappers K'naan, Snow tha Product, Riz MC and Residente, inspired by Yorktown (The World Turned Upside Down) from the musical Hamilton, and reworked, 'Immigrants, we get the job done' is a multilingual rap performed on a moving train that tells the in/visible immigrant story in the US (see: www.youtube.com/watch?v=6_35a7sn6ds). The full lyrics can be found online, and there are many ways to use this material in the social justice classroom.

Talking points and activities

- Explore and analyse the various narratives, including the storytellers, their methods and lyrics, and the research stories within them.
- Examine the train metaphor portraying the immigrant story from diverse global perspectives and as a symbol of mobility, rapid change and transitions. Different carriages represent distinct stories, sometimes overlapping and intersecting like biographies and histories.
- Discuss the flag metaphor, particularly in the context of the US flag appearing in a sweatshop segment. Explore the role of pledging allegiance in US institutional life, alongside the hiddenness of its makers in the video.
- Explore racialization processes and how individuals are identified based on various markers. Consider the effectiveness of these markers in connecting with the audience and its message.
- Analyse the use of multilingualism, linguistic hybridity and their representation in the performance. Reflect on our experience as listeners when we switch the subtitles on and off.

- Identify various livelihoods represented, such as seasonal fruit picking, sweatshops, construction, healthcare and labour, and examine their connection to racialized capitalism.
- Examine the use of spectacle and events in the video, including war, fence building and Immigration and Customs Enforcement (ICE) raids, and their role in shaping specific narratives.
- Discuss the intended audience and goals of the video, and evaluate its success in achieving these objectives. Consider how these elements collectively reveal processes of migrantization, racialization, identification and categorization, their influence, and their consequences.

A final part of this puzzle of the politics of storytelling is how we move from passively consuming stories to something more. The constant exposure to dehumanizing images and stories of lives at risk can be distressing. Students often question how to cope with these stories in these turbulent times, and so a final feature to explore here is the shift from spectating to witnessing as a political act in the classroom. There are different ways of thinking with these questions around absorbing and acting on information and coping with being overwhelmed. Hannah Jones' concept of 'violent ignorance' is immensely valuable in acknowledging, naming and confronting the desensitization that occurs when we choose to look away from painful knowledge. In this way, she shows us that 'by ignoring violence, we become implicated in that violence continuing' (Jones, 2021: ix). Giroux's (2020: 201) concept of 'manufactured illiteracy', as explored in Chapter 1, provides another helpful analytic frame and refers to the deliberate process by which individuals and institutions are conditioned by the cultural apparatus to be passive, apathetic and disconnected from political and social issues. Boler's (1999) concept of witnessing, as discussed in Chapter 3, urges us to go beyond either turning away from or being mere spectators of the experiences of migrants and refugees, consuming images, narrative or events without taking active responsibility or considering our own implication in the issues at hand. Instead, as witnesses, we recognize the political and ethical consequences of how we see and interpret the world, as well as the potential impact our perspectives and actions may have on others. We also critically engage with the historical, social and political factors that shape ways of knowing and relating. The position of knowledge holding proposed earlier offers a further helpful lens, where we can avoid the pitfalls of over-reliance on the tragic victim frame through recognition of live experience as productive of knowledge and a form of epistemic justice.

Exploring violent ignorance and manufactured illiteracy politically and pedagogically as witnesses and knowledge holders helps us understand how turning a blind eye to certain issues is a form of passive violence. Thinking along these terms also helps us better understand that the 'political now' is not unprecedented, and doing this work reveals the politics embedded in both everyday life and social structures. This then exposes the unsettling emotions that arise when engaging with different perspectives and multiple standpoints, and challenges the notion of neutrality and objectivity, as the ways these ideas around knowing are intertwined with existing power structures comes to be revealed. Exploring ignorance through the lens of emotions in the political classroom and shifting from spectating towards witnessing help us move from 'what is' to 'what if' and lay the foundations for a politics of hope.

Teachable moment: spectating from the English Channel and the politics of knowing

On 10 August 2020, a BBC reporter reports on small boat crossings live from the English Channel, tracking an overcrowded dinghy. The reporter tells us: 'The sea is choppy ... It's pretty overloaded there, they're using a plastic container to try to bail out the boat, so obviously is pretty overloaded, and it's pretty dangerous.' He gets closer and shouts: 'Are you okay? Are you alright? Where are you from?' They reply: 'Syria.' He then tells us: 'They say they are from Syria.' He goes on to ask (switching between the people and us the viewer): 'How many people? ... They say they are okay; there are some women but majority men. Where are you going? ... their destination is Dover, obviously; it seems to be safe at the moment. We will shadow it and see how the situation develops' (see: https://twitter.com/BBCBreakfast/status/1292706269774651392?s=20).

On 11 August 2020, a Sky News reporter also reports live from the English Channel as they approach a dinghy with about ten people on board. The reporter shouts: 'Hello, are you okay?' Waving at the people on the dinghy, she gives a thumbs up. She then asks: 'Where are you coming from?' They shout back: 'Iran. Afghanistan. Please don't film us.' The Sky News team then let the dinghy drift past, letting us, the viewer, know, 'We are getting closer to the white cliffs of Dover; we will obviously stay with the boat to make sure it gets safely to shore', then commenting on 'how unsettling it is to see "migrant boats" up close' (see: https://twitter.com/SkyNews/status/1293102560438607872?s=20). When this reporting aired, it was condemned as voyeurism, treacherous, exploitative, inhumane, unethical, a blood sport and even snuff-film journalism. Like some grotesque reality game show, these live reports pull us into the border spectacle as passive spectators. We are left asking: how could people see this unfold before them, and why did they not help?

Activities

Show the video clips from both the BBC and Sky News reporters in class. Divide students into groups, and provide them with a set of guiding questions, such as: how is the situation portrayed in each report? What emotions and ethical considerations are elicited by the reporters' actions and words? How do these reports affect the viewers' perceptions of the migrants' journey? Encourage group discussions, and later have groups share their findings with the class.

Challenge students to generate ideas together and design a responsible reporting guide or code of ethics for journalists covering migration-related stories to ensure humane and ethical reporting. Discuss these guidelines as a class, and reflect on their potential impact for knowledge production.

Reflective task

As teachers, it is vital that we take steps to prevent inadvertently perpetuating voyeurism while critically examining it. We should constantly scrutinize our decision-making processes for selecting teaching materials. But how can we involve others in these decisions? Is there guidance we can draw on? These concerns are central to my practice, and I most often (re)turn to resources like the RISE Australia (2015) manifesto, '10 things you need to consider if you are an artist – not of the refugee and asylum seeker community – looking to work with our community', and the Refugee Hosts-run ProTestimony website (available at: www.refugeehistory.org/blog/2017/8/23/protestimony) to guide my choices. Both resources tackle challenging questions about participation, voyeurism, testimonial injustice, representation politics, dignity and respect, and a more extensive discussion of these resources can be found in Chapters 6 and 7.

Talking points

- To what extent does this reporting and visual representation of migration reveal characteristics of violent ignorance, including sensationalism, dehumanization and the perpetuation of simplistic 'crisis' and securitization narratives?
- Are there circumstances when controversial photographs and reporting should be excluded from reporting and dissemination, including in our classrooms? And are there cases when they should be included?
- What insights about the politics of spectating and witnessing emerge from this teachable moment? How do these dynamics shape our understanding of migration and ways of knowing and relating?
- When we shift our focus from the spectacle itself to the reporters engaged in spectating, what does it reveal about processes of migrantization and racialization?

The reporting and visual representation of migration can indeed be seen as a form of violent ignorance. The selective use of images that focus solely on 'crisis' and sensationalize the suffering of migrants perpetuates racist stereotypes and dehumanizes them. This type of reporting generally overlooks the underlying structural factors and systemic injustices that contribute to people feeling compelled to undertake a dangerous passage, reducing the issue to oversimplistic narratives. The repeated display of certain images in the media not only creates but also fuels a politicized spectacle of the border, capturing dramatic moments that evoke emotional responses from viewers. However, these images also shape depoliticized understandings and perceptions of migration, influencing public opinion and policy debates. It is therefore crucial to critically analyse the ethical and political implications of using such visuals that may contribute to the voyeuristic consumption of suffering, the objectification of migrants and the reinforcement of stereotypes. Engaging with the complexities of migration requires moving beyond the spectacle and actively seeking diverse narratives, challenging dominant representations and amplifying the voices of migrants themselves, and this can be our first step as witnesses towards better listening to, and learning from, people as knowledge holders.

From theory to practice: resources and activities for engaging with the politics of knowing

The Migration Museum (see: www.migrationmuseum.org) explores the movement of people to and from Britain. It is part of a broader project to build a permanent Migration Museum to capture this history of movement across the ages. The online website curates multiple resources in various formats. Encourage students to explore the 'poetry of migration' section. Have students select a poem or story that resonates with them and analyse the narrative's construction. Prompt students to critically examine how the narrative portrays migration, identity and cultural diversity. Discuss how these narratives challenge dominant knowledge production related to migration.

This Associated Press mini-documentary 'Adrift' provides an investigative report into how a boat drifted from West Africa across the Atlantic to be found off the coast of Tobago (see: https://apnews.com/article/adrift-investigation-migrants-mauritania-tobago-documentary-002537539099). Inside were the decomposing bodies of more than a dozen Black men; no one knew where they were from or what brought them there. The two-year investigation includes interviews with relatives and friends, officials, and forensic experts, as well as police documents and DNA testing. It found that 43 young men from Mauritania, Mali, Senegal and possibly other West African nations had boarded the boat; only some of them have since been identified, but many remain unknown. Watch the documentary and discuss the impact of storytelling and investigative reporting on our (public) understanding of migration politics. Encourage critical thinking about how knowledge is produced and presented in the media, and what shifts when knowledge is learned through multiple voices.

Forensic Architecture is a research agency located at Goldsmiths University that conducts investigations into human rights violations (see: https://forensic-architecture.org/category/migration). These encompass acts of violence perpetrated by states, police forces, militaries and corporations. Forensic Architecture collaborates with various organizations within civil society, including grass-roots activists, legal teams, international non-governmental organizations (NGOs) and media organizations, undertaking investigations on behalf of communities and individuals impacted by conflicts, police brutality, border regimes and environmental violence. Ask students to read and analyse the case study, considering the ways in which data, evidence and narratives are used to document violations. Encourage students to discuss the role of organizations like Forensic Architecture in challenging official knowledge production and holding power structures accountable.

Refugees Deeply is an independent platform for journalism and community engagement in matters concerning refugees and migration worldwide (see: https://deeply.the newhumanitarian.org/refugees). It combines investigative reporting with compelling storytelling and uses collaborative methods to create an online space for learning and sharing knowledge. Challenge students to work collaboratively to create their own multimedia storytelling project about migration issues. They can use resources from Refugees Deeply for inspiration. This project could include written narratives, visual elements and interactive components. The goal is to encourage students to actively engage in knowledge production and storytelling that challenges mainstream narratives.

This chapter closes with suggested approaches and prompts that invite reflection on emotional dimensions and challenges in teaching migration when engaging with racialized and dehumanizing politics. These approaches highlight the need to address affect in the classroom and explore how discomfort, rage, apathy and empathy can be harnessed for political engagement. The prompts also emphasize the ethical and political responsibility we share in the classroom.

From theory to practice: feeling through the politics of emotions

- Moving beyond the headlines: consider strategies for moving beyond superficial understandings and media narratives to develop a nuanced and critical understanding of migration and its political implications. Reflect on how to encourage students to engage with deeper complexities and challenge simplistic narratives.
- Addressing affect: explore ways to acknowledge and address the range of emotions that emerge in the classroom when discussing migration and related issues. What pedagogical approaches can facilitate constructive discussions recognizing the politics of emotions?
- Harnessing discomfort: consider how discomfort can be productive in the political classroom. How can we encourage students to acknowledge and critically engage with discomfort for it to develop into transformative learning experiences?

- Channelling rage at injustice: consider appropriate approaches to channelling students' rage and anger towards injustice into meaningful action. What examples of activism and social movements can we learn from each other to inspire and guide us?
- Piercing apathy: explore strategies to overcome apathy and disengagement when discussing migration and related issues. How can we create a sense of urgency and foster a commitment to social justice? What pedagogical techniques can help students develop a sense of agency and empower them to take meaningful action?
- Developing politicized empathy: reflect on an understanding of empathy that is informed by political consciousness. How can empathy be cultivated in the classroom while recognizing power dynamics and structural inequalities? What educational practices and resources can help students develop active empathy?

Concluding comments

Our lives, world views and perspectives are shaped by the political realities that surround us, and politics acts as a lens through which we perceive and comprehend the world. Putting to one side scrutiny and debate over whether politics should be included and discussed in the classroom, this chapter has explored various aspects of the politics involved in the teaching of migration, including the 'culture wars' creep into the classroom and the political imperatives that have a firm grip on migration discourse that influence the attention we give to certain political issues while ignoring others. Through the example of the AU, we explored alternative ways to do the politics of migration in the classroom as interruptive and disruptive of the politics of inclusion and access, and of the university as a space of learning *with* and not limited to learning *about*. Politics is emotional and emotions are political. As teachers, we bear an ethical and political responsibility to support our students and each other as we collectively navigate the emotional entanglements, investments and consequences of learning about migration. This chapter has suggested different pedagogical devices to resist dominant narratives by working with alternative narratives, confronting ignorance and manufactured illiteracy through counter-stories and counter-empirics, shifting from being spectators to witnesses, and recognizing knowledge holders as knowledge producers. Chapter 5 turns to what we need to help us ethically and politically navigate learning about migration in the 'political now'. It suggests that the conceptualization of building better migration literacies is central to ensuring that we cannot claim ignorance or turn away from what we know and to equipping us with the pedagogical tools to do the work of disruption so we hopefully feel less helpless.

5

Migration Literacies

Introduction

Thus far, *Developing a Critical Pedagogy of Migration* has explored the value of critical pedagogy in making power visible by questioning assumptions about knowledge, examining the past to comprehend the present and placing ethical and political consequences at the centre of critical discussions and debates about migration across various domains and spaces. Introduced in Chapter 1, critical literacy provides a way to begin dismantling deep-seated assumptions of knowledge and to transform pedagogical practices that may often perpetuate oppression and exclusion (Muller and Bryan, 2020: 34). Language and word choice play a pivotal role in developing critical literacies and shaping our understanding of migration. In this chapter, we delve deeper into the concept of 'migration literacies' as a pedagogical device to better understand not only the language of governance structures but also how this comes to semantically organize and structure dominant migration knowledge in research and teaching. Building better migration literacies aims to disrupt and transform migration-related knowledge production by exploring how state thinking shapes so much of what we know and how we talk about migration, revealing not only the power-blind logic of the omission of certain politics of migration governance, but also the intricate interconnections and intersections between the historical and contemporary 'mechanisms of human disqualification' that perpetuate the disposability of certain individuals over time (Dhar, 2021: 65).

Migration literacies

There is a growing body of knowledge that highlights the importance of critical literacy and critical media literacy in how we talk about and absorb information about migration-related issues, particularly in relation to the portrayal of refugees and migrants (see Philo et al, 2013; Crawley et al, 2016; Crawley and Skleparis, 2018; Czymara and van Klingeren, 2022).[1]

As explored in Chapter 1, critical literacy refers to the ability to critically analyse and interpret texts, including written, visual or spoken forms of communication. It involves questioning and challenging the underlying assumptions, biases and power dynamics contained within, and it encourages us to consider multiple perspectives, evaluate evidence and engage in reflective and critical thinking. Critical media literacy, on the other hand, has a more specific focus on the analysis of media messages, including news articles, advertisements, television programmes, films, social media and other forms of media content, and involves understanding how the media constructs meaning, influences public opinion and shapes our understanding of the world (Kellner and Share, 2007; Funk et al, 2016; Share et al, 2019). Critical media literacy emphasizes the ability to deconstruct media messages, identify media techniques and biases, and evaluate the credibility and reliability of sources. It also encompasses the understanding of media production and the impact of media on society. Al-Jazeera's decision in 2015 to no longer use the term 'migrant' in its coverage of the humanitarian crisis is an example of media training the lens of critical literacy on itself. Both critical literacy and critical media literacy are directly implicated in critical pedagogy approaches – for example, Giroux emphasizes the role of the cultural apparatus in his public pedagogy (see Chapter 1) – and both involve posing questions about systemic and structural issues of power, hierarchies of oppression and social injustice.

As many of the examples and cases in *Developing a Critical Pedagogy of Migration* have already explored, when it comes to media reporting about migration issues, the 'political now', with its increasingly dangerous xenophobia, polarizing debates and 'culture wars'-type framings, means that we need critical literacy and critical media literacy more than ever. As an example, the language used in media reporting on Ukrainian refugees since the Russian invasion in February 2022 reveals a persistent narrative of racialized othering. When Russia invaded Ukraine, reporting tended to focus on geographic and ethnic similarities, depicting Ukrainians and 'Europeans' as culturally similar, with references to physical attributes like 'blonde hair and blue eyes', emphasizing their geographic, cultural and physical proximity as Europeans. However, two contemporary comparisons unsettle these claims. First, proximity only applies to certain cases. As Leila Hadj Abou and colleagues (2022) point out, Italy is closer to Tunisia and Libya than it is to Ukraine, but arrivals from these countries in Italy were met with a far less welcoming response from across Europe. Second, in April 2023, the widely reported UK government evacuations of British citizens from Sudan following intense clashes between Sudan's military and the country's main paramilitary force showed predominantly people of colour boarding evacuation planes. No mention was made about physical or cultural proximity, despite the (also unacknowledged) deep colonial histories between

Britain and Sudan. These examples prompt us to consider questions about who is framed as most deserving and how colonial ties or European ties are selectively emphasized or evoked in migration debates. Critical media literacy offers some answers to understanding what is happening, and racial literacy offers more.

With its roots in critical race theory, Lani Guinier (2004: 110) defines racial literacy as a 'tool of diagnosis, feedback, and assessment' that provides us with 'the capacity to decipher the durable racial grammar that structures racialized hierarchies and frames the narratives' deeply embedded in nation states. Racial literacy signals a deep awareness and attentiveness to the ways that racialized hierarchies mirror the distribution of power and resources in the society more generally. Debbie Bargallie and Alana Lentin (2020) argue that race is fundamentally a political project, serving as a technology of rule that is crucial for upholding and reproducing the status quo. In racially literate teaching, it is therefore essential to grasp the histories of racialization as conceptualized by those whose lives are impacted by the oppressive and exploitative practices associated with racial rule that underpin racialization (Bargallie et al, 2023: 2). By centring the experiences and knowledge of those most affected by racial rule, teachers can foster anti-oppressive pedagogies.

> **Problem posing: racial literacy**
>
> Begin by posing this problem: what is racial literacy? How do we become racially literate? Ask students to write down their attempts at definitions, reading aloud reflections to each other in small groups before sharing their analysis with the wider class one at a time for discussion. Can they connect racial literacy to everyday lives? Do they see themselves as in need of better racial literacies? What does racial literacy reveal about power? Student notes are a great basis for class discussion about possible action; can students identify strategies for developing racial literacy in smaller groups and together as a class? You can also revisit their reflections at the end of your class or course and ask what is clearer about racial literacy and what remains unanswered.

Racial literacy should not be reduced to the co-option, commodification or depoliticization of cultural awareness that has come to characterize certain post-Black Lives Matter initiatives and generic equality, diversity and inclusion (EDI) programmes and awareness trainings. Abolitionist scholar-activists Bettina Love and Deena Simmons describe EDI as a form of 'management of inequalities' that should be rejected when it fails to confront systemic racism. Racial illiteracy, they argue, cannot be addressed solely through allyship, EDI training or difficult conversations that target individual ignorance or individual and interpersonal dynamics, or that overlook the deep-rooted racism originating from slavery and colonialism.[2] From a pedagogical standpoint, racial literacy involves anti-racist practices that enable students to become racially literate in various forms of racial representation. It equips them with the skills to navigate and challenge the complex dynamics of race in society, and to develop a deep understanding of, and engagement with, structural inequalities. Eduardo Bonilla-Silva's (2012) concept of racial grammar is instructive; he describes this as 'akin to a grammar that structures cognition, vision, and even feelings on all sort of racial matters. This grammar normalizes the standards of white supremacy as the standards for all sort of social events and transactions' (Bonilla-Silva, 2012: 173). Racial grammar is not only transactional and communicative but also dynamic, adapting to the current context. It emphasizes that the invisible structures and practices associated with white supremacy are just as influential as the visible aspects. These structures also shape discursive practices about migration and are, paradoxically, particularly visible in the absence of 'race-talk', colonial histories and imperial legacies that shape migration governance, as explored in Chapter 2.

Building on the concept of racial literacy, *Developing a Critical Pedagogy of Migration* argues that we need 'migration literacies'. Building migration literacies should help us to uncover the invisible grammar underpinning the semantic organization of deeply embedded racial, colonial and governance histories that have come to influence the field and structure all sorts of migration matters in different ways. For example, by developing migration literacies, we can enhance our understanding of migration as a phenomenon intricately connected to governance and deeply rooted in colonialism (Mayblin and Turner, 2021; Scheel and Tazzioli, 2022) and coloniality (Quijano, 2000). As introduced in Chapter 2, coloniality is understood as the haunting effects of Britain's and the West's unresolved colonial past in the present. It is an 'ongoing cultural structure that reinforces the idea that the West is identified with civilization and that whatever is outside of it is barbarism' (Fregoso Bailon and De Lissovoy, 2019: 359). This legacy means that coloniality pervades our lives as learners, influencing the books we read, our research practices, the cultural structures around us and our built environments, as well as our common sense and our perceptions of ourselves and others (Maldonado-Torres, 2007; Kumashiro, 2009). By cultivating migration literacies, we actively engage with and challenge these enduring colonial legacies in our knowledge production and everyday lives, making it a crucial aspect of a critical pedagogy of migration (Collins, 2022; Piccoli et al, 2023).

Another reason we need better migration literacies is because disciplinary grammar plays a vital role in the adoption, uncritical or otherwise, of official categories and discourses in migration studies, as suggested by Abdelmalek

Sayad's (2004) notion of 'state thinking'. The categories that dominate migration research and policy work often reveal the very coloniality that sustains the ordering and stratification of racialized migrants (Bakewell, 2008). By developing better migration literacies, we enhance our ability to recognize and question the power dynamics and resource distribution that these narratives often obscure within societies. By revealing this invisible grammar, we also open up the possibility of new categories. This work is crucial to avoid reproducing the 'international migration narratives' (IMNs) that Antoine Pécoud (2015: 3–4) defines as 'the growing corpus of international reports and publications on migration, by IOs (International Organisations) and other international entities' that have proliferated since 2000 and that aim to 'produce a global and consensual discourse on a topic that is the object of bitter disagreements'. IMNs have evolved to encompass a fairly stable set of core arguments around a problem–solution framing (Wee et al, 2018). They are effective because while claiming neutrality and objectivity, effectively depoliticizing debate, they perpetuate harmful assumptions and colonial practices. IMNs also remain immune to critique, and as such come to be invisibilized, due to their supposed evidence-based foundation. Depoliticization occurs because of the 'rhetorical strategies employed by various social actors to either open up or close down the appearance of an issue as being political' (Wood, 2016: 524) and thus extends into the realm beyond the state. Depoliticized IMNs surround us in the cultural apparatus in multiple, problematic ways to the extent that they have entered everyday language. They have also been co-opted in the humanitarian sector and in the world of migrant advocacy work. Through critical engagement with these narratives in our teaching and research, we can work harder to render them visible, prevent them from acquiring self-evident meaning, and avoid complicity in perpetuating the processes of migrantization and racialization we seek to reveal and dismantle. This is what Paulo Cuttitta (2018: 4) calls repoliticizing work: 'revealing and reviving the political (that is the plural and conflictual) character of politics'. Building better migration literacies is one way to do this work through critical awareness of migration governance as a semantic organizing framework that reproduces the status quo.

A further reason we need better migration literacies is because they connect to the everyday experiences of migration and the concepts and ideas we use to describe them. How we talk about migration in teaching and learning often means that we draw from a catalogue of highly mobile, and often de-racialized tropes that have been used for decades to mark out communities of colour in everyday contexts, as well as in political debate that fuels the immigrant imaginary (Sian, 2022). The ways we describe, discuss and analyse social phenomena (labelling them as 'crises'), populations ('migrants', 'refugees', 'expatriates', 'indigenous', 'second generation' and so on), settlement experiences ('integration', 'assimilation', 'absorption', 'segregation', 'host societies' and so on) and their effects ('inclusion', 'exclusion', 'belonging' and so on) are all influenced by historical, cultural, political and economic factors. However, the prevailing grammar of migration, much like racial grammar, renders invisible underlying assumptions and power dynamics. Better migration literacies expose the normalization effects of the immigrant imaginary and the semantic institutionalization of international migration narratives in all aspects of our lives.

A final reason we need to be building better migration literacies is because doing so is an act of refusal and resistance. It calls for challenging default perspectives and acknowledging the potential dangers of uncritical learning. Developing robust migration literacies opens transformative opportunities to critically examine and reshape how we talk about migration, as has been the intended focus of the problem posing and reflective tasks, topic-based and reflective case studies, teaching activities, and talking points in this book so far. We can do this refusal work by locating colonial ties, revealing coloniality and naming relations of power. We can do this by refusing the default tropes that make us complicit in advancing the norms of migration management through the subtle reproduction of colonial knowledge. We can do this by insisting on clear and conceptually precise language that enables critical engagement with these narratives and their perpetuation of inequalities. We can do this refusal and resistance work by identifying alternative categories and by shifting our focus from 'what is' to exploring 'what if' scenarios.

Reflective task

Reflect on your teaching practice and learning context, and consider how adopting different strategies might bring about transformation. What might happen to your pedagogic practice if you:

- Explore an approach to teaching migration that deviates from serving state interests and, instead, seeks to challenge normative frameworks and problematic world views.
- Embrace a stance of refusal and resistance against perpetuating categorization processes rooted in colonialism, and actively seek alternative vocabularies to facilitate discussions on migration.
- Actively incorporate a migration grammar that challenges dominant governance and disciplinary orientations while critically examining their impact on our classrooms.

Developing better migration literacies serves as a valuable tool for disrupting prevailing depoliticized tropes, fostering the creation of new vocabularies that repoliticize how we talk about migration and that centre ethics and politics. It enables the establishment of socially just classrooms that amplify counter-stories and counter-empirics, challenge dominant narratives, and feel radical enough to suggest new ways of talking about migration. How might we go about this work? The remainder of this chapter explores practical approaches for building a pedagogical toolbox to cultivate better migration literacies, ultimately helping us to avoid not only seeing and thinking like the state, but also teaching like the state.

Using migration literacies to problem-pose colonial idioms in migration governance

> **Problem posing: migration management**
>
> Begin posing this problem: what does migration management mean? Who are the main actors? Who is considered as needing to be 'managed'? Can migration ever be fully 'managed'? What are the limitations of attempting to control the movement of people? These questions set the baseline for unpicking foundational understandings of the concept of management and how it relates to migration. Divide students into small groups, and assign each one of the following questions:
>
> - Who holds responsibility for managing migration? Is it solely the domain of nation states, or do international organizations and civil society also play a significant role?
> - What are the underlying motivations and interests of governments, international bodies and other stakeholders in managing migration? How do these interests impact policies?
> - What ethical considerations come into play when managing migration? How do human rights and humanitarian concerns intersect with migration management?
> - How does the public perception of migration management impact policies and decisions? Are there disparities between public opinion and government actions?
>
> Engage in a class-wide discussion to compare the insights from different groups. Encourage students to identify common themes, conflicting ideas and complexities related to migration management discourse and migration literacies. Challenge students to come up with new ideas and propose actions or initiatives they can take to address specific challenges they have identified, such as advocacy for policy changes, awareness campaigns or community engagement.

'Migration management', 'managed migration' and 'migration governance' are terms used by a wide range of state and non-governmental actors that have entered the language of research and teaching, even though, as

Martin Geiger and Antoine Pécoud (2010) suggest, what we are referring to is perhaps less clear. Global migration governance refers to how states' responses to international migration are shaped and regulated through norms and organizational structures. Migration management encompasses a wide range of governmental initiatives relating to the cross-border movement of people.

The term 'management' in the context of migration implies a technocratic approach to solve a neutral organizational problem. Such rhetoric focuses on efficiency, performance and achieving goals, optimizing outcomes, and making recommendations for best practices. In this way, it appears politically neutral, reducing migration and humanitarian matters to technocratic matters despite doing deeply politicized work (Vanyoro et al, 2019). Migration management is also selectively applied to certain racialized migrant populations, aiming to monitor, control, order and contain their movements. We can see the coloniality of contemporary migration governance again here: far from being benign, today's racialized migration control practices were fine-tuned in the colonial era in attempts to constrain mobility pre- and post-independence (Sadiq and Tsourapas, 2021; Bradley, 2023), leading directly to the emergence and continuance of state migration management policies today (see Chapter 2). The concept of 'imagined spatiality', as proposed by William Walters (Geiger and Pécoud, 2010: 10), is a significant aspect of migration governance. It perpetuates the colonial logic of migration governance, as it frames irregular migration as an external 'problem' to receiving states. This perspective overlooks the internal factors that drive people's movement, such as the demand for cheap labour and punitive detention regimes. Segmented migration management, which categorizes migrant populations in Western contexts, perpetuates colonial tropes of selection, facilitation and constraint in migration governance. These approaches prioritize and favour certain populations or movements while regulating, surveilling and excluding others. Moreover, the language of governance and management, with its technocratic rhetoric, further obscures the role of migration management policies in migrant deaths and fails to acknowledge the risks and political nature of so-called 'solutions' (see Case Study 3.4).

It is important to critically examine how managerial discourse is replicated across academic research, as scholars often prioritize policy-relevant research influenced by migration governance actors, such as donors, international and intergovernmental organizations (IGOs), political parties, NGOs, and states (for a fuller discussion about the policy-research pipeline, its relation to 'impact' and the politics of refusal, see Chapter 6). This allows those same actors to justify interventions, shape migration narratives regarding what migration is and how it should be addressed (Geiger and Pécoud, 2010: 1–2), and evade accountability for the political consequences of migration management policies. The IOM serves as an illustrative example of colonial governance within the context of migration management, and pedagogically, with the following case study, we can think about the language of migration management and the kinds of work it does to present migration as a problem to be solved. According to its website, the IOM works 'to help ensure the orderly and humane management of migration, to promote international cooperation on migration issues, to assist in the search for practical solutions to migration problems and to provide humanitarian assistance to migrants in need, including refugees and internally displaced people'.[3] Its 12-point strategy, adopted by the IOM Council in 2007, sets out its approach, incorporating technocratic international migration narratives around security, reliability, delivering cost-effective services, orderly management, expert advice, technical cooperation, building national capacities, bilateral cooperation, implementation, maximization, spreading best practices, data compatibility and sharing, supporting global dialogue, developing effective policies, coordinated responses, programme development, and delivery. Three main pillars of resilience, mobility and governance underpin this approach. Notably, compassion is not prominently highlighted in any of these narratives. The IOM is not a supra-state organization, but it does actively engage in domestic policy, such as training customs officials and implementing biometric technologies. For example, Ruben Andersson (2014) offers an incisive account of the key role played by the IOM in the development of a 'national' Mauritanian migration policy. IGOs like the IOM have also become embedded in information campaigns designed to dissuade and prevent irregular migration and human trafficking (Andersson, 2014; Pécoud, 2015), which is another example of the increasingly central role they play in directing, facilitating and regulating migration.

Case Study 5.1: IOM and WAKA Well

In 2019, the IOM launched WAKA Well, an advocacy campaign promoting 'safe and informed migration', raising awareness about the risks and reducing the vulnerabilities associated with irregular migration. The campaign, launched on Facebook in 2022,[4] targets young people in Western African countries and uses the slogan '*Waka well, fa kwan pa so*', which we are told translates to 'Use the right process to travel' in pidgin. Using various forms of media, including testimony, song, poetry, music and video advice from elders, it seeks to engage with its audience and promote what it calls 'orderly migration'. Border control measures, including initiatives like WAKA Well, are often framed and presented as acts of saving lives, reflecting a phenomenon described as 'humanitarianization' in migration management (Pallister-Wilkins, 2022). Critical scholars (for example, Achiume, 2019; El-Enany, 2020; Mayblin, 2017, Mayblin and Turner 2021) argue that IGOs have long reflected racialized migration management and colonial biases, undermining their claimed humanitarian aims. Megan Bradley (2023) reveals the IOM's involvement in historical colonial practices, moving colonists out of newly independent states and support for white migration in apartheid-era South Africa, highlighting its role in global migration governance and border surveillance despite its human rights rhetoric. Scholars like Paolo Cuttitta and Polly Pallister-Wilkins have highlighted how moral sentiments and humanitarian arguments are increasingly deployed by policy makers to justify and enhance restrictive migration and border policies, a phenomenon discussed in Chapter 4. In her work on humanitarian borders, Pallister-Wilkins (2022) observes ways that human rights discourse fails to acknowledge its colonial legacies and how historical power structures continue to shape contemporary humanitarian practices, underscoring the need for a critical examination of the humanitarian approach in migration governance.

Talking points

- Using the IOM as an example, what does the term 'migration governance' reveal or obscure about the historical continuity between the past and present?
- Considering WAKA Well, how is West African migration portrayed as a problem and a solution, and for whom is this framing intended?
- How can we resolve the tensions between human rights rhetoric and migration governance in the cases of WAKA Well and the IOM's Missing Migrants project (see Chapter 3)? How do both initiatives operate within the same governance framework while seeming depoliticized?
- How can we reintroduce political dimensions into the language of governance?
- What would be the consequences of renouncing the term 'migration management' in our discourse on migration, both within and outside the classroom?

A second key area we can explore to build better migration literacies is to look more carefully at the coloniality of the idioms of migration governance. Let us turn our analysis to the notion of 'integration', a widely used term in policy and scholarly discussions, largely referring to the adjustment and settlement experiences of immigrants, particularly in European research. Despite lacking a clear scholarly definition, it is often understood in common-sense ways and tends to focus on narrow determinants and practical outcomes like housing, jobs, education and language. It is also often presented as an assumed goal in policy discourse and academic research, portraying migrants' 'integration' as a rational and achievable aspiration. As a central feature of migration governance narratives, integration-related research is favoured by policy makers seeking to address a state-defined problem through integration policies. It is also, arguably, another example of the grammar of migration that has entered everyday discourse and been co-opted by the very individuals targeted for integration by the state, as well those advocating on their behalf. This pervasive nature of governance-speak is also in part related to a critique of the NGO-ization of resistance, where 'apolitical' NGOs play a central role within a system that shrinks democratic and public services, doing the work of governments. The concept of integration encompasses various colonial assumptions about the ordering, sorting and governing of racialized others, and from the perspective of migration literacies, it is important to critically examine and consider whether and how we might impose constraints on the notion of integration. It is to this question that the discussion now turns.

Integration assumes a static society where immigrants are viewed as 'foreign elements' requiring adaptation and assimilation into a well-defined society with clear boundaries and cohesive social and cultural systems. It fails to acknowledge the evolving nature of societies, characterized by fluidity, diversity and shifting social, cultural and political structures influenced by globalization, interconnectedness and transnationalism. When used by governments, integration appears to be framed by the assumption that all social relations happen within what Peggy Levitt (2012) described as the national container, with the so-called 'receiving state' fundamentally distinct from migrants. It fails to recognize that people simultaneously stay connected to other places at the same time, as if to be 'integrated' mimics traditional claims to citizenship, where acquiring one requires relinquishing another. Therefore, the analytical value of integration becomes questionable when considering that not all migrants settle permanently, have permission to do so or sever their transnational ties.

Integration implies that a so-called 'majority' 'host' population has already achieved some kind of success in relation to wider social inequalities and that it somehow exists without its own problems. As Anna Korteweg (2017: 440) observes, 'as long as media and political debates continue to use the language of immigrant integration and academics follow this practice, we end up implying that all of those labelled immigrant are newcomers who cannot make claims for recognition of systematic barriers that are put in the way of full participation', despite many of these barriers also applying to people not categorized as immigrants. This might also be framed as the dispensation of integration, which Willem Schinkel (2018:4) describes as 'white' citizens constituting 'a perfect negative image' of those who are excluded, so that any 'problems' that do emerge come from those on the outside of society. As such, society is, then, imagined as a pristine pure domain that is without problems, carving a line between those for whom integration is not an issue at all and those who 'need' integration. What does the language of integration suggest about a status quo? What does it obscure and illuminate about societal troubles?

Integration assumes a society that is free from racism and discrimination, placing the burden of adaptation solely on racially marginalized migrants (Vanyoro et al, 2019), while absolving the so-called 'host society' of any responsibility for adaptation across various domains. In cases where migrants fulfil all the so-called 'requirements' of integration yet integration outcomes fall short, the question of blame arises. Scheel and Tazzioli (2022: 11) suggest that the integration paradigm problematizes not so much the mobility of individuals labelled as 'migrants' but rather their mere presence, which is often marked by intersecting factors of race, class and gender. In this framing, integration research runs the risk of becoming 'immigrant research', overly focusing on individuals rather than examining the systemic factors that shape settlement outcomes. It tends to overlook such issues as spatial and state segregation, the fear of engaging with local populations, and the embedded hostility within immigration policies. Monish Bhatia's (2020) insightful work on the bureaucratic permission of the state to be cruel is particularly relevant in this context. Engaging with these critical perspectives in the classroom becomes crucial in questioning and challenging the separation of empirical observations from normative assumptions of desired end goals (Spencer, 2022: 219).

In his provocation on integration, Willem Schinkel (2018: 12) argues that 'measuring immigrant integration is a thoroughly neo-colonial practice. It comes out of a history in which the encounter with the other first emerged and emerged by way of a raced work of cultural classification and form with the context of dominance.' Through the colonial lens, migrants arrive not in an empty or neutral space but in metropolitan spaces that are already 'polluted' by racial power relations with a long colonial history, colonial imaginary, colonial knowledge and racial/ethnic hierarchies linked to a history of empire (Fanon, 1967). In other words, migrants arrive in a space of power relations that is already informed and constituted by coloniality. Through this lens, integration is provided as the 'solution' for a 'problem' that is created by the same colonial powers (Pécoud, 2015). Following the work of Alana Lentin (2015), the focus instead needs to be on not what integration is but what it does, that is, how it too functions as a technology of governance precisely because it operates on an inherent division of 'us versus them', relying on naturalized binaries like migrant–citizen (Hadj Abdou, 2019) and perpetuating the notion of societies comprised of insiders and outsiders.

Problem posing: integration

Building better migration literacies requires more radical approaches and engagement with language. We can begin by posing this first problem: what is integration? When is it a problem, and when is it a solution? What stops it? What is segregation? When is it a problem in society, and when is it a solution? What causes it? Students can collaboratively create and reach a consensus on definitions using a think–pair–share model. They can further explore the usage of these terms in readings, articles and editorials, examining the contributors and their perspectives.

We can then pose this second problem: why is integration such a dominant concept in migration teaching? How does the concept of integration relate to you? Building on the first activity, students can reflect on its dominance and use, selecting a key academic article. They may also reflect on their own positioning in the 'integration' narrative: is it expected of them?

Finally, we can pose this third problem: whose interests are served by integration discourse (and not, say, a segregation discourse)? What happens if 'we put constraints on our use of the language of "integration" and instead develop language and concepts to address continuing inequalities and the social, political, and economic conflicts that shape our world today' (Korteweg, 2017: 436)?

Posing these problems in this way means examining the concept in question, asking students to share their knowledge and locate the concept in their own lives (and if it is absent, then to consider why that is). The problem of inequality and unevenness, visibility and invisibility in migration governance is then raised directly through structured and participatory dialogue that combines open questions, academic content and everyday experience. This dialogue can be effectively levelled up into an action-oriented discussion, with more complex classroom talking points framed around a series of 'what if' questions: What if we reconsider integration as differential inclusion to understand how immigrants are already members of a given society, albeit in different ways than other populations within a given state? What if we approach integration as a category of practice, analysing its power dynamics and social inequalities, and examining its political and ethical dimensions in state governance? What if we challenge traditional perspectives that focus on the so-called 'integration contract', that is, adhering to 'host society' rules to produce integration and inclusion, yet ignore segregation as a more authentic descriptive reality? What if we investigate how integration shapes borders, critically mapping the concept of what an integrated society should or could look like, and assessing its potential beyond policy makers' imagination? What if we explore the ways in which integration activates, reactivates, inscribes and reinscribes borders and boundaries for people moving into and around a given state? What if we assess the

> beneficiaries and those adversely affected by this discourse, aiming to repoliticize and disrupt established understandings? What if we come up with new categories and use alternative frames? What might they be, and what might they change?

Two final aspects are obscured when we fail to apply 'integration' as a colonial category. One relates to the affective experience of settlement and the already-felt experiences of belonging and participation of people who are deemed the subject of integration work or of needing more integration. How does the discourse of integration differentiate between people moving through a place, seeking to settle and those who have settled? Josie Gardner and colleagues (2022: 9) write about refugee women supporting other refugees as informal and voluntary hosting through community service. I have also written extensively about these kinds of community practices in my research with refugee community organizations in Glasgow (Piacentini, 2014, 2015, 2016, 2017, 2018a, 2018b). Such community determined 'integration' work most often centres around the transmission of the kinds of invaluable information people desperately need to settle. This is the kind of local and transnational networking that is crucial for supporting newly arrived people in any given place and often reactivates and reinscribes the norms of the place of departure in the new place of settlement. This practice is commonplace and well documented, but because community-held knowledge may not always be considered as serious knowledge, it risks being overlooked. From the perspective of people who have settled on their own terms, we can challenge who gets to define integration and flip the narrative of state-prescribed, normative forms of top-down integration that fail to locate integration within the context of racialized hostility.

The second aspect about integration as a category is temporal: if it is about bringing people into a society, then it presupposes that they are still somehow on the move and as such renders people settling and those with parents who may be immigrants as still mobile (Schinkel, 2018). A case in point here is the use of generational markers ('second'/'third generation'), suggesting a 'journey towards', rather than a destination of, belonging and participation.

From theory to practice: problematizing the 'second generation'

Generational markers are a common feature in migration teaching and learning, most often employed to depict the transformations experienced by ethnically marked populations over time (Hesse and Sayyid, 2006: 22). However, they can also contribute to the marginalization of individuals within a national imagined community (Elrick and

Schwartzman, 2015; Dahinden, 2016; Anderson, 2019) and to the immigrant imaginary (see Chapter 2). As Scheel and Tazzioli (2022: 13) observe, 'the fact that not all newcomers or their children are problematized as "migrants" in need of integration indicates that the label migrant refers to a racialized subject'. The prevalence and uncritical adoption of generational markers also reveal deeply ingrained and invisibilized processes of racialization and migrantization, rooted in colonial and assimilationist perspectives, which perceive the descendants of migrants born as citizens in other countries as an enduring, out-of-place 'problem' to be addressed (Chimienti et al, 2019). By employing this trope in the categorization of populations, particularly those racialized as 'non-white', we confine individuals to a liminal space. This is precisely because the very notion of 'second generation' suggests a group of people considered as not belonging in the country in which they were born and grew up, as people perceived as 'foreign' who are both tasked with accounting for themselves and discriminated against on the same grounds.

Activities

Conduct a search for the term 'second-generation migrants' on academic platforms like Google Scholar or other repositories. Choose any article and examine the definitions and categorizations provided by the authors, as well as the rationale behind their classification and any underlying assumptions. What do you find? Reflect on the implications of these findings for knowledge production and the reproduction of the migrant. What alternatives could you use?

Talking points

- How does 'second generation' operate as a label of exclusion?
- Why does it have such purchase in policy discourse and academic research?
- When we reframe it as a colonial trope of the semantic organization of racialized people, how does its meaning change?

Building 'migration literacies' through keywords

Raymond Williams (2015: 15) emphasized two crucial criteria for identifying significant words: their relevance in specific activities and their indicative role in shaping forms of thought. Developing better migration literacies requires critically engaging with both criteria. Critical migration scholars have been at the forefront of this endeavour; for example, the New Keywords Collective (Tazzioli and De Genova 2016) emphasizes the need to deconstruct seemingly banal and routine fixtures of dominant political language to unveil their hidden assumptions, challenge their perceived transparency and reintroduce a political dimension that is often stripped away. This work can be understood as a necessary epistemic intervention (Stierl, 2022), interrogating the semantic organization of migration discourse to reveal its colonial underpinnings. Examining keywords in their historical context also reveals their continued relevance and lasting impact on migration discourses and debates. By using these keywords as a pedagogical framework, teachers and students gain a deeper understanding of the historical context and governance aspects of migration. The following activity provides a way to show how history repeats itself and why we need to be careful and 'care-full' when talking about migration. Its main objective, however, is to critically reflect on the origins and development of migration-related keywords, using suggested resources that explore keywords commonly encountered in classrooms and academic discussions that go beyond simple dictionary definitions by also incorporating historical perspectives. This activity encourages reflection on the significance of word choice and the importance of cultural histories and etymology.

From theory to practice: working with keywords

Teaching resources

- Das, N., Melo, J.V., Smith, H. and Working, L. (2021) *Keywords of Identity, Race, and Human Mobility in Early Modern England*, Amsterdam: Amsterdam University Press. This collection of essays examines certain key terms that featured in English debates about migration and empire in the 16th and 17th century, highlighting issues of identity, race and belonging throughout that period.
- Casas-Cortes et al (2015) 'New keywords: migration and borders', *Cultural Studies*, 29(1): 55–87.
- Tazzioli, M. and De Genova, N. (2016) (eds) 'Europe/crisis: new keywords of "the crisis" in and of "Europe"', New Keywords Collective. Available at: https://www.researchgate.net/publication/297367783_Europe_Crisis_New_Keywords_of_the_Crisis_in_and_of_Europe_-_New_Keywords_Collective_2016_edited_by_Martina_Tazzioli_and_Nicholas_De_Genova
- De Genova, N. and Tazzioli, M. (2022) (Coordinators and Editors), co-authored by: Aradau, C., Bhandar, B., Bojadzijev, M., Cisneros, J.D., De Genova, N., Eckert, J., Fontanari, E., Golash-Boza, T., Huysmans, J., Khosravi, S., Lecadet, C., Macías Rojas, P., Mazzara, F., McNevin, A., Nyers, P., Scheel, S., Sharma, N., Stierl, M., Squire, V., Tazzioli, M., van Baar, H. and Walters W., 'Minor keywords of political theory: migration as a critical standpoint: A collaborative project of collective writing', *Environment and Planning C: Politics and Space*, 40(4): 781–875.
- Sitholé, T., Crawley, H., Feyissa, D., Tapsoba, T.A., Meda, M.M., Sangli, G., Yeoh, S.G. and Phipps, A. (2022) 'The language of migration', *Zanj: The Journal of Critical Global South Studies*, 5(1–2): 14–26.

Activities

Before beginning, discuss together what students consider to be keywords in migration studies. Then, ask them to select one keyword to research from the aforementioned resources. This can be an individual or group task, and it can be non-assessed or assessed:

- Consider the keyword etymology. Ask students to summarize the historical background of their chosen keyword from their readings.
- Explore which aspects of the keyword's history surprise students when viewed from a contemporary perspective.
- Discuss how an etymological analysis can enhance understanding of the term and shed light on its historical significance.
- Encourage students to reflect on how their chosen keyword relates to current examples, issues or concerns, and how they can connect these keywords to their personal lives.
- Invite students to share any questions or thoughts they have about the keywords for class discussion.

Talking points

- Why do we rely on prevailing semantic representations of migration without examining their shared meanings, especially from the perspective of migrants themselves?
- What types of discomfort do these representations produce, and how can we harness this discomfort to drive action and change?
- In what ways do keywords in migration governance reinforce the existing order? Also consider how they manifest in activism and social justice efforts, challenging and facilitating change.
- How can we balance the need for clear comprehension with a critical examination of problematic keywords, ultimately contributing to improved migration literacies and potentially radical approaches to repoliticizing the grammar of migration?

Metaphors, metonyms and migration literacies

Metaphors and metonymies play a significant role in shaping how migration has come to be discussed and understood. They possess important explanatory power, but the way that 'common sense' works means that we often fail to notice or think little of them (Kumashiro, 2009). They become actors themselves in the politics of knowing and relating, pushing us to view the world through their lenses. They serve to establish legitimacy, communicate political arguments, convey ideology through political myth and evoke emotional responses (Charteris-Black, 2006), and can be found in scholarship, media reporting, political language, policy debates and the classroom. A significant body of research has evidenced the use of metaphor and metonymy in political and media discourse about migration and migrant populations, such as 'parasites', 'scourges', 'animals', 'natural disasters' and 'criminality', highlighting their highly problematic and deeply harmful effects (see Santa Ana, 1999, 2013; Charteris-Black, 2006; Musolff, 2016; Ahrens and Fleithmann, 2020; Hart,

2021; Taylor, 2021; Catalano and Waugh, 2022). The water metaphor, for example, is historically rooted in xenophobia and stands out as particularly problematic and racist, labelling people on the move as 'floods' or 'tidal waves'. Extreme examples, such as the *LA Times* on 3 September 2015 announcing, 'Today's much larger crisis could be the first gush of a human tsunami that will swamp the continent', often pass as mainstream reporting, further perpetuating negative and dehumanizing narratives. While seemingly softer metaphors like 'flows', 'influx' or 'waves' may be more accepted, and feature even in critical scholarship, they still evoke images of uncontrolled movements that dehumanize individuals by assimilating them into a singular body that needs to be controlled (Kainz, 2016). Water metaphors convey notions of navigating through and around obstacles, causing long-term damage to infrastructure and impacting the well-being of individuals. They also evoke a sense of destructive power. Describing the movement of people as flows or streams naturalizes metaphorical framings, perpetuating the perception of an accumulating threat where a trickle can develop into a flow and eventually a tsunami. Water metaphors also map neatly onto the notion of the nation state as container, wherein flows signify the threat of a 'build-up of pressure' (on education, healthcare systems, housing, employment and notional and national resources) that will ultimately reaching a 'critical point' (Charteris-Black, 2006: 577).

Teachable moment: Europe as a garden and the rest of the world as a jungle

Josep Borrell, EU High Representative for Foreign Affairs and Security Policy and one of the EU's most senior diplomats, made a speech to aspiring diplomats at the College of Europe in Bruges on 13 October 2022, using an extended metaphor of 'Europe as a garden' and the 'rest of the world' as a jungle. In a scripted speech, he said:

> Bruges is a good example of the European garden. Yes, Europe is a garden. We have built a garden. Everything works. It is the best combination of political freedom, economic prosperity and social cohesion that humankind has been able to build – the three things together. And here, Bruges is maybe a good representation of beautiful things, intellectual life, wellbeing. The rest of the world – and you know this very well, Federica [Mogherini, Rector of the College of Europe and former High Representative for Foreign Affairs and Security Policy) – is not exactly a garden. Most of the rest of the world is a jungle, and the jungle could invade the garden. The gardeners should take care of it, but they will not protect the garden by building walls. A nice small garden surrounded by high walls in order to prevent the jungle from coming in is not going to be a solution. Because the jungle has a strong growth capacity, and the wall will never be high enough in order to protect the garden. The gardeners have to go to the jungle. Europeans have to be much more engaged with the rest of the world. Otherwise, the rest

of the world will invade us, by different ways and means. (See: www.eeas.eur opa.eu/eeas/european-diplomatic-academy-opening-remarks-high-representat ive-josep-borrell-inauguration_en).

The comments were widely criticized for the colonial undercurrents and racist connotations contained in the metaphorical imagery of the garden/jungle: the garden needing to be carefully tended for it to flourish and nourish; the reference to building 'high walls' in the context of the increasingly tangible realization of Fortress Europe; and the jungle as uncontained, unexplored and mysterious, representing a pervasive threat from 'outside' that needs to be civilized through order, containment and control. Two things are worth noting: the framing of European states as prosperous systems without reference to their roots nourished in their former colonies; and the civilizational turn that has most recently been reproduced in reporting on the war on Ukraine. Borrell released a statement a few days later, stating that his comments were misinterpreted and not racist nor neocolonial, while doubling down on the notion of Europe as under threat from outside 'invaders'.

Further reading and resources

- 'European Diplomatic Academy: opening remarks by High Representative Josep Borrell at the inauguration of the pilot programme', 13 October 2022. Available at: www. eeas.europa.eu/eeas/european-diplomatic-academy-opening-remarks-high-represe ntative-josep-borrell-inauguration_en
- 'Josep Borrell: on metaphors and geo-politics', 18 October 2022. Available at: www. eeas.europa.eu/eeas/metaphors-and-geo-politics_en
- 'European Forum Alpbach: keynote speech by High Representative/Vice-President Josep Borrell at the panel discussion on "Crises: failing to see the long-term wood for the short-term trees?"', 28 August 2020. Available at: www.eeas.europa.eu/eeas/european-forum-alpbach-keynote-speech-high-representativevice-president-josep-borrell-panel_en

Talking points

- How do we understand this jungle/garden metaphor in terms of colonial discourse around the hierarchy of superior and inferior racialized populations?
- What links can we make to what Liz Fekete of the Institute of Race Relations has called 'civilizational racism' in the Eurocentric notion of hierarchies (Fekete 2023)?
- How do we understand this through the current lens of EU consensus building in favour of the further militarization of EU borders, the pursuit of 'culture wars' and historic revisionism?

Militaristic/war metaphors are also very common in media reporting and can increasingly be found in polarizing political rhetoric that gives legitimacy to invader/protector tropes and managed migration approaches (see Hart, 2021; Mujagić, 2022). Evidence of this can be found in Suella Braverman's comments about Knowsley and 'Stop the Boats' campaigns discussed in Chapter 2. Donald Trump's anti-Mexican speech in his official

'White House statement from the President regarding emergency measures to address the border crisis on May 30, 2019' (available at https://trumpwhitehouse.archives.gov/briefings-statements/statement-president-regarding-emergency-measures-address-border-crisis/) provides a perfect illustration of mixing militarized/securitization/water metaphors, where he refers to 'being invaded', 'illegal aliens draining our welfare system', 'people pouring across borders' and 'lawlessness'.

As we have seen, the media plays a key role in shaping public perception through politicized visual and textual language. Drawing specifically on Stuart Hall's work on moral panics, Encarnación Gutiérrez Rodríguez (2018: 19) argues that the deeply politicized visual and textual vocabulary used by the media in the 21st century in contemporary Europe has resulted in the 'refugee' becoming a 'floating signifier'. Critical understanding of metonyms, or the use of associated images or terms to represent broader concepts, is equally important for building better migration literacies. They too are directly implicated in migration governance and contribute to the construction of the racialized Other through racist vocabulary and imagery used to rationalize new forms of migration governance. Metonymies are also effectively used in reporting on racialized populations, when race and place are spatially coded, imbuing places with new meanings (Elliott-Cooper, 2018). The 'Stop the Boats' campaign (see Chapter 2) and reference to 'channel crossers' are both examples of the English Channel becoming a racially coded space. The infamous 'taking back control' slogan of the Brexit Leave campaign is another example of metonymic racism, conveying racialized threats while denying overt racism. Similarly, the term 'asylum seeker' has become a metonymic synonym for illegality and criminality; it is a legal and administrative category that has become burdened with negative connotations and tends to be used in a degrading and dehumanizing manner. Such administrative distinctions and categorizations hold significance in terms of individuals' ability to live with dignity and freedom.

In the context of 'culture wars', metaphors and metonyms both migrantize and racialize certain populations, naturalizing perceptions of difference and embedding essentialism. These linguistic devices contribute to a broader repertoire of 'racial grammars': socially acceptable ways of discussing race and migration that often appear de-racialized. Metaphors and metonymies can also be used to justify harsher migration governance. For instance, compassion is often invoked to justify stricter immigration policies and crackdowns, using moralistic framings of 'evil people smugglers' and 'smuggling business models', and framing individuals as naive, desperate and vulnerable, and in need of protection. The humanitarian gloss on bordering practices (Pallister-Wilkins, 2022) is a metonymic example, where compassion and moral duty come to signify stricter border governance, a rhetorical device increasingly characteristic of European leaders' speeches.

Importantly, building better migration literacies requires us to equally consider how migrants use metaphors and metonymies themselves to describe their life experiences, in contrast to their usage in media reporting and by politicians. Counter-metaphors can provide deeper insights into their experiences and the social, cultural and emotional dimensions of migration. Theresa Catalano and Linda Waugh (2022) highlight the ways in which migrants are affected by metaphors and metonymies in media and policy discourse, their understanding of how these devices are employed, and the potential for resistance through counter-stories and the repurposing of metaphors with alternate meanings. They observe how migrants use metaphorical devices like 'journeys' to capture a sense of hope for a better life and opportunities; 'water' comes to represent mobility; and militaristic metaphors come to symbolize fear and angst. Incorporating these perspectives helps counterbalance the dominant narratives perpetuated by the media and politicians, which often prioritize security concerns, economic impacts or cultural anxieties. Recognizing and critically engaging with these rhetorical devices is essential for developing a more nuanced understanding of migration and its racial dimensions, as well as for fostering better migration literacies, and we must be vigilant of the use of figurative language in teaching and learning resources, and how we talk about migration.

From theory to practice: working with metaphors and metonyms

Better scrutiny of metaphors and metonymies means that we confront them when we encounter them, question the underlying assumptions they carry and seek to disrupt the uncritical ways in which they are used and reproduced. In class, you can begin with some example news headlines and ask students to search together for more based on a particular metaphor commonly used in 'culture wars' language to suggest division or threat. You can take the example of militaristic metaphors in this instance, but the activity can be replicated with other metaphors, including animals, disease and water/natural disasters:

- location (where): fronts, battle, front line, battlefield, battle lines, battleground, fault lines, barricades, crosshairs, territory, war zone, face-off, outpost, fortress;
- actions and outcomes (what): marching, fighting, winning, losing, truce, armed with, defeat, threaten, under attack, under siege, besieged, onslaught, destroys, protecting, invading, occupying, triumph, victory, weaponize, instability, disruption, breaking entry, gaining entry, tearing down, ticking timebomb, rampant; and
- agents (who and how): warrior, combatant, armies, casualties, enemy, invaders, brigade (as in pro-immigration brigade).

Example headlines

- 'Army on alert at French ports to stop migrant invasion. Soldiers are on standby to patrol northern French ports amid growing tensions about an army of migrants intent on reaching Britain', *The Express*, 7 September 2014.
- 'As Cameron preaches abroad about slave labour migrants besiege the Tunnel to join our black economy and MPs demand send in the army', *Daily Mail*, 29 July 2015.
- 'In the heart of England: shock pics that prove UK's migrant invasion is out of control. The astonishing scale of Britain's immigration crisis was laid bare by dramatic photos of a gang of illegals cutting their way out of a lorry on a road in the heart of the English countryside', *The Express*, 11 June 2015.
- 'The south coast is under invasion. It would be difficult for anyone who believes in laws and borders not to resent these illegal Channel crossings', *The Telegraph*, 11 November 2022.
- 'Locals go to war over accommodation centres for 5,000 new boat migrants: government has a "fight on its hands" as councils across Britain push back on plans to fill old RAF bases and prisons with incoming asylum seekers', *Daily Mail*, 29 March 2023.

Talking points

- What narrative is implied by portraying migration as a battleground or invasion, and what are its mental images and consequences?
- In what ways is the battle metaphor used in various contexts, including media, policy and public discourse, and how does it influence public perception and policies?
- How does the battle metaphor justify restrictive migration policies and the development of anti-migrant ideologies?
- What aspects are overlooked by such metaphors/metonyms, such as socio-economic realities, experiences of escaping poverty, encounters with racism or forced displacement, and what are the political implications?

Writing prompts

Select a headline or short text and identify the figurative language used, including implicit, explicit and intentional elements. Then, rephrase the text by either removing the metaphor or substituting it with a different one. Analyse the impact of these changes on the text and its communicative effectiveness for social justice work. Discuss the challenges posed by metaphorical/metonymic language and how it connects to the rhetoric of 'culture wars'. Stumbling blocks in rewriting are okay. This is one step towards developing power awareness through better migration literacies.

Concluding comments

The chapter has explored how migration governance narratives not only prescribe problems but also offer depoliticized technocratic solutions. It has argued that migration governance language needs to be analysed as a tool of coloniality in order to better understand its power in sustaining deep inequalities. The chapter has suggested building better migration literacies as a pedagogical framework to do the work of critically examining the in/visible semantic organization and institutionalization of migration management narratives through language, policy categories and metaphors in order to repoliticize our disciplinary grammars, interrupt dominant narratives and reject de-racialized and ahistorical accounts (Tejeda et al, 2003). Building better migration literacies enables us to challenge the erasure of historical and contemporary violence, and to confront the underlying injustices and inequalities in ways of knowing and relating. Recognizing this grammar in structuring how we teach about migration also helps us better understand the processes of migrantization and racialization that shape how migration experiences are produced and maintained. Better migration literacies can also be effective in working towards a decolonized curriculum because they acknowledge and confront the legacy of colonial thinking (Gebrial, 2018: 29). Migration literacies alone do not eliminate the normativity of migration governance in teaching and everyday life, but better literacies create space for critical discussion that can lead to the disruption of dominant narratives and vocabularies in the 'political now'. This has real pedagogical impact, as it transforms how we engage with knowledge and helps build critical resistances in classrooms to dominant solutions–focused migration governance narratives that also shape how we navigate the policy–research landscape and the knowledge that is valued there and considered 'impactful', 'serious' and therefore 'useful'. This raises questions of ways to refuse and what other tools we can develop to help us do this work of refusal, so we move closer to 'what if'. It is to these concerns that we turn in Chapter 6.

6

Impact and Refusal

Introduction

A central aim of this book is to think about useful ways of connecting pedagogy with the social and political task of social justice, anti-oppression and anti-racist resistance through disruption and transformation. While the quest for 'useful' and impactful research with real-world relevance is now (largely) taken as given, even if it is problematic as we will go on to explore, it remains largely under-researched and consequently poorly understood in relation to teaching practice. Our pedagogical aims are to create autonomous, critical and civically engaged students, to develop as ethical teachers, to draw on critical, anti-oppressive and anti-racist pedagogies, and to instil in learners a commitment to social justice. These too are impacts. Henry Giroux and bell hooks remind us that teaching is an act of hope, and so it is with this in mind that we need to be thinking about impact in terms of what *could* be. First, this chapter explores what the search for policy-relevant 'useful research' about migration means in practice and for building better migration literacies. Second, it explores how to think about impact as pedagogic practice through resistance and refusal, as well as collaboratively developed manifesto writing between students, teachers and practitioners, as approaches that offer both possibilities and rewards.

The search for impact and policy relevance

Problem posing: impact

Begin by asking students to define the term 'impact' within the context of HE: what could impact mean in the classroom? Once you have established a working understanding, encourage them to consider its different interpretations, such as

> social, academic or personal impact. You can ask students to explore the underlying assumptions associated with the concept of impact in teaching. Ask questions like: who defines impact in teaching? What criteria do we use to measure impact? What are the consequences of these definitions and measurements? You can go on to discuss the power dynamics within the teaching environment. Encourage reflection on the roles of teachers and students, institutional structures, and how societal expectations of impact may vary. Extend this further to challenge students to reimagine impact in teaching and consider how teaching practices can promote social justice, equality and inclusivity. Explore alternative ways to measure impact, such as personal intellectual growth, critical thinking and social engagement and mobilization. Finally, identify pedagogical practices that align with their vision for a more socially responsible, equitable and transformative educational experience.

The notion of 'impact' in academic research refers to the demonstrable contribution that research makes to society and the economy.[1] It encompasses both academic impact, which relates to theoretical and methodological advancements, and economic and societal impact, which relates to knowledge exchange, public engagement and contributions to society and the economy at various levels. Much of what has come to be designated and measured as impact boils down to 'making a difference', with a push for research to be more outward looking and made more accessible to policy makers, the media and the public in order to have influence (Colley, 2014). The UK-mandated research impact agenda has also influenced research in mainland Europe, introducing new approaches to incentivizing, monitoring and rewarding research impact achievements (Bandola-Gill and Smith, 2022). Previous chapters have explored how a central feature of the 'political now' is the privileging and prominence of certain knowledges over others. As Maurice Stierl (2022) and Lorenzo Piccoli and colleagues (2023) sharply observe, there is a direct pipeline between migration studies and policy research, with migration studies scholars deeply implicated in both the reproduction of migration governance and the production of a migration policy landscape. Replicating the way international migration narratives work (see Chapter 5), this happens because, first, policymaking requires a problem to be solved and, second, policy relevance means that policy categories are often privileged, both of which push academics towards specific research questions and specific types of evidence to solve specific kinds of problems (Hadj Abdou and Pettrachin, 2021).

We would be right to ask whether research or politics take primary position in this imagined mutual relationship (Scholten, 2018). Evidence shapes policy action, and policy makers search for knowledge claims that map neatly onto their predetermined policy agendas and plans, influencing which knowledge claims are explored and which are ignored, how questions might be determined by funding schemes and how evidence is to be obtained, the form it takes and how it is used. This is further complicated by political agendas. For example, in 2022, the UK Home Office, having long relied on the trope of welfare as a major pull factor for asylum migration, failed to acknowledge its own 2020 (Home Office, 2020) research that drew on extensive evidence showing welfare policies and labour market access have little or no impact on migration decision making. Another example is the research-intensive period since the summer of 2015 that marked a turning point in European migration scholarship, where academic expertise and insights became highly sought after in media and political discussions (Stierl, 2022). As a result, the subfield of migration and border studies has experienced significant growth, fuelled by the technocratic demand for managed migration 'solutions' and research agendas addressing the migration 'crisis' and what can be done about it (as discussed in Chapter 5). Following directives set out by EU state governments, university research offices, policy makers and think tanks have cohered around a managerialist solutions-focused approach to the 'migration problem' that seeks to 'make an impact'.

When it comes to the policy–research pipeline, we can and should be asking: who is impact for? To whom is it useful? Who decide what constitutes 'good' or 'bad' impacts (see Pelkmans, 2013)? How is impact understood and shaped by relations of power and control? If it is good for policy makers and think tanks, can it be good and useful for the people who are subject to policies that are focused on reducing net migration or developing offshoring policies as an effective migration management tool? And if it is good and useful for people categorized as migrants, can it be good and useful to policy makers? How does the impact agenda interrogate dominant power when the Western research agenda on migration-related matters increasingly sees both academia and policy-directed research as aligned? These important, searching questions are closely tied to a deeper inquiry into how research and policy interact, not just in the field of migration studies but in the many disciplines interested and invested in migration.

As already explored in Chapter 5, the search for policy relevance also shapes migration literacies and informs how we talk about migration. Oliver Bakewell (2008: 434–5) suggests that this quest has 'encouraged researchers to take the categories, concepts and priorities of policy makers and practitioners as their initial frame of reference for identifying their areas of study and formulating research questions'. The issue at hand is the unreflective and unproblematized use of social categories, as well as reductive constructions of the migrant and of refugee figures, which has led to an intellectual crisis in the use of key concepts in migration research and teaching. Lorenzo Piccoli and colleagues (2023) describe this as a semantic institutionalization of migration governance that has shaped the field. Our failure to challenge the uncritical adoption, or indeed conflation, of categories of practice and analysis in our teaching and in research priorities that create statistical migration spectacles is a sure way to reproduce normative migration tropes and ethnicized differences, as well as reinforce the logic of the migration apparatus. These kinds of conflations stop us from both reading the world and reading the word in the classroom because they legitimize the common-sense grammar and vocabularies of migration that make us not only see and think like the state, as James Scott and Abdelmalek Sayad caution, but also talk and teach like the state. As discussed in Chapter 5, these vocabularies seep into our learning oftentimes undetected and unquestioned, and make us implicated, at best, and complicit, at worst, in the kinds of dehumanization and racialization of migrants that we, as critical scholars and students, seek to avoid.

> **Reflective task**
>
> Do you carefully and 'care-fully' consider the categories you employ in your teaching when discussing matters related to migration, and do you reflect on their potential influence on ways of knowing and relating? How do you actively challenge and disrupt disciplinary norms, and to what extent can these established norms be questioned? Furthermore, what conversations are taking place within your field regarding problematic processes of categorization?

Of course, framing matters, and if migration is only treated as a problem, or as a crisis, then impact can only really be measured by the extent to which it offers a 'solution'. Moreover, solutions are increasingly expected to be delivered as silver bullets of immediate and usable advice, partly because 'research with "impact" privileges immediate recommendations over the less quantifiable "outputs" of vision or dreams' (Bhattacharyya, 2013: 1415). Recommendations are themselves part of the managerial governance narrative that Antoine Pécoud's work on international migration narratives (see Chapter 5) skilfully explores. They have become part of an approach to research that has very effectively colonized and, as a result, depoliticized much of migration research and teaching. The policy–research pipeline and push for impact also involves the academic researcher taking on a kind of technocratic 'technical adviser' role (Giroux, 2021), performing 'outreach' to demonstrate academic usefulness. Framing migration as a problem requiring a solution and then reproducing this framing to demonstrate impact mean that we fail to understand migration as a feature of broader social-political developments or as a symptom of historical and contemporary Western interventions in foreign countries, as Hadj Abdou and Pettrachin (2021) and Andersson (2018) have argued.

A last point to make is that demonstrating 'academic usefulness' brings pressures. Funding applications demand impact statements before research has begun. The UK Research Excellence Framework places a financial premium on impact case studies that set out in detail the kinds of changes and benefits that research has had on society, the economy, public policy and practice, the environment, and the quality of life. While writing this book, I received internal communications from my institution outlining the financial consequences and monetary value for HE institutions of 'impact case studies', advising staff that 'one 4-star academic output is worth £8k per annum, whereas one 4-star impact case study is worth £74k per annum'. It is no wonder that in her blog on the imposed linearity, velocity (it can also be speeded up but never, it seems, slowed down!) and force with which ideas are pushed out in the world, Ali Phipps (2017) describes impact as feeling like 'a fist connecting with a face. It brings to mind the forcible contact of one object with another.' Ruben Andersson (2018: 226) also describes being 'stared down' by the 'wheel of impact' in his office, a 'telling mandala of today's neoliberal academia … replete with colour-coded "pathways" to this holy academic grail, represented as a black bull's eye'. Of course, many academics are already deeply committed to doing 'really useful research' and working closely with non-academic partners and communities, seeking out the very real-world application and transformations that the impact agenda promotes. However, they may also be doing this in their own, co-determined ways, and this complicates the push, and therefore pressure, for policy relevance.

Working in institutions that aspire to, celebrate and reward research-led teaching, the impact agenda can manifest itself in the classroom in very similar ways. While impact in the context of research is focused on reaching wider audiences, teaching supports the development of a wide community of scholars, and in the classroom, we contribute to public debate with hundreds or thousands of students over our academic careers. There is a growing emphasis on fostering collaborative learning between students and communities, raising ethical considerations, responsibilities and the implications of impactful teaching that involves collaboration among academics, students and non-HE partners. The challenges posed by the COVID-19 context further highlight the need to address these concerns as community organizations navigate a wider range of enduring challenges in their work and interactions. Simultaneously, there is a growing demand for innovative teaching practices that move beyond traditional lecture-based models and towards an engaged public pedagogy, grounded in a sense of civic responsibility beyond the confines of academia. The critical-pedagogical literature is quiet about the place and nature of impact in relation to learning and teaching, and we can explore its intersection in different ways.

First, the knowledge produced through research finds its way into the curriculum, shaping students' understanding of various subjects. The danger here is that policy-relevant knowledge can then determine what matters most in the classroom (hooks, 1994). Second, critical pedagogy connects classroom learning with the experiences, histories and resources that each student brings. In the context of an engaged public pedagogy, the collective body of knowledge in the classroom should extend beyond solely translating research outcomes. As we will explore further below and in Chapter 7 and have already explored in earlier case studies in previous chapters, what constitutes knowledge must also encompass student experiences, emotions, practices, local knowledge and alternative learning communities, both formal and informal, and both face-to-face and in virtual spaces. This recognizes that knowledge is produced not only within the confines of research institutions but also within and from the everyday experiences and social interactions of individuals, and informs what we understand by impact and impact ownership in the classroom. Third, just as the search for policy-relevant research involves power struggles and contestation over what knowledge is considered as 'really useful', the critical classroom is also a site where students and teachers grapple with and challenge predetermined hierarchies of power. Critical pedagogy recognizes that learners bring valuable experiences, perspectives and knowledges to the collective learning process, and these too are sites where knowledge is contested. We are also reminded that learning is never neutral or apolitical but rather embedded in systems of power and influenced by social dynamics. In the critical classroom, we are encouraged to work towards dismantling hierarchical power relations through relationalities that foster critical thinking, dialogue and the co-construction of knowledge. If we are to take seriously our responsibility as researchers for critically engaging with the policy–research pipeline, then we must also take this seriously as teachers in the classroom.

Reflective task

Which criteria inform our choices when selecting course materials, and do we openly discuss these in the classroom? How do we engage pedagogically with the influence of the policy landscape on what we teach, how we teach and what we may unintentionally leave out? Do our teaching practices inadvertently mirror the prioritization of policy categories and concerns? Is it possible to actively resist the impact of the policy–research pipeline in our teaching, or should we focus on improving our ability to resist participating in it?

Resistance, refusal and counter-stories as impact

Refusal can reveal itself it many ways in our research and teaching. It may be connected to rejecting the close relationship between research funding and the impact agenda, as outlined earlier. It may be connected to the slow machinery of funding agencies, with their goal-oriented agendas and high risk of failure of applications, which work against the very immediate and pressing nature of the times we live in and the urgency of learning about phenomenon as they occur in real time. It may be an act of solidarity with partners and communities beyond the academy who struggle to find acceptance in the conventional world of funding bids, data collection, academic authorship and publication. It may be adopting a political position of non-engagement with research that perpetuates epistemic violence, especially where the research pipeline is direct and evident. Refusal may be connected to a rejection of 'inclusion' agendas that change little about power structures, leaving research hierarchies firmly intact. It may be found where we ask ourselves: are we doing the research just because we can (Hagen et al, 2023)? Is it research 'that needs doing' because of its intellectual and social value (Edwards, 2022)? Or, is it something else besides research that is needed? More is not always better, and it can sometimes be about refusal of the unquestioning right to know. As Tuck and Yang (2014: 811) argue, some communities are simply over-coded: 'simultaneously hyper-surveilled and made invisible by the state, by police, and by social science research'. They place the university at the heart of the problem of colonial knowledge-production practices, describing it 'a colonial collector of knowledge as another form of territory' (Tuck and Yang, 2014: 814). Finally, building better migration literacies (see Chapter 5) is also generative of refusal, as we confront and challenge in our classrooms the narratives of migration governance, the rational technocratic language of migration management and the uncritical reproduction of colonial tropes of sorting and classification.

Case Study 6.1: RISE: Refugees, Survivors and eX-detainees

RISE: Refugees, Survivors and eX-detainees (RISE) is the first and only welfare and advocacy organization in Australia entirely governed by refugees, people seeking asylum and ex-detainees. As such, it views those who seek assistance from RISE as members, not clients. RISE has a list of '10 things you need to consider if you are an artist – not of the refugee and asylum seeker community – looking to work with our community' (RISE Australia, 2015). The title is presented here in capital letters in the way it is on their website. You do not miss this message.

You feel the emphasis, the urgency, the seriousness and the weight of what they are saying, and their frustration with extractive approaches to knowledge production. This list is sharply worded; it pulls no punches. It centres the reader's discomfort by putting us on the spot. It questions false claims to neutrality and exposes limited understandings of the biases we bring when our practices are self-serving. This is not just a list of key points to consider; it is also a manifesto for action:

1. Process not product. We are not a resource to feed into your next artistic project. You may be talented at your craft but do not assume that this automatically translates to an ethical, responsible and self-determining process. Understand community cultural development methodology but also understand that it is not a full-proof methodology. Who and what institutions are benefiting from the exchange?
2. Critically interrogate your intention. Our struggle is not an opportunity, or our bodies a currency, by which to build your career. Rather than merely focusing on the 'other' ('where do I find refugees' etc.) subject your own intention to critical, reflexive analysis. What is your motivation to work with this subject matter? Why at this time?
3. Realise your own privilege. What biases and intentions, even if you consider these 'good' intentions, do you carry with you? What social positionality (and power) do you bring to the space? Know how much space you take up. Know when to step back.
4. Participation is not always progressive or empowering. Your project may have elements of participation, but this can just as easily be limiting, tokenistic and condescending. Your demands on our community sharing our stories may be just as easily disempowering. What frameworks have you already imposed on participation? What power dynamics are you reinforcing with such a framework? What relationships are you creating (e.g. informant vs expert, enunciated vs enunciator).
5. Presentation vs representation. Know the difference!
6. It is not a safe space just because you say it is. This requires long term grass-roots work, solidarity, and commitment.
7. Do not expect us to be grateful. We are not your next interesting arts project. Our community are not sitting waiting for our struggle to be acknowledged by your individual consciousness nor highlighted through your art practice.
8. Do not reduce us to an issue. We are whole humans with various experiences, knowledge and skills. We can speak on many things; do not reduce us to one narrative.

9. Do your research. Know the solidarity work already being done. Know the nuanced differences between organizations and projects. Just because we may work with the same community doesn't mean we work in the same way.
10. Art is not neutral. Our community has been politicized and any artwork done with/by us is inherently political. If you wish to build with our community your artistic practice cannot be neutral. (RISE Australia, 2015)

Talking points and activities

- Divide students into small groups and assign each one of the ten points to discuss and summarize its key themes and principles. Share your feedback and consider together how these points collectively function as both resistance and creation, encouraging students to reflect on how these themes apply to their own practices.
- Ask students to choose a point from the manifesto and relate it to a real-life scenario from their practices. Consider how we can apply the principles from the manifesto to improve our practices. Discuss together how it can be used to unlearn and improve community engagement practices, and to rethink how impact is determined and realized.
- Take Point 6, which highlights that declaring a space as safe requires long-term work, solidarity and commitment. Divide students into small groups and provide them with scenarios in which they are tasked with creating and maintaining a safe space for a community. Conclude with a class-wide discussion on the challenges and responsibilities of maintaining safe spaces and fostering long-term commitment in community engagement. (See also the discussion on safe spaces in Chapter 3).
- Focus on Points 7 and 10, which address emotions and the inherently political nature of art. In small groups, consider how refusal to be reduced to a project or an issue is tied to emotions and ethical considerations. What might be the implications for our practices?

Many have written about refusal, and we can learn from their praxis. Moe Ani Nayel (2013), in 'Palestinian refugees are not at your service', talks about a repeated refusal to give up time and privacy in refugee research. Jamie J. Hagen, Ilaria Michelis, Jennifer Philippa Eggert and Lewis Turner (2023), in 'Learning to say "no": privilege, entitlement and refusal in peace, (post)conflict and security research', focus on the possibility and necessity for active refusal in multiple research contexts, and the complexities of refusal in form and mode. In sharing their report, 'Mission accomplished? The deadly effects of border control in Niger', Border Forensics (2023) tweeted the measures they took to ensure that infrastructures supporting migratory mobilities remain hidden from the gaze of the state as a refusal to perpetuate further state violence. Alison Phipps, Piki Diamond, Chaz Doherty, Sophie Nock and Tawona Sitholé have co-written 'A short manifesto for decolonizing language education' as a pledge to 'unsettle the arrogance of ignorance derived from institutional authority which can often lead to the fragmentation of bodies of knowledge, giving rise to a misguided elitism that, in turn, creates tensions and contradictions between theory and practice' (Phipps 2019: 4). Eve Tuck (2009), in her article 'Suspending damage: a letter to communities', writes about communities' refusal to be framed as depleted and calls instead for a reformulation of how and with whom research is framed, designed, conducted and used.

> **Problem posing: refusal**
>
> Begin with posing the problem: what does refusal look like when learning about migration? Ask students to note down what they understand by refusal and, substantively, what might be being refused. Can they identify together what the work of refusal might relate to? Can they explore together how this work of refusal, be it our own or others', shapes the politics of migration knowledge production and problematizes impact. Discuss the concept of refusal as an act of resistance. You could probe further, asking: who has the authority to distribute or refuse knowledge? What might be the consequences of refusal? What alternatives exist for rejecting or resisting knowledge practices? You can highlight refusal as an act of critical consciousness, ethical care, doing good harm and being political. Discuss how refusal is rooted in a commitment to meaningful education, critical thinking and humanization. Explore its potential to empower students individually and collectively to challenge oppressive systems. You might also explore innovative models, curricula and practices that promote alternative ways of knowing and relating that push against normative notions of impact.

To ensure an anti-oppressive approach to impact in the classroom, it is crucial to not only move beyond passive consumption of information but also search out alternative knowledges that disrupt the dominant stories we are told. With this idea of clamouring for different kinds of impact in mind, several questions already explored in this book can guide our thinking: how can we prioritize and centre the contemporary and historical words and experiences of those whose perspectives we draw from as an act of epistemic justice? What 'good harm' might arise from challenging our default ways of knowing? How can we acknowledge and respect different sources and modes of knowledge production, including those passed down through generations through storytelling, poetry, music and song? And what kinds of impact might they have on how we understand the 'political now' through the lens of history?

Case Study 6.2: 'Curating Discomfort'

Public pedagogy takes place online, in print and in public spaces. The Hunterian Gallery at the University of Glasgow offers an excellent case study of the relationship between discomfort and public pedagogy, as well as what a politics of refusal can look like in the public sphere. In 2019, it established its 'Curating Discomfort' project, with funding from Museums Galleries Scotland, the national development body for Scotland's museums. The main aim of Curating Discomfort is to redress and correct historical power imbalances present within the museum and its endeavours. Serving as an initial step towards transformation, Curating Discomfort refuses by actively disrupting existing museum practices to create fresh frameworks and narratives related to its curated collections. It represents the start of an ongoing process of embedding anti-racist practice into every aspect of the museum's work. The museum has free entry and shares several resources online: podcasts, blogs and visual records of its development and work. Using this example, students may be encouraged to examine the role of dominant institutions, including sites of national and cultural heritage, in constructing and reinforcing particular knowledge claims and ideologies.

Further reading and resources

- The Curating Discomfort website is available at: www.gla.ac.uk/hunterian/about/achangingmuseum/curatingdiscomfort/
- The Curating Discomfort introduction video is available at: https://youtu.be/yYPzLlCST-8
- A blog from Zandra Yeaman, Hunterian Gallery Curator of Discomfort, is available at: http://hunterian.academicblogs.co.uk/curating-discomfort/

Talking points

- Having engaged with the resources, consider the ways in which such initiatives are practices of the refusal and disruption of traditional practices that create alternative narratives and frameworks, as well as their effectiveness.
- Reflect together on the usefulness of using discomfort as a tool for promoting critical thinking and questioning dominant knowledge structures in cultural sites.

- Encourage students to reflect on the broader implications of embedding anti-racist practices and refusal in knowledge production within cultural institutions and its potential to respond to 'culture war' ideologies, particularly regarding issues related to historical narratives, power dynamics and anti-racist practice.
- Lastly, encourage students to take this learning with them into other cultural institutions and reflect on how it might be applied and what it might change.

Curating discomfort falls into the disrupting and interrupting work of storytelling and counter-stories (see Chapters 3 and 5) but this time at an institutional level. Such acts of refusal through narrative, however presented, can help build better migration literacies, urging us to develop a critical approach to 'voice' that confronts and seeks to dismantle the structural barriers facing people who are often not listened to or ignored. In the context of migration studies, narratives are deeply connected to embodied and emotional forms of knowledge, allowing us to confront uncomfortable truths about restrictive migration regimes, the migration–industry complex, racism and xenophobia, and the tangible impacts of political boundaries. Such narratives also illuminate the legacies of racialized capitalism, colonialism, slavery and empire, providing a deeper understanding of historical and contemporary contexts. Various forms of storytelling, such as autobiographical writing, visual art, and in-person and virtual accounts, can help redress affective numbness (Zembylas, 2023a), address feelings of anger, cultivate resistant anger, and foster active empathy (Zembylas, 2023b: 718).

It is also crucial to critically consider the purpose and impact of presenting counter-stories, and how these are selected. Literature on critical race theory identifies four main aims of counter-narratives that map neatly onto critical pedagogic approaches: providing new and often untold narratives to understand power dynamics; reconstructing dominant narratives on race to combat silencing; fostering activism; and serving as a means of disruption and transformation (Blaisdell, 2021). It is within the aim of fostering activism that critical-pedagogic approaches can disrupt and transform. We must also acknowledge the power relations within which counter-stories and community actions have emerged, as well as the privileges afforded to certain perspectives. Importantly, as Blaisdell observes, counter-stories and community-facing pedagogy are not only about providing alternative perspectives but also about tearing down the master narratives.

From theory to practice: refusing dominant narratives

An engaged pedagogy (bell hooks) means building the classroom as a collaborative community where students feel able to share their counter-stories, experiences and perspectives, and engage with non-dominant narratives. A public pedagogy (Henry Giroux) emphasizes the significance of alternative voices, histories and counter-stories as legitimate narratives that challenge dominant narratives, offer alternative perspectives and decentre power and voice. How might we do this?

- Incorporate diverse voices and sources in the curriculum, including literature, memoirs, documentaries, music and guest speakers from our communities to explore the intersectionality of migration experiences and life stories in terms of race, gender, class and other forms of oppression in various forms.
- Analyse and challenge dominant migration narratives by considering refusal and questioning the uncritical use of migration governance language in how we talk and learn about migration.
- Connect beyond the classroom, either in person or online, with communities and organizations, and consider what work is needed to tear down master narratives and the role of the classroom in this action. Chapter 3 explores how we can do this through breaking free of the classroom and identifying alternative learning spaces.
- Develop better migration literacies by critically examining counter-stories and their contextual influences through reflective writing or journalling to help deepen personal connections to the counter-stories.
- Reflect on the ethics of engaging with others and centring alternative voices as knowledge holders. Where we are connected to community organizations, invite them to review curricula, provide feedback on representation and explore scope for their engagement with the classroom on their terms. When we have key topics we want to cover, invite their views on the questions that matter most to their work that we can tackle in the classroom. Chapter 7 provides a case study of 'the world*ing* classroom' that explores in detail the ethical questions and complexities faced in collaborative curriculum development, offering insights into practical challenges and solutions.

Manifestos as critical pedagogy: from 'what is' to 'what if'

Critical pedagogy extends to interventions in the world, calling for action to disrupt deeply entrenched inequalities and injustices. As discussed throughout this book, there are various approaches and forms of intervention around impact and refusal within critical pedagogy, including engaged pedagogy, public pedagogy, anti-racist pedagogy and the pedagogy of discomfort, which aim to challenge oppressive systems and create transformative learning experiences. In exploring these approaches, the focus shifts to how we can actively engage in this work and advocate for different forms of impact that foster critical resistance within justice-oriented classrooms. One such method is through the creation of learning manifestos as a means for us to articulate values, beliefs and commitments to social justice, and to participate in radical possibilities and envision alternative futures.

> **Problem posing: the manifesto**
>
> Begin by asking students to think deeply about what angers, enrages or upsets them most about the world. This could be related to social injustices, inequalities or any other pressing issues.
>
> Pose the following problem to the students: how might a manifesto channel these emotions? Ask students to envision the kind of world they believe could eradicate these oppressions. What does that world look like, and what are its defining features? Challenge students to think about how they would write about this ideal world in a manifesto format. What principles, values and calls to action would be included in their manifesto?

Manifestos publicly express collective intentions, motives or views. They serve as affective, compelling and powerful tools for advocating radical social change. They also offer an action-oriented framework for embracing emotions like rage, passion and hope as valid forms of knowledge creation and expression. As Breanne Fahs (2019: 34) tells us, manifestos 'simultaneously create and destroy', and by generating discomfort, igniting hope and promise, and stimulating dreaming and imagining, they should inspire the envisioning of alternative futures. Whatever emotions fuel our writing and thinking of and with manifestos, their radical vision and urgency of message take direct aim at the status quo and, in this sense, align with the goals of critical pedagogy. However, while aspirational, manifestos should also provide practical guidance and actionable principles for initiating change (see Case Study 6.1). As a pedagogical tool, they constitute a distinct departure from traditional academic writing and allow for a critical exploration of learning and teaching outside the confines of established conventions and practices. Therefore, in this sense, manifestos hold significant pedagogical value in the critical migration classroom, as they help us translate abstract ideas about social justice learning and teaching into action-oriented principles. In essence, they offer a way to do academic work otherwise.

Engaging in the collective process of writing manifestos enables us, through a shared commitment to imagine change, to actively participate in academic work and invest ourselves in practical ways that extend beyond individual efforts. Collaborative writing activities in the critical migration classroom can also extend beyond students to include community experts, fostering writing-to-learn and writing-for-change approaches. We can use a manifesto for migration learning and teaching to reconnect with community-driven, socially just praxis and serve a diverse range of learner communities, while recentring politics in migration studies in its broadest sense. Some students, particularly those marginalized by intersecting oppressions, may be more attuned to the radical approach required in writing manifestos. This reveals a paradox, as Fahs (2019) observes, where the manifesto genre can disadvantage privileged students and advantage those from lower-status groups who face multiple intersecting oppressions, creating a reversal of the usual dynamics in the academic context. There is also an irony about writing manifestos within the 'neoliberal-imperial-institutionally-racist-university' (Joseph-Salisbury and Connelly, 2021: 1), a space built upon the legacy of colonialism that upholds colonial and racist principles rooted in Enlightenment thinking that perpetuates hierarchies based on race, gender, class and ability. However, if we follow the arguments of this book, there is no doubt that in the critical classroom, the 'political now' compels us to directly confront all structures that sustain racism and oppression, and our manifesto writing needs to forge the micro with the macro; this is where the collective task of manifesto writing can provide another action-oriented framework to move from 'what is' to 'what if'.

From theory to practice: writing manifestos together

A manifesto is an argument for doing things differently and doing them better. It is often set up in opposition to some 'thing' that is not good enough or that is demanding of some kind of change. A manifesto presents an opportunity to say that we stand up for some things and stand against others.

Start with the 'why'

In the classroom, explore the purpose and impact of a manifesto for a migration-related social justice cause, emphasizing the link between history and biography, and how it can take the form of an engaged public pedagogy. Discuss its intent, its role in advancing the cause and how it can lead to meaningful changes, both within and outwith the classroom. Consider its potential legacy and the broader impact when shared.

Write about the 'what'

There are many pedagogical approaches to fostering collective thinking and writing. Begin with individual reflection, then progress to think–pair–share with evolving prompts that gain in complexity. Part of this work can be an exercise of knowledge holding, telling and sharing what we know about a given topic and what we do not know, what we feel about a given topic, and why we care, while encouraging discussion on beliefs and self-reflection. Some suggestions to get started might be:

- What are our guiding principles and values?
- What do we stand for and oppose in the context of migration?
- How do we envision change and connect it to our core values?
- What aspects of learning transformation do we aim for, and what is our call to action?
- Who is our intended audience, and what emotional impact do we aim to create?
- Whose voices are marginalized, and whose voices dominate the discourse?

Start writing!

Recognizing students as 'purveyors of knowledge' (Fahs, 2019: 38), our engagement with migration must go beyond individual learning. Challenging prevailing narratives becomes the collective responsibility of the classroom community, where we hold each other accountable for our actions and perspectives (hooks, 1994). Moreover, our conversations and learning about migration directly impact the development of building better migration literacies. You could develop guiding principles that reflect the arguments within this book as a flexible starting point for classroom discussions and manifesto writing. Following bell hooks, encourage students to break free from traditional academic writing conventions, to write with passion and urgency, to be engaging and daring, to be thought provoking, and to inspire curiosity.

Reflect

Think together about what happens to knowledge in this learning space. Reflect on how our perspectives and understanding have evolved in the critical classroom. Have we re-evaluated our approach and engagement with concepts, leading to a transformation of knowledge? Consider what actions we plan to take with the knowledge we have gained. How will we apply it to create a positive impact in the world, emphasizing both knowledge creation and practical application?

I want to now set out an example of collaborative manifesto building and writing. In 2018, I organized a workshop bringing together a collective of academics, activists, practitioners from third sector and civil society organizations, and masters-level students all working in the area of migration.[2] Our goal was to critically engage with our pedagogy and discuss approaches to teaching about migration in the 'political now'. Our workshop aims were threefold: (1) to identify teaching approaches that are agile and responsive to the 'political now', as well as ethical and responsible, both inside and outside of the classroom; (2) to begin thinking through the value of a pedagogical roadmap for classrooms as somewhere to try to make sense of current events and what this might look like; and (3) to make new teaching and learning connections between what, where and how we teach, and between the experiences and expectations of students and communities.

That day was highly productive, sparking lively discussions and deep self-reflection on our goals in the critical classroom, as was recognizing the limitations of our approaches. We used simple techniques, such as flip-chart paper on walls and coloured post-it notes, to capture our reflections, ideas and questions for ourselves and each other. We encouraged one another to express thoughts on what we felt worked in our teaching, our aspirations for improved practices and our commitment to fostering a more socially just learning environment. These notes were then organized under general categories of 'ethical teaching', 'ethical research' and 'ethical practice', and supplemented with additional workshop notes that were later shared among participants. However, our aspirations extended beyond that day, aiming for a greater impact that would be meaningful and beneficial to those present in the room and others we would encounter in the future. As a result, we collectively decided to craft a manifesto of practice to guide us in our pursuit of better, socially just teaching and research. Drawing inspiration from RISE Australia and Saga Weckman's advice on doing research with Finnish Gypsies (1998), I initially created a draft manifesto and shared it with all participants. This draft initiated an online discussion, where we collectively shaped its content. Once the final version was agreed upon, we adopted the manifesto as a set of guiding principles for ethical pedagogy, guiding our work in our respective fields. Importantly, this manifesto belongs to all who were part of the workshop, and we have shared it as an openly accessible, collaboratively written resource for a broader community of learners (Piacentini et al, 2021 [2018]). It marks the initial step in our ongoing collective praxis, serving as a mechanism to enhance our collaborative work.

Case Study 6.3: A manifesto for a critical pedagogy of migration

Our aim is to foreground ethical pedagogy in our practice.

The term 'Ethical' is used here in the sense of being mindful of the outcomes of and larger intersections of our practice and then implementing this with conviction to challenge binaries, boundaries and engage as many as possible. This relates to education contexts within the academic institution and within real-world settings in the context of collaborative work with partner organizations and communities, and so takes us into and outside of the classroom. Within the framework of our manifesto for change, we commit to a re-centring of ethical practice in teaching, learning and research. We commit to active learning and reflexive research practice that acknowledges and confronts defaults and what feels uncertain and uncomfortable. We seek to foreground the concerns of communities and the third sector, and reflect this in what we teach, how we teach, in developing research ideas, drafting research questions, and identifying methodological approaches.

In our Teaching and Learning we commit to:

- Re-centring fundamental principles of humanity, justice, and equality in our teaching practice. We ask ourselves: Do we make time to do this? How might we do this? How might this connect to real-world contexts in the 'political now'?
- Checking our 'defaults' and 'go-to's' in our teaching. We ask ourselves: Where are my starting points historically, culturally, politically, socially? What are my motivations for selecting this subject matter and why now and why me? Whose stories do I include? Whose do I omit? Whose stories am I aware of? Why? What place do my politics and values have in how I teach and the decisions I make about what I teach? How does my practice privilege certain knowledges over others? Do I encourage others in the learning space to do the same?
- Ethically inviting partner organizations and communities into our learning space. We ask ourselves: Do we talk to research partners and communities about ways to include them in our teaching, to bring out-of-class learning into the class? How can we be creative about innovative learning strategies that can also provide spaces for building networks between the student community and real-world practice (campaign work, volunteering). Are we working with partners to identify opportunities to develop curricula together? Are we making space and time for these conversations to develop? Are we action-oriented collaborators in the classroom? How are we risk aware? Are we creating safe spaces for dialogue but also brave spaces where students may express controversial and challenging views and are asked to be accountable and be challenged by partners, where they may feel discomfort, vulnerable and unsafe as we confront together the challenges of teaching, learning and researching migration in the 'political now'?
- Moving beyond the headlines: We cannot lose context, we must historicize our teaching practice, ensuring students understand the

historical context, while being responsive to the 'political now'. We commit to pushing back against knowledge only delivered in easily accessible bite-size chunks. We commit to ensuring that we integrate space for slow and reflective learning on 'how we got to this point' and thinking on 'where this could go next' in our teaching programmes.
- Building better migration literacies. We ask ourselves: What words and labels do we use? How do we frame debates? What tropes are we trapped in? How do we support each other in understanding these frames? Critical self-reflexivity means we must also turn these questions on ourselves and consider the frames we use and the ethics of our practice in our language, metaphors and selection of material for teaching.
- Using ongoing evaluation and feedback as an active learning process. Don't leave it until the end of a module. As we teach, check in. Ask students and remind them to ask themselves whether the topic is useful and relevant, and how. Do we do enough sense checking? Has thinking changed over the course of learning? What are we still wondering about in the classroom? Are we proposing independent research that is viable academically but also ethically sound and beneficial to research partners and communities? Do we need more spaces for connections between learning and practice, in both in and out of class contexts?

In our Research we commit to:

- Asking ourselves what use is our research going to be to the organization or communities we work in service to and being explicit about who research is for and who benefits. We will ask you what is needed and whether it is more research, other types of work or action. We will ask ourselves are we extracting, collaborating, co-producing, exploiting?
- Defining together what is meant by a meaningful collaborative relationship. Setting clear expectations of each other can be critical to understanding what constitutes a meaningful relationship, why such an approach is necessary, what it might look like in practice, and the underlying ethics involved. We will ask what is the appropriate role of researchers in this organization or community? What is the appropriate role for partners in the research project? What are the roles for partners in the educational context? What methods are we using to decide and evaluate this together? How do we co-create brave spaces for critical discussion and reflection on what is needed for our collaborations to happen in meaningful ways? How can we be better action-oriented collaborators?
- A collaboration that means more than simply gaining access. We will work towards integrating collaboration over the long-term,

including co-writing with partners on different research outputs and dissemination, building this into project plans from the beginning. We commit to moving the status of research partners from 'research resource' to co-producers of knowledge and writing this into proposals for funding. We commit to using existing resources and knowledge about collaboration, but most importantly asking questions of our research partners and being led by their expertise. Remember we might move on after our research is over, but our partners will continue to live its consequences.

- Slowing things down: the 'political now' is pressing and urgent, but the development of relationships and of collaborative work needs time and planning. Factoring in time to our ethical approach creates space for reflection on the salience of the proposed research. Different institutional contexts often operate on different timeframes, discussing and writing this into research proposals, exploring together a range of platforms for realistic dissemination together is good practice.
- Thinking about what language we privilege in our writing. The writing for 'academic'/'non-academic audience' can feel like a false divide. Our communities are also our experts. Instead, we commit to writing with clarity and precision, to communicating complex ideas in accessible ways that do not exclude, presuppose a hierarchy of knowledge or privilege one audience over another. We commit to not making assumptions about knowledge and focusing on accessibility, not on dumbing down.
- Earning our right to be in the field! Building relationships requires a position of solidarity and commitment. We will prioritise the building of trust in researcher relationships, not only for the duration of the project but beyond. We will know who we are contacting and do our homework regardless of the specific research issue we want to explore. We will do everything we can to make sure partner organizations also get to know us so that any decision to collaborate is informed across all parties.
- Not presuming that knowledge is free: the risks and costs, be they financial, time, emotional labour and other, to our communities and research partners need to be recognized and addressed both by the researchers and research institutions/universities. To make this mutually beneficial we think of resources beyond what we need from partners to include the resources we can offer, for free or 'in kind'. However this is framed, we commit to ensuring reciprocity and moving away from entitlement. This needs to be part of the conversation when developing the research relationship and applies to teaching and researching.

Concluding comments

In this chapter, we have explored the question of impact, acknowledging its importance in understanding the policy–research pipeline and the resulting implications for knowledge generation and pedagogical practices. Using our developing migration literacies, we can critically engage with what we understand by impact and different practices of resistance, including acts of refusal, foregrounding counter-stories and adopting dynamic pedagogical approaches like manifesto writing. These efforts are not limited to finding alternative perspectives but focused on tearing down the dominant narratives, disrupting and transforming what and how we learn along the way. By embracing innovative pedagogical methods that push us towards thinking 'what if', we can cultivate critical thinking skills, foster active empathy and encourage students to become active participants in shaping migration-related debates. In conclusion, through a careful engagement with the knotty question of impact in migration research and teaching, as well as the relationalities it centres and sidelines, we can develop a more nuanced understanding of migration dynamics, challenge prevailing narratives and promote social justice in a learning environment that better reflects the complexities and realities of migration experiences. These concerns are not limited to the classroom but extend and connect beyond, and Chapter 7 focuses on the kinds of connections we want to nurture in how we can teach migration otherwise.

7

Connections

Introduction

Chapter 6 explored the intricate connections between impact and the critical-pedagogical classroom, the forms it can take and how it may be refused and rebuilt in meaningful ways. It identified the importance of incorporating the diverse perspectives of students, teachers, refugees, migrants, activists and community organizations, recognizing that none of these positionalities are necessarily mutually exclusive. Building upon these insights, this final chapter explores what this kind of connecting work can or should involve so that we achieve the potential benefits for all when we actively foster and cultivate learning opportunities that extend beyond the confines of the classroom. The central focus of this chapter is on connections: the power of establishing meaningful connections in the pursuit of transformative education and the ethics and politics of building connections. It explores the significance of forging connections at every stage of curriculum design, including the development of course materials, supporting student projects that want to connect to communities, the implementation of connected teaching methodologies and building connected classrooms. The chapter concludes with reflections on the ideas covered across the book, pulling together the connecting threads of this critical pedagogy of migration.

Connecting in with communities beyond the university walls

Engagement with communities outside of the classroom demands of us a shift in thinking from the abstract to the 'real': engaging with real people, real places and real problems. It also provides an opportunity to think about our positionalities as teachers and students in relation to the communities we seek to learn with, to demonstrate our interconnectivity and to better understand why we need knowledge that comes from multiple sources (hooks, 1994; Giroux, 2020). This can be discomforting, as we are forced out of what can feel like the limiting (and in some sense comforting) boundaries of the classroom and campus, and beyond what constitutes 'serious knowledge'. According to Cann and DeMeulenaere (2020: 110), establishing such connections can also give rise to 'discordant communities', where conflicts stemming from differences emerge but ultimately result in profound and powerful learning experiences for all involved, thereby influencing their perceptions of legitimacy. The pedagogical challenge lies not only in creating these diverse spaces initially but also in nurturing a sense of community that embraces differences, allowing discord to surface and generate learning opportunities (hooks, 2003, Cann and DeMeulenaere 2020). Discord, as an extension of discomfort, creates opportunities for difficult conversations that push into and create new learning spaces, and so, in this sense, discord is also generative. Many of us in the classroom are involved in organizations outside the academy and so will be constantly negotiating our academic identities, positionalities and knowledges. We should equally be attentive to the 'realness' of the social worlds and experiences of social inequalities of our students, especially those who face marginalization because of wider social categorization processes and interlocking forms of oppression. This also means avoiding assumptions that students and teachers are not themselves part of multiple communities of practice that will equally be shaped by racialized, gendered and classed identities. Thinking about connections as relational and spatial is a helpful way to explore how the global is constituted in the local in how we understand and navigate our everyday lives.

First, thinking relationally about connections, meaningful relationships develop when we value knowledge, wisdom and experience as expertise rather than simply as testimony. They develop where we make clear that we work in service to communities (Joseph-Salisbury and Connelly 2021) with mutually understood and realistic expectations of each other. Connections grow when, together, we commit to learning carefully and 'care-fully', and where genuine collaboration can lead to a transformation of the ideas we hold of ourselves and others. Practising meaningful research relationships means taking and making time to get to know each other, and being clear on what we need to know and how we value each other, both in abstract and in tangible ways. These foundations are going to be central to building positive, meaningful ways of working together when research and teaching in the 'political now'. Second, thinking spatially about connections offers potential to develop a critical pedagogy of place, focused on our location in our social worlds and how they are shaped by power and politics (Eppley, 2019; Gruenewald, 2003a). Place has an extended understanding here, encompassing both geographic sites and students' backgrounds and experiences of local life in order to understand what happens there (Gruenewald, 2003b). As such, a critical pedagogy of place necessarily problematizes the limits of the classroom, extending beyond it, linking histories, subjectivities, politics and cultures, and offering ways to create or rediscover new spaces for learning that are non-extractive and non-exploitative of other people; here, we can recall the example of the city walk in Chapter 3 that raised important ethical and political questions about how we design place into our learning.

From theory to practice: developing ethical knowledge ecologies

Consider the following questions:

- How do we find out about life-wide learning spaces beyond our classroom?
- How can we actively bridge the gap between traditional university learning spaces and spaces that challenge conventional boundaries of knowledge and expertise?
- What practical steps and concrete actions can we take to create, nurture and engage with connections to a diverse range of communities and experts who operate outside formal academic spaces in meaningful ways?
- When should we incorporate ethics into these relationships, and how can we prioritize ethical considerations effectively?
- How can we proactively address the political dynamics inherent in these relationships, shaping the nature of our connections in ways that align with our shared learning goals and values?

Activities

The aim here is to map knowledge ecologies. Start by defining key terms related to the prompts, such as 'traditional university learning spaces', 'diverse range of experts', 'non-academic partners', 'community learning', 'political dynamics' and so on. Divide the class into small groups to think about each term and prompt. Provide each with a large sheet of paper or a digital collaborative platform and guide them to create a visual map or diagram that represents their ideas for addressing the prompt. The map should include key concepts, actions and connections. Following the group discussions, have each group share their visual 'connecting' maps with the whole class. During their presentations, emphasize practical steps and actions highlighted in their maps, and compare different approaches to each prompt, encouraging students to identify common themes, innovative ideas and potential challenges. Conclude by having students work together to create an action plan using the insights and practical steps from their group maps. This plan should outline concrete actions for bridging traditional and non-academic spaces, building meaningful connections, integrating ethics, and addressing political dynamics.

When we make a distinction between academic and non-academic spheres of experience and practice, we also make a distinction about knowledges: what constitutes valued knowledge and, indeed, who the holders of such knowledge are. Within the field of refugee and migration studies and the work of, for example, third sector and advocacy organizations, we are also in an important moment of accountability for extractive research practices and for perpetuating testimonial injustice. As discussed in this book, the academic–non-academic and academic–activist distinctions are in many cases a false binary and very often connected in complex and interesting ways (Joseph-Salisbury and Connelly, 2021). Intellectual labour and knowledge production are not limited to the university, and while we can and should be critical of the capital-producing conditions of the neoliberal university, many academics and students would describe themselves as activists, working closely with communities in different ways. Work that takes place outside of the academy also informs research and teaching, revealing how one can be both academic and activist in both those spaces. Indeed, in their writing about anarchist pedagogies, Noterman and Pusey (2012: 195) observe that there is no 'outside' to the university. Michele Lancione, speaking about his campaign to get Frontex off campus (see Stierl, 2023), effectively illustrates this point: dangerous connections can also develop that are far removed from anti-oppressive social justice work and that can constitute a form of violent ignorance. Lancione's activism offers a powerful and neat critical analysis of the problem with the policy–research pipeline, the demand for impactful research, the relationships that develop from them, the space for radical responses, the politics of refusal and the kinds of deep and uneasy discomfort produced through difficult and controversial connections. He forcefully reminds us that policy-defined problems are of course never neutral and data are never harmless, and that the question we should be asking ourselves is: are we doing research or providing a service to the state (Stierl, 2023)?

Being radical in this connected learning space, then, requires more than studying radical ideas. Chapter 4 offered the case of the Asylum University as an exploration of experimentation around those very questions of what we define as learning spaces, who is included and where they exist. Another radical approach is for knowledge that exists outwith the academy to be accepted, accredited and celebrated as expertise (Joseph-Salisbury and Connelly, 2021). The connected classroom is one place where this work can begin and where we can find ways to redefine where we see the locus of knowledge production. A connected classroom offers an opportunity to fold in ways of knowing and relating through negotiation, advocacy work, migrant resistance and struggle that emerge in cities and towns in ways that are local and transnational.

In the connected classroom, students and teachers actively engage with each other in relational ways and learn from the city around them, that is, from the people who occupy the city or town, especially those who might not necessarily be considered as belonging to the city. Coalition building, resisting and disrupting are all vital in the fight for epistemic and testimonial justice in the classroom; they help us to expose power and politics, and reveal the ethics of our practice, pointing to what Linda Dittmar and Pamela Annas (2017: 2) call 'teaching against the grain', that is, offering 'renegade possibilities that can in fact occur in any place where teaching and learning aim to embody transformative praxes'. The rest of this chapter focuses on two areas of a pedagogy of connections and coalition building: the first explores 'connecting in' from the perspective of third sector practitioners; and the second focuses on 'connecting across' through cross-border teaching.

Connecting in from the perspective of third sector practitioners: 'You don't know me but ...'

The current landscape of the neoliberal university and its impact agenda, as discussed in Chapter 6, imposes increasing demands on staff to establish meaningful collaborations with non-academic partners. These collaborations can often be reduced to two specific forms: (1) inclusion as a community partner on funding proposals to address predetermined research questions; and (2) designation as a 'community partner' to showcase knowledge exchange activities or provide evidence of impact. HE institutional pressures frequently result in a barrage of requests or invitations from often ill-prepared faculty and students to organizations asking they be named as project partners on research proposals, provide placements or internships, grant access to individuals for research projects, or contribute to sessions without compensation. Such requests are also too often characterized by a lack of any meaningful existing relationships and little consideration for sustaining these relationships in the long term. With these issues in mind, I put the following question to community experts in the field: if we are committed to making social justice a central focus as scholar-activists, what should define our approach to each other, and what principles can guide our collective decision making so we work better together?

Case Studies 7.1 and 7.2 offer some responses and can be used in the classroom in different ways, as discussion documents, as reflective pieces or as a set of principles for building better ethical practice.[1] First, we hear from Zoë Holliday, who, at the time of writing this response for the workshop that was the foundation of this book, was a coordinator for the Refugee Survival Trust, a Glasgow-based charitable organization set up in 1996 that campaigns against the destitution facing refugees and people seeking safety in Scotland.

Case Study 7.1: Collaborating ethically: Example 1

Before choosing and approaching an organization to work with, it is important to understand their day-to-day activities and how they align with your research interests. Consider whether their work relates to the research you want to conduct and if they have access to the people you wish to engage with. It is surprising how often requests are made to organizations that are unrelated to their areas of focus or expertise. Additionally, assess how the organization's work aligns with the curriculum you teach. Determine if your proposed research or outputs would be useful to the organization and frame your proposal in a way that highlights the benefits they would gain from your collaboration. Consider any potential risks your research may pose to the organization and find ways to minimize these risks. If there is a possibility that your research outcomes may not favour the organization, think carefully about the potential impact on their reputation. It is crucial to be mindful of the costs involved for the organization. Placements and collaborations may incur additional expenses such as desk space, overhead contributions, and use of resources. If you can cover these costs or offer compensation, your proposal may be more favourably received. Flexibility is key, so be prepared to adapt your project proposal or request to address concerns or risks raised by the organization. Also, be flexible in accommodating their working practices and demands on their time. Demonstrating your willingness to work within their constraints can enhance the likelihood of successful collaboration.

When your collaboration involves people seeking asylum and refugees, it is crucial to consider what refugees, people seeking asylum, and migrants would gain from participating in your research or bringing their experiences into the classroom. Compensation should be offered when appropriate, such as providing payment or a meaningful role that can enhance their CV and future employment prospects. Additionally, assess whether what you are offering has the potential to bring about positive changes for participants and their communities. If the answers to these questions are no, then you need to re-evaluate and adapt what you are offering. Consider the risks involved in their participation, not only in terms of direct risks such as identification or potential impacts on their asylum claims, but also the potential distress caused by repetitive or sensitive questioning. Reflect on the purpose and necessity of the information you seek. If certain information is not needed or serves no purpose, perhaps you should hold back and prioritize the safety and well-being of the participants. It's vital to create a safe and respectful space for discussions with guest speakers who share their expertise and experiences. The critical classroom should be discomforting in its ability to challenge established knowledge and power dynamics, but it must never be exploitative. Prioritize building meaningful relationships before engaging in sensitive discussions to understand the emotional experiences of both speakers and listeners. Active empathy and responsibility are essential in creating an environment that fosters mutual understanding and respect. Finally, always consider alternatives. Perhaps the kind of data you seek are available in open access repositories. Or the voices you want to hear are already available on other platforms. While it may not always be possible, strive to ensure that your work reflects the voices and perspectives of refugees in meaningful ways. (Zoë Holliday)

Next, in Case Study 7.2, we turn to Dylan Fotoohi, who, at the time of the workshop, was a Development Officer for Family Integration at the Scottish Refugee Council, and Gary Christie, Head of Policy & Communications of the Scottish Refugee Council. They speak about their experience of, and frustration with, extractive approaches to 'collaboration'.

Case Study 7.2: Collaborating ethically: Example 2

"So, you don't know me. But here's a bit about the research I am planning to do. I've already drafted a letter of support from you for my application to [delete as appropriate: ESRC, AHRC, Horizon 20:20] You just need to sign it today by 5pm. And can you get me [enter number] refugees to talk about [enter research question far removed from current preoccupations of refugees or organization]. Oh, and please cost your time to the project and note it as 'in-kind' support in the letter. I'll never bother you again after that."

Okay, at the Scottish Refugee Council we haven't received exactly such a request. Nevertheless, it is a synthesis of some of the less positive experiences and transactions (or extractions) we have had with academics seeking to collaborate with us as a civil society organization working directly with refugees and advocating with and on their behalf. Some of these concerns can equally be applied to teaching as well as conducting research. From our perspective, bridging the gap between academia, communities, and the third sector can be beneficial for all parties. Generating and advancing academic and theoretical knowledge, especially if done with the aim of bringing about positive social change, is advantageous and meaningful. However, to ensure that academic activities and their impact communicate with and contribute to the priorities of non-academic partners, it is essential that the subject matter, methodology, ethics, and the products of academic endeavour are informed by the concerns of communities and the third sector. See us not just as gatekeepers, tick boxes and research subjects but as partners. Involve us meaningfully in the development, design, and implementation of all of your academic activities.

It's our day job to speak to refugees and communities, to engage with policy makers and other practitioners. We know what's happening on the ground. We can bring in real-world policy 'relevance'. We have both the knowledge and the expertise. We are already listened to in many fields. However, two real-world issues we all face are time and resources. Creating time to make this meaningful engagement happen is challenging both for third sector organizations and academia. We also need to understand that we may work to different timeframes. A policy window for change in the fast moving political and policy arena of migration may have come and gone by the time that academic paper is published. Resources will always be a challenge for the third sector. A day out of the office is a day away from advocating for our client group, writing a press release or meeting with civil servants. Our key beneficiaries are refugees not academics. Think about longer-term requests and build us into funding bids.

We have had some excellent, productive, and impactful collaborations with a range of academic institutions. From being consulted and invited to lecture on some modules, to a long-standing programme of placements for student social workers. From academics and Masters' students embedded in our organization that have had practical impact on our work; to involvement in larger scale collaborations that have produced new knowledge and policy change. These have all had one thing in common. They have all been planned, mutually beneficial and meaningful to both parties. We have been very happy to be bothered again by these academics. (Dylan Fotoohi and Gary Christie)

These responses give us much to reflect with. What Zoë, Dylan and Gary have to say might make us feel discomfort or unease as we see our own practices reflected back. If we want to create ethical, epistemically just and meaningful connections in teaching and research, we must listen and reflect on the obligations we have to the communities we work in service to when building a pedagogy of connections. While one might question the relevance of their reflections to teaching, we do well to remember two things: first, developing research projects and ethical supervision of student projects are important components of a socially just pedagogical practice; and, second, we can take these words and apply them to teaching because bringing experts into the classroom requires the same concerns with ethical engagement as good research practice, as discussed in Chapter 3.

Based on the insights from Case Studies 7.1 and 7.2, we can establish five guiding principles for a better, more collaborative pedagogy and practice: pragmatism and managing expectations; valuing time; acknowledging power; affective awareness and 'care-fullness'; and reframing expertise and expanding knowledges. These principles, in themselves another form of manifesto, can be used to shape classroom discussion, help with project planning and encourage us to build ethically and politically careful and 'care-full' connections.

Concerning, first, pragmatism and managing expectations, wherever they take place, social justice conversations require a thorough understanding of how collaborative working can serve as a catalyst for bringing about meaningful transformation. We need to be not only reflexive but also honest and realistic about why we want to work with community organizations or groups, as well as why they may want to work with us, and we do well to remember that the terms of that collaboration will mean different things. Can we clearly explain what we are doing differently in terms of our learning focus and purpose? If we are committed to actively involving expert voices in shaping the learning experience, then we must remember that collaboration also encompasses emotional investment and intellectual labour, which also have their limits. Setting out those limits better and earlier in any social justice conversation helps manage expectations.

Second, concerning how we value time, when 'connecting in' to communities, time takes on a particular significance. It encompasses more than the mere presence in the physical classroom space; it also involves the allocation of time away from other important commitments and tasks. Ethical engagement with the politics of time means consideration of how time is valued differently, compensated for and respected in collaborative endeavours. Creating a flexible and responsive learning environment better accommodates different schedules and time constraints, allowing for meaningful participation, without unduly burdening any individual or group. We must also communicate this with students. Compensation for time will depend on the specific context and resources available, and may involve financial compensation, particularly when it involves a contribution of time and expertise outside of regular commitments. Acknowledging and valuing the time and effort invested by community partners through the attribution and recognition of expertise are also important forms of compensation that disrupt how and where knowledge is valued.

Third, concerning acknowledging power, within the shared space of the classroom, we each of us hold different social positions. We must both recognize the power dynamics inherent in these positions and consider how we wield that power because it can often be obscured or go unnoticed, leading to unequal interactions and outcomes. We must critically examine our intentions behind bringing people into the classroom space and whether our actions and teaching practices reinforce or disrupt these power dynamics. Recognizing and interrogating power dynamics within the classroom and taking a position of working in service to communities help us better achieve a transformative educational experience that promotes social justice.

Fourth, concerning affective awareness and 'care-fullness', we must recognize, validate and take seriously the range of emotional responses our requests for classroom collaboration and pedagogic input can evoke, including scepticism, suspicion, weariness, reluctance or refusal to participate. Power imbalances can contribute to people feeling marginalized or exploited within learning settings, especially if our focus is learning *about* rather than learning *with*. As has been explored in this book, merely declaring the classroom or research project to be anti-oppressive, just or 'safe' is insufficient. We can practise affective awareness and 'care-full-ness' by fostering a culture of active listening and learning. When working with communities, we can provide space for individuals to express their needs and boundaries, and be transparent regarding the intentions and objectives of the research or classroom project, acknowledging the emotional impact of dialogue and respecting community partners' autonomy and agency in deciding their level of involvement.

Fifth, concerning reframing expertise and expanding knowledges, migrant communities and advocacy groups possess valuable knowledge that has been developed, shared and passed down through generations; they are already very well equipped with knowledge and information, and are listened to as experts. When community partners and experts enter the classroom, be clear that we are seeking their expertise as knowledge holders, not just their testimony, and this holds a privileged place in our learning space. In the classroom, practising epistemic justice involves recognizing and accrediting this expertise. Provide meaningful recognition and attribution. Ensure that the knowledge we get access to from 'connecting in' is appropriately cited and recognized within the curriculum learning materials and discussions. This begins the work of interrupting practices of knowledge extraction, amplifying and valorizing marginalized perspectives through dialogue and reflection.

> **Reflective task**
>
> Reflect on the notions of testimonial justice and epistemic justice covered across this book. Discuss how these concepts relate to recognizing and valuing the expertise and knowledge of community partners and experts. How do you ensure that voices are heard and listened to, respected, and integrated into the collaborative process? Consider what happens to a request to work collaboratively with our communities when we flip the narrative, decentre our needs and practise testimonial and epistemic justice:
>
> - Instead of approaching them with the question, 'How can you help me?' ask, 'How can I help you?'.
> - Instead of telling them, 'Here's what I need to know', ask, 'What do you need to know?'.
> - Instead of emphasizing 'Here's how you will benefit', ask, 'What do you hope to gain by taking part?'.

It is too easy to claim to be an activist 'out there' but to fail to look at the structures that we work within. What is interesting to think with here is that although the classroom is *of* the institution, by asking these questions, we can locate ourselves *beyond* its control and capture. Through the work of listening, connecting in and refusing, we can show our students, each other and our communities that we are not just here accepting everything: that we do not just talk about critical thinking and non-extractive approaches to research and learning in our seminars but take active stances both 'out there' in the world and within our institutions. Therefore, in response to the earlier question about what should characterize our approach to centring social justice in our pedagogy, one answer might be: a commitment to ensuring proximity to, and embeddedness in, struggle, to being accountable to the communities we serve and to adopting radical approaches of learning *with*, studying *with*, thinking *with*, and knowing *with*. Such a commitment means that, together, we create spaces and opportunities to 'connect in' to each other and cross boundaries that challenge norms about who gets to be the expert, whose knowledge counts where and why.

From theory to practice: 'Nothing about us without us is for us'

There are many fantastic resources available to guide ethical approaches in collaborative work, challenging the privileged status of academic knowledge and prompting us to confront uncomfortable questions about our motivations and intentions, as well as how we become complicit in perpetuating dominant knowledge hierarchies. Engaging with critical work on decolonizing methodologies already referred to in this book is an excellent place to start. Building on the RISE manifesto (Chapter 6) and Zoë's and Dylan and Gary's words in this chapter, the following resources offer further practical tools to acknowledge and correct harmful practices. The intention here is not to simply offer additional ethical and political guidelines, as if they were mere checklists. Instead, the goal is to shed light on the complexities of representation and participation. By actively using these tools and seriously considering the questions they raise, we are compelled to work towards establishing a classroom that is socially just, fair and ethical. In doing so, we move closer to achieving our objectives of reciprocity, respect and mutual benefit.[2]

ProTestimony (Refugee Hosts nd), curated by Hari Reed and collaborators, and hosted by Refugee Hosts, is an online exhibition of Reed's research into how humanitarianism has been changed by Calais. The questions and dilemmas raised may be applied more expansively to research and teaching about refugee-related matters. Protestimony addresses discomforting questions about participation, voyeurism, testimonial injustice, the politics of representation, dignity, respect and what might be considered morally right or wrong.

The blog 'How can academics support migrants rights groups/cause? To begin with, forget that you are an academic' by Eiri Ohtani (2017), a migrant rights campaigner and activist, offers advice to academics and students who want to support or get involved in migrant rights groups or activism.

Caroline Lenette has written extensively about decolonizing methodologies and developing social justice-oriented collaborative research practices. Her two books – *Arts-Based Methods in Refugee Research: Creating Sanctuary* (Lenette, 2019) and *Participatory Action Research: Ethics and Decolonization* (Lenette, 2022) – are excellent places to start thinking through many of these questions.

Connecting across through cross-border learning: the world*ing* classroom

Teaching and learning practices do not need to be limited to institutional or indeed national borders. Technology can play a significant role in facilitating these spaces by enabling connectivity and collaboration across distances. How might we do this work? This second case example introduces the 'world*ing* classroom' as a kind of blueprint for developing connected cross-border teaching practice.

As a university faculty member, it is common to receive emails seeking potential research collaborations, especially in the context of impact and the push for, and rewarding of, more collaborative and interdisciplinary work, expected at an increasingly accelerated 'add names, stir and serve' pace. In 2015, I received one such email, introducing Danish academics who were seeking Scottish partners for a multidisciplinary research network about 'grass-roots refugee solidarity initiatives' in various North European cities. The network was multidisciplinary, seeking to bring together diverse perspectives from anthropology, sociology, critical geography, political science and international relations. The slow machinery of funding bodies meant that the conversation that began in 2015 was eventually funded during 2017–19 as the Helping Hands Network. Over that two-year period, we met four times for three-day field visits in Copenhagen, Nijmegen, Glasgow and Hamburg, visiting 25 different solidarity-focused initiatives, including pop-up distributions centres for clothing, bicycle recycling, community cafes, health centres, homework clubs and community groups. We learned about the practice of solidarity work and what remained behind when the 'crisis' subsided. We talked about place and space, and connected the 2015 moment to histories and memories, to the local to the global and the present to the past. The formally funded period of research came to an end in June 2019, but the academics from Glasgow (myself included) and Nijmegen were keen to continue working together, building on the research relationships and friendships that had formed.[3] We had gained a deeper understanding of our respective cities and identified similarities and differences in terms of working-class and community solidarity, activism and narratives related to colonial histories. As researchers and teachers, we began dreaming together, envisioning possibilities for cross-border teaching and building on our work together. Our goal was to create a learning space that went beyond the local context and engaged with the current political debates and events within our respective historical frameworks. We were particularly interested in learning from each other's experiences and enriching our understanding of solidarity work through mutual exchange.

We needed to determine how to bring this vision to life and make it a reality, and so we started where we were; modelling the research network approach of openness to learning and finding commonalities in translocal spaces with our respective communities, we began with the lenses of place, history and memory. A serendipitous funding call between our institutions meant that we could meet face to face in Glasgow and Nijmegen. Bringing together masters' students, community activists and academic staff from both institutions in a collaborative learning space, we conceptualized the notion of a 'world*ing* classroom'. The term 'world*ing*' reflected our ongoing and generative process of linking diverse positionalities, academic disciplines and places, and acknowledged the significant relational context and content that connected our sites. Together, we identified a focus on borders, hospitality and asylum from different geographical and societal perspectives, and identified the relevant points in our respective curricula to integrate our connected classroom. At the core of our world*ing* classroom was a commitment to community-driven pedagogy, that is, building an innovative and dynamic online learning environment where students, lecturers, community partners and activists could engage with migration-related issues from multiple perspectives. This approach situated knowledge and experiences within a broader translocal and global context, fostering the co-creation of academic knowledge. Additionally, it supported an active, socially just pedagogy that challenged preconceived notions of agency and action. The 'what' and 'how' of this work can be summarized in two main steps:

1. Preparation: our in-person workshops in both places were central to bringing community partners and activists with whom we had long-standing relationships along with us to collaborate, including during inception, classroom design and delivery. We invited current students to share their comments about our project ambitions and feasibility, and their perspectives on student learning. Both students and partners pushed us to explain what we wanted to do and why, holding us accountable for all the claims we were making (And this was challenging!). The workshop discussion was mapped by a visual facilitator to keep track of our processual decision making. This visual representation served as a reference point as we reflected on our pedagogical interventions during the subsequent stages of the project.
2. Co-producing the course material: having decided our substantive focus, we developed a comprehensive set of resources that reflected the practices and approaches of each site involved. Due to institutional limitations, we were unable to provide students from both universities with access to a single shared virtual learning environment (VLE). As a workaround, we duplicated the resources and made them available to both groups of students. Clear guidelines were provided on how to engage with the materials in a translocal manner. We recorded a video for each site about the historical context and current practices related to shelter/hospitality. Additionally, we curated a diverse range of materials that were relevant to the topic and spoke to the specific sense of place. These materials included published papers, student theses, opinion pieces and commentaries from activists, and photography. We also formulated guiding questions to prompt meaningful discussions among the students.

If we consider the world*ing* classroom as a model or blueprint for constructing translocal connected classrooms, the following discussion on gains and lessons can serve as a valuable pedagogical tool to proactively anticipate, and navigate, the potential challenges that may arise. First, the gains. Students experience the dynamic creation of collaborative spaces in local and translocal contexts with a unique real-time learning experience.

They also gain valuable critical thinking skills as they learn about one place through the lens of another place, as well as skills in navigating intercultural knowledge and experiences. Learning of colonial legacies and the coloniality of migration governance was shocking and surprising; for many, it was a confrontation with their sense of national progressiveness and it produced discomfort. As teachers, we were able to engage with international education systems and teach about places from diverse perspectives while piloting community-led teaching practices spanning local and international boundaries. Our partners, who are actively involved in the project, gain insights into alternative approaches to organizing solidarity work and building cross-national alliances. The knowledge and experiences of migrants are also key, and migrant-led organizations and community groups are integral to the learning space as experts. This approach brings diverse expertise directly into the educational setting, reshaping the relationship between the university and civil society, and fostering a more authentic and multidirectional exchange of knowledge and ideas.

We also learned several lessons. First, creating such a classroom requires a significant commitment of time and resources from everyone involved. In its first iteration, we dedicated ample time for planning, discussions and reflections about delivery. We also relied on the participation and time of others involved in this process, and a small amount of funding for our workshops meant that we could compensate participants for their time. It is worth noting that out classroom first took place before the COVID-19 pandemic, when online platforms like Zoom were not necessarily as widely used or considered mainstream. With increased accessibility of online meeting spaces, we now have a better understanding and knowledge of how to effectively and more time-efficiently work in virtual environments. However, we still need to consider how we compensate partners for their time online.

Second, the need for careful attention and consideration to language in a cross-border, translocal and multilingual setting needs to be recognized. English emerged as the primary language of instruction due to the practicalities of our English-speaking and English-taught courses at the Scottish and Dutch universities. However, we are aware that this choice could inadvertently reinforce racialized linguistic hierarchies, a key feature of coloniality. A shared language facilitated communication, but it also presented challenges: there were disparities in, and discomfort around, language proficiency within the classroom; we had incorrectly assumed shared understandings of concepts and migration-related ideas; we experienced some translation issues, including potential mistranslations; and there were communicative difficulties due to accents and language barriers. We have since produced materials in multilingual formats, for example, Dutch-language resources alongside brief English-language summaries, to try to rebalance the reliance on English and incorporate materials from Dutch-speaking activist organizations.

Third, the experiences and responses of students in the connected world*ing* classroom raised important reflections regarding how we locate colonial histories and legacies within the learning space. In our very first iteration of the world*ing* classroom, one Dutch student remarked: "We don't have as many issues for racism here as you seem to do in Scotland." This observation could very easily have been presented in the opposite direction, as it reflects a denial, or amnesia, that is deeply ingrained in mainstream narratives in both sites. It speaks to a more general lack of awareness of colonial histories and their ongoing influence, as well as the structural role that race and racism continue to play in Dutch/Scottish societies. Students have repeatedly expressed shock and shame at learning of their respective colonial histories in their sites of learning. Confronting these challenges to self-identities and addressing racial dynamics, the classroom can be deeply unsettling and requires ongoing preparatory work with students. One practical activity could involve encouraging students to reflect on their unlearning of historical narratives and anonymously sharing these reflections with each other, using an online discussion board or a shareable Google doc, in order to stimulate discussion and prepare for discomfort. Activities like making empire visible (see Chapter 2) can also support some of this work of locating the present in the past.

Teachable moment: racism in the classroom

Language and how we talked about race, racism and racialization also surfaced as an issue in our world*ing* classroom. In one instance, a student in one location used a racialized term, 'coloured', to describe people of colour, seemingly without recognition of, or attention to, its racist connotations. Students reported their disappointment with faculty staff's failure to address the issue in their feedback. We followed up with what we had named 'a restorative discussion' to address everyday racism and explore possibilities for anti-racist action in the classroom. However, the session did not meet the students' expectations; in their words, the discussion became a confusing and unsatisfactory debate about what Alana Lentin calls 'not racism', and this reinforced for them a Scottish/Dutch exceptionalism in relation to colonial and imperial histories. They felt that academic staff dominated, and the conversation became hostile, without a clear conclusion or indication of next steps. While the intention was to create a space for discussion, on reflection, the discomfort and dissatisfaction did not sit well with us. We were perhaps defensive, but we also felt that when trying to address the question of language and translation, and the dominance of English as a colonial legacy itself, this discussion was shut down or dismissed by some of the students. The outcome fell short of the desired goal. The complexity of managing such multilingual conversations online and across two contexts posed significant challenges for everyone involved.

The cross-institutional, cross-language and cross-disciplinary nature of the world*ing* classroom does not excuse or explain away racism but provides a critical context that demands our collective confrontation. This proved to be a very discomforting situation for everyone involved, and we continue to reckon with these complexities. The aim of the world*ing* classroom was to build a space where all participants are exposed to the positionalities of their knowledge claims and critically reflect on their value and relevance beyond their individual classrooms. This moment reveals that racial literacy should be foregrounded in world*ing* classroom preparation, as should our challenge to the exceptionalism often associated with so-called 'progressive' nations. Taking practical steps to address this issue, key texts that examine exceptionalism and racial dynamics have now been incorporated into the curriculum.

Talking points

- How could we have proactively addressed the discomfort and power imbalance in the learning environment by actively involving students in co-creating and shaping the restorative space? What specific strategies or approaches might have facilitated this collaborative effort, ensuring that student voices and concerns were foregrounded?
- Where is the space to consider language and its effects in this example?
- What alternative approaches or actions, or specific changes in our methods, communication or facilitation, might have led to a more positive and productive experience for all students involved and better racial literacies?

A fourth lesson of our world*ing* classroom has been that acknowledging personal and disciplinary positionality is a crucial aspect of teaching migration because it is a field of multidisciplinary perspectives that may conflict with one another. The issue of homogeneity and heterogeneity in the classroom also needs to be addressed as we think about whose views are privileged and whose are marginalized, and why that is. Bringing multiple perspectives and voices together is an inherently political and ethical task that comes with responsibility to and for each other. Having non-academic partners play central roles in the connected classroom, helping to build the curriculum, bringing knowledge as experts and engaging with students as facilitators, offers some ways through disciplinary differences and a framework to place their knowledge and expertise at the centre.

The world*ing* classroom model offers many riches. It provides the opportunity to begin a pedagogic process that leads to important learning outcomes, such as: seeing and understanding issues from various perspectives though critical literacies; developing intercultural competencies; and situating knowledges and experiences in a broader translocal context. The pedagogical principles and technologies developed in the world*ing* classroom can be replicated and adapted. It is also a very enriching and enjoyable experience; there is an excitement every year we come to teach this connected session as we review materials, talk about our communities of students and bring our own hopes for transformative learning to our shared educational space. Even with the challenges, it has achieved what we hoped it would, that is, bringing different expertise directly to bear in the educational setting, and in this way has the potential to interrupt and reconfigure the relationship between the university and civil society, making knowledge exchange a truly multidirectional process. However, the world*ing* classroom also raises important questions about pedagogical discomfort. It highlights the necessity of acknowledging and confronting historical legacies of racism, colonialism and empire in understanding migration-related issues. It emphasizes the need to critically examine power dynamics, racial hierarchies and the language used in the classroom to ensure that teaching and learning spaces are inclusive, anti-oppressive and socially just. It also requires that we find ways, as bell hooks suggests, to cope with conflict. By recognizing and addressing these issues, the world*ing* classroom has become a transformative space for critical engagement and meaningful learning.

Concluding comments

This chapter has been about connections. It has focused on how we build connections with different communities of experts and learners who we also work in service to, with suggested approaches that require of us to unlearn what we understand by socially just and anti-oppressive practice. Such connections mean that we, as academics and students, are held to account in important ways by our communities, so that we can together interrupt how we see the world and build really useful knowledge. We need to nurture and nourish connections to advance social justice causes in ways that disrupt and transform. We can also connect through collaborative teaching practices and approaches that push us towards new and challenging ways of thinking about how the local is constituted in the global and how we locate the 'political now' in its historical context of colonial legacies and imperial ties. Connected classrooms are important reflexive spaces of unlearning, where we challenge our assumptions, reconsider power dynamics and develop resources together. This work can be uncomfortable but ultimately productive in disrupting and transforming our perspectives, in decentring and recentring knowledge, and in challenging the dominant migration narratives that have come to shape so much of how we talk about migration. It is here that we can pull together the threads of connections woven through the book.

Reconnections

Developing a Critical Pedagogy of Migration opened with three key ideas that shape its work: critical pedagogy is a necessary confrontation with neutrality and power in the classroom; interrogating migration knowledge requires developing critical literacies as a beginning point; and learning is not limited to the classroom, and knowledge comes in multiple forms. It then set out three key interventions the book hopes to make on how we learn and teach migration: the 'political now' can only be located in its historical context; discomfort is a welcome and necessary way to 'do good harm'; and building better migration literacies are necessary to disrupting and transforming learning. These were set out as separate concerns, but this is of course a superficial distinction; as the pages of the book have shown, they intricately fold into each other, as these last few pages will set out.

This book's approach has been rooted in an understanding of critical pedagogy that is embedded in politics and ethics through necessity. Doing the work of critical pedagogy in migration teaching, and doing it better, requires of us an openness to discomfort and a commitment to challenging the knowledge hierarchies we bring with us and draw upon as teachers and as students in the classroom, as only then can we create transformative spaces for learning. Extending the theme of this last chapter, and bringing this book to its conclusion (on these pages anyway), there are many connections we can make. *Developing a Critical Pedagogy of Migration* has argued that we must recognize the connections between the 'political now' and the colonial legacies and imperial ties that continue to haunt our present. Essential for developing a critical consciousness and building migration literacies is understanding: the historical context and the ways in which colonialism and imperial ties continue to influence knowledge production; the framing and semantic institutionalization of migration governance; and the ways in which border technologies of surveillance, control, containment, sorting, classification and settlement, as well as the legacy of colonial idioms, can be both hidden and revealed in migration governance language (see Chapter 5). By critically examining these legacies, we can connect more deeply to the biases embedded in dominant narratives, in the construction of the immigrant imaginary and in the reproduction of colonial ideologies in how we teach and learn about migration (see Chapter 2). Making these connections is necessary for building migration literacies to help us develop our praxis, that is, to make us better equipped to confront the uncritical reproduction of colonial governance technologies and the semantic institutionalization that shapes so much of our ways of knowing and relating (see Chapters 2 and 5).

The 'political now' is also deeply connected to our emotions, bringing with it ethical and political implications, as well as consequences for the discomfort and vulnerabilities we feel through our experience of conscientization (see

Chapters 3 and 4). It is in developing a critical pedagogy of migration that we open ourselves to the affective investments and emotional entanglements of the work of social justice teaching so that we can indeed 'do good harm' (see Chapter 3). Doing good harm is a necessary outcome because pursuing transformative education disrupts established systems and beliefs, and this necessitates an emotional response that can be difficult and discomforting, and one that may even be resisted. Doing good harm is productive of transforming not only how we see, describe and understand the world but also what we can do to change it. In this sense, it too is connected to critical engagement with the 'political now' and our reckoning with history (see Chapter 2) and is a central connecting feature of engaging with the ethical and political pedagogy advocated in this book. It requires that we become better witnesses by placing passive empathy and ignorance to one side, and critically engaging with the literacies we need to cut through the noise, recentre power, overcome race-blindness, name violence and manage our affective investments and, in many cases, our feeling of being overwhelmed (see Chapters 3 and 4).

Doing good harm is also a vital driver and outcome of building the kinds of migration literacies we need to interrupt and expose the depoliticized dominant narratives of migration governance that reproduce so much injustice and harm (see Chapter 5), both purposefully and explicitly. Building better migration literacies involves developing a deep understanding of migration beyond the narrow lens of policy and legal frameworks as depoliticized tools for talking about migration. Better migration literacies require connecting the lived, and live, experiences of migrants through storytelling and counter-stories, counter-empirics, and knowledge holding as forms of serious knowledge. It requires working with alternative ways of doing epistemic justice to the epistemic violence of dominant discourses that are reductive or stereotypical and that frame migration as a problem to be managed (see Chapters 5 and 6).

Better migration literacies are also about how we build our communities, and they lay the foundations for developing different kinds of praxis within and outwith the classroom as we 'connect in' and 'connect across' different communities of learners and experts (see Chapters 1 and 6). Meaningful connections emerge through collaborations that are social justice oriented, demanding of us a critical unlearning of what constitutes useful knowledge, where we look for it, who holds it and how we can build it together (see Chapter 7). Reading the world to read the word means that we no longer accept the silencing of the legacies of colonialism, the problematic hegemony of migration governance, the harmful reliance on metaphors and metonyms, or our positions as spectators to the violence of borders and divisive 'culture wars'. Reading the world helps us identify and make space for refusals to happen and for refusals to reorientate our practice (see Chapter 6). We can connect our refusal to accept social injustice to those interrupting and disrupting spaces that counter-stories and practices of witnessing offer to us. However, this also demands that we practise openness to doing academic work otherwise, where rethinking what constitutes 'serious knowledge' offers opportunities to dismantle dominant ways of knowing, not just as presenting alternative perspectives but as ways to tear down established practices and build new ways of working in the classroom (see Chapters 4, 5 and 6). Connections also rely upon new ways of imagining how things could be, the 'what if'. Manifestos for learning offer us a pedagogical device, a pedagogy of possibilities, where we commit to struggle where we are and dream the impossible. These connections urge us to develop an engaged and public pedagogy, and ethically and politically informed praxis (see Chapter 6).

In line with the traditions of anti-oppressive and anti-racist practice, the work that *Developing a Critical Pedagogy of Migration* calls for in the classroom is interruptive and disruptive. It involves an ongoing and difficult practice of unlearning. It is about dismantling our own complicity in sustaining the immigrant imaginary, or in reproducing migration governance as the dominant or default way to talk about migration. It is about imagining beyond in order to challenge and transform what we understand about really useful knowledge, the location of expertise and the holders of that knowledge. It is about work that demands practices of resistance, of working in service to, and in solidarity with, our communities to dismantle systems of oppression. This means that we connect deeply with each other to foster spaces for dialogue, reflection and critical questioning, allowing for the exploration of alternative perspectives and the reimagining of possibilities. This is doing good harm; this is a pedagogy of hope.

Developing a Critical Pedagogy of Migration has been about approaches we can adopt to change how we read the world to read the word in order to then shape and mould how we teach and learn about migration so that we, and the next generation of scholars and activists, teachers and learners, can challenge the dominant dehumanizing narratives that have come to characterize how we talk about migration. *Developing a Critical Pedagogy of Migration* offers the reader a roadmap, with practical tools and strategies for building the critical classroom. The hope of this book, through its problem posing and reflective tasks, theory to practice teaching activities, case studies, teachable moments, talking points and suggested activities, is that it offers the reader a practical toolbox to start the work of building the critical classroom. It requires an ongoing commitment to ethical and political praxis. Ultimately, building the critical classroom is a continual process of learning and unlearning, critically engaging with the complexities of migration and social justice, dismantling and rebuilding, disrupting, and transforming. This is only the beginning.

Notes

Chapter 2

1. Indeed, it produced an opposite response. On 7 March 2023, in her speech at the House of Parliament introducing the (then) Illegal Immigration Bill 2023, Suella Braverman doubled down on her hard line stance on immigration, insisting "we need to stop the waves of illegal migrants breaching our borders ... Yesterday's laws are simply not fit for purpose ... They will not stop coming here until the world knows if you do come to Britain illegally you will be detained and swiftly removed" (source: www.hansard.parliam ent.uk/commons/2023-03-07/debates/87B621A3-050D-4B27-A655-2EDD4AAE6 481/IllegalMigrationBill). Any internet search of Braverman speeches provides extensive evidence of her particular brand of divisive, dangerous rhetoric.
2. Migrantization categorizes and prioritizes individuals as migrants through state processes, focusing on the migrant population as the primary unit of analysis (Dahinden, 2016; Anderson, 2019). In contrast, de-migrantization broadens the perspective to include various segments of the population, including migrants. Racialization involves structuring social relations based on attributes like biology and culture, assigning individuals to social groups believed to reproduce these characteristics (Miles and Brown, 2003).

Chapter 3

1. For examples, see: the British Sociological Association's 'Statement of ethical practice' (available at: www.britsoc.co.uk/bsa_statement_of_ethical_practice.pdf); the International Sociological Association's 'Code of ethics' (available at: https://www.isa-sociology.org/en/about-isa/code-of-ethics/); the American Sociological Association's 'Code of ethics' (available at: https://www.asanet.org/wp-content/uploads/asa_cod e_of_ethics-june2018a.pdf); the Australian Sociological Association's 'Code of ethics' (available at: https://tasa.org.au/content.aspx?page_id=22&club_id=671860&module_ id=357739); the National Health and Medical Research Council (NHMRC's) 'National statement on ethical conduct in human research (2007) – updated 2018' (available at: www.nhmrc.gov.au/about-us/publications/national-statement-ethical-conduct-human-research-2007-updated-2018); and UK Research and Innovation's (UKRI's) 'Core principles on ethics' (available at: https://www.ukri.org/councils/esrc/guida nce-for-applicants/research-ethics-guidance/framework-for-research-ethics/our-core-principles/).
2. Some resources I work with include 'Hidden stories' by the Association of Visitors to Immigrant Detainees (AVID) (available at: https://aviddetention.org.uk/sites/defa ult/files/images/Hidden%20Stories_WEB.pdf) and 'Voices from detention' by Bail for Immigration Detainees (available at: https://www.biduk.org/pages/voices-from-detention).
3. See: https://missingmigrants.iom.int/methodology

⁴ UNITED for Intercultural Action is a European network against nationalism, racism and fascism, and in support of migrants, refugees and minorities. See: https://unitedagainstrefugeedeaths.eu/about-the-campaign/about-the-united-list-of-deaths/

⁵ For Abolitionist Futures, see: https://icopa2018.wordpress.com/information/safer-spaces-statement/
For Sisters Uncut, see: www.sistersuncut.org/saferspaces/
For the Anti-Racist Forum, see: www.antiracistforum.org/safer-space
For the Safer Spaces Poster Project, see UniArts Helsinki. Available at: www.uniarts.fi/en/guides/student-initiative-creating-safer-spaces/

Chapter 4

¹ See www.unherd.com/about-unherd/.
² See www.academyofideas.org.uk/about-the-academy-of-ideas/.
³ On 6 November 2023, in a Politics Hub Sky News interview, Conservative Peer Baroness Sayeeda Warsi accused Suella Braverman of actively 'fighting culture wars' and creating fires rather than putting them out after branding pro-Palestinian demonstrations 'hate marches' (source: https://www.youtube.com/watch?v=lKUQLCWP3jA).

Chapter 5

¹ See also Migrant Voice (available at: www.migrantvoice.org/toolkit) and the Ethical Journalism Network (available at: https://ethicaljournalismnetwork.org/resources/guidelines-ethical-migration-reporting).
² I am indebted to Sean Cameron Golden's (2023) article directing me to this invaluable 2020 online talk organised by Haymarket books "Abolitionist Teaching and the Future of Our Schools". Available at: www.youtube.com/watch?v=uJZ3RPJ2rNc&t=2521s
³ See www.iom.int
⁴ See Waka Well, available at: www.wakawell.info/en

Chapter 6

¹ Economic And Social Research Council www.ukri.org/councils/esrc/impact-toolkit-for-economic-and-social-sciences/defining-impact/
² The manifesto, which includes a full listing of the manifesto collective made up of academics, students, community organizations, advocacy groups and activists, is available at: https://criticalpedagogymigration.wordpress.com/

Chapter 7

¹ I am indebted to Zoë, Dylan and Gary for their consent to use a version of their reflections from papers submitted to a workshop on critical pedagogy approaches. Their views are based on their many years of experience working in the refugee/asylum sector.
² See: https://refugeehosts.org/2017/12/12/protestimony/
³ My fellow academics from University of Glasgow and Radboud University were Gareth Mulvey, Kolar Aparna, and Joris Schapendonk.

References

Achiume, T. (2019) 'Migration as decolonization', *Stanford Law Review*, 71(6): 1509–74. Available at: https://ssrn.com/abstract=3330353

Adu-Gyamfi, J. (2015) 'Ethical challenges in cross-cultural field research: a comparative study of UK and Ghana', *African Social Science Review*, 7(1): Art 3. Available at: http://digitalscholarship.tsu.edu/assr/vol7/iss1/3

Ahmed, S. (2004) 'Declarations of whiteness: the non-performativity of anti-racism', *Borderlands*, 3(2).

Ahmed, S. (2014) *The Cultural Politics of Emotion* (2nd edn), Edinburgh: Edinburgh University Press.

Ahrens, J. and Fliethmann, A. (2020) 'Metaphors of migration: an introduction', *On_Culture: The Open Journal for the Study of Culture*, 10. Available at: http://geb.uni-giessen.de/geb/volltexte/2020/15785/

Albtran, A., Al-Dubaee, S., Al-Hashimi, H., Beja, M.N., Gilson, N.F., Izzeddin, A. Kirkwood, S., Mansaray, A., Mpofu, S.D., Ní Raghallaigh, M., O'Reilly, Z. Smith, K. M. and Zamir, M. (2022) *Research Involving People of a Refugee Background: Considerations for Ethical Engagement*, Dublin: University College Dublin.

Anderson, B. (2019) 'New directions in migration studies: towards methodological de-nationalism', *Comparative Migration Studies*, 7(36): 1–13.

Anderson, B. and Blinder, S. (2015) 'Who counts as a migrant? Definitions and their consequences', Migration Observatory Briefing, University of Oxford, Centre on Migration, Policy and Society.

Andersson, R. (2014) *Illegality, Inc.: Clandestine Migration and the Business of Bordering Europe*, Oakland, CA: University of California Press.

Andersson, R. (2018) 'The price of impact: reflections on academic outreach amid the "refugee crisis"', *Social Anthropology*, 26(2): 222–37.

Aparna, K. and Kramsch, O. (2018) 'Asylum university: re-situating knowledge-exchange along cross-border positionalities', in G. Bhambra, D. Gebrial and K. Nişancıoğlu (eds) *Decolonizing the University*, London: Pluto Press, 93–107.

Aroa, B. and Clemens, K. (2013) 'From safe spaces to brave spaces: a new way to frame dialogue diversity and social justice', in L. Landreman (ed) *The Art of Effective Facilitation*, Sterling, VA: Stylus, 135–50.

Avalos, N. (2021) 'Decolonizing the classroom: settler colonialism, knowledge production, and antiracism', in A. Desai and H.N. Nguyen (eds) *Global Perspectives on Dialogue in the Classroom*, Cham: Palgrave Macmillan, 23–32.

Back, L. (2007) *The Art of Listening*, London: Berg.

Bakewell, O. (2008) 'Research beyond the categories: the importance of policy irrelevant research into forced migration', *Journal of Refugee Studies*, 21(4): 432–53.

Bandola-Gill, J. and Smith, K.E. (2022) 'Governing by narratives: REF impact case studies and restrictive storytelling in performance measurement', *Studies in Higher Education*, 47(9): 1857–71.

Bargallie, D. and Lentin, A. (2020) 'Improving racial literacy: what will it take?', Croakey Health Media. Available at: www.croakey.org/improving-racial-literacy-what-will-it-take/

Bargallie, D., Fernando, N. and Lentin, A. (2023) 'Breaking the racial silence: putting racial literacy to work in Australia', *Ethnic and Racial Studies*. doi:10.1080/01419870.2023.2206470.

Benson, R., Duffy, B., Murkin, G., Hesketh, R., Hewlet, K., Gottfried, G. Page, B. and Skinner, G. (2021) 'The four sides in the UK's culture wars', King's College London. Available at: https://kclpure.kcl.ac.uk/portal/en/publications/the-four-sides-in-the-uks-culture-wars

Besley, T. (2012) 'Why read Giroux?', *Policy Futures in Education*, 10(6): 594–600.

Bhambra, G.K. (2017) 'Brexit, Trump and "methodological whiteness": on the misrecognition of race and class', *British Journal of Sociology*, 68(S1): 214–32.

Bhambra, G.K. and Holmwood, J. (2021) *Colonialism and Modern Social Theory*, Cambridge: Polity.

Bhambra, G.K., Gebrial, D. and Nişancıoğlu, K. (2018) 'Introduction: decolonizing the university?', in G.K. Bhambra, D. Gebrial and K. Nişancıoğlu (eds) *Decolonizing the University*, London: Pluto Press, 1–16.

Bhatia, M. (2020) 'The permission to be cruel: street-level bureaucrats and harms against people seeking asylum', *Critical Criminology*, 28: 277–92.

Bhattacharyya, G. (2013) 'How can we live with ourselves? Universities and the attempt to reconcile learning and doing', *Ethnic and Racial Studies*, 36(9): 1411–28.

Blaisdell, B. (2021) 'Counternarrative as strategy: embedding critical race theory to develop an antiracist school identity', *International Journal of Qualitative Studies in Education*, 36(8): 1558–78.

Boda, P.A., Nusbaum, E.A. and Kulkarni, S.S. (2022) 'From "what is" toward "what if" through intersectionality: problematizing ableist erasures and coloniality in racially just research', *International Journal of Research & Method in Education*, 45(4): 356–69.

Boler, M. (1999) *Feeling Power: Emotions and Education*, New York: Routledge.

Boler, M. and Zembylas, M. (2003) 'Discomforting truths: The emotional terrain of understanding difference', in P. Trifonas (ed) *Pedagogies of difference: Rethinking education for social change*, New York: Routledge Falmer, 110–36.

Boler, M. and Zembylas, M. (2016) 'Interview with Megan Boler: from "feminist politics of emotions" to the "affective turn"', in M. Zembylas and P. Schutz (eds) *Methodological Advances in Research on Emotion and Education*, Cham: Springer, 17–30.

Bonilla-Silva, E. (2012) 'The invisible weight of whiteness: the racial grammar of everyday life in contemporary America', *Ethnic and Racial Studies*, 35(2): 173–94.

Border Forensics (2023) 'Mission accomplished? The deadly effects of border control in Niger. Report'. Available at: www.borderforensics.org/investigations/niger-investigation/

Bradley, M. (2023) 'Colonial continuities and colonial unknowing in international migration management: the International Organization for Migration reconsidered', *Journal of Ethnic and Migration Studies*, 49(1): 22–42.

Browne, S. (2010) 'Digital epidermalization: race, identity and biometrics', *Critical Sociology*, 36(1): 131–50.

Brunger, F., Russell, T. and Wall, D. (2020) 'Decolonizing research ethics: best practices for the ethical conduct of research involving indigenous peoples', in A.S. Iltis and D. MacKay (eds) *The Oxford Handbook of Research Ethics*, Oxford Academic. https://doi.org/10.1093/oxfordhb/9780190947750.013.47

Burns, N., Mulvey, G., Piacentini, T. and Vidal, N. (2022) 'Refugees, political bounding and the pandemic: material effects and experiences of categorizations amongst refugees in Scotland', *Journal of Ethnic and Migration Studies*, 48(17): 4066–84.

Cann, C.N. and DeMeulenaere, E.J. (2020) *The Activist Academic: Engaged Scholarship for Resistance, Hope and Social Change*, Goreham, ME: Myers Education Press.

Casas-Cortes, M., Cobarrubias, S., De Genova, N., Garelli, G., Grappi, G., Heller, C., Hess, S., Kasparek, B., Mezzadra, S., Neilson, B., Peano, I., Pezzani, L., Pickles, J., Rahola, F., Riedner, L., Scheel, S. and Tazzioli, M. (2015) 'New keywords: migration and borders', *Cultural Studies*, 29(1): 55–87.

Catalano, T. and Waugh, L. (2022) 'Metonymies of migration. Media discourse about and by migrants', in M. Brdar and R. Brdar-Szabó (eds) *Figurative Thought and Language in Action*, Amsterdam: John Benjamins Publishing Company, 215–36.

Charteris-Black, J. (2006) 'Britain as a container: immigration metaphors in the 2005 election campaign', *Discourse & Society*, 17(5): 563–81.

Chimienti, M., Bloch, A., Ossipow, L. and de Wenden, C.W. (2019) 'Second generation from refugee backgrounds in Europe', *Comparative Migration Studies*, 7(40): 1–15.

Clark-Kazak, C. (2017) 'Ethical considerations: research with people in situations of forced migration', *Refuge: Canada's Journal on Refugees*, 33(2): 11–17.

Colley, H. (2014) 'What (a) to do about "impact": a Bourdieusian critique', *British Educational Research Journal*, 40(4): 660–81.

Collins, F.L. (2022) 'Geographies of migration II: decolonizing migration studies', *Progress in Human Geography*, 46: 1241–51.

Colombo, M. (2020) 'Who is the "other"? Epistemic violence and discursive practices', *Theory & Psychology*, 30(3): 399–404.

Crawley, H. and Skleparis, D. (2018) 'Refugees, migrants, neither, both: categorical fetishism and the politics of bounding in Europe's "migration crisis"', *Journal of Ethnic and Migration Studies*, 44(1): 48–64.

Crawley, H., McMahon, S. and Jones, K. (2016) *Victims and Villains: Migrant Voices in the British Media*, Coventry: Centre for Trust, Peace and Social Relations, Coventry University.

Cuttitta, P. (2018) 'Repoliticization through search and rescue? Humanitarian NGOs and migration management in the Central Mediterranean', *Geopolitics*, 23(3): 632–60.

Czymara, C.S. and van Klingeren, M. (2022) 'New perspective? Comparing frame occurrence in online and traditional news media reporting on Europe's "migration crisis"', *Communications*, 47(1): 136–62.

Dahinden, J. (2016) 'A plea for the "de-migranticization" of research on migration and integration', *Ethnic and Racial Studies*, 39(13): 2207–25.

Das, N., Melo, J.V., Smith, H. and Working, L. (2021) *Keywords of Identity, Race, and Human Mobility in Early Modern England*, Amsterdam: Amsterdam University Press.

Davies, H.C. and MacRae, S.E. (2023) 'An anatomy of the British war on woke', *Race & Class*, 65(2): 3–54.

Davies, T., Isakjee, A., Mayblin, L. and Turner, J. (2021) 'Channel crossings: offshoring asylum and the afterlife of empire in the Dover Strait', *Ethnic and Racial Studies*, 44(13): 2307–27.

Davis, D. and Steyn, M. (2012) 'Teaching social justice: reframing some common pedagogical assumptions', *Perspectives in Education*, 30(4): 29–38.

Davis, M. (2018) '"Culture is inseparable from race": culture wars from Pat Buchanan to Milo Yiannopoulos', *Media/Culture Journal*, 21(5).

Davison Hunter, J. (1991) *Culture Wars: The Struggle to Define America*, New York: Basic Books.

De Genova, N. (2018) 'The "migrant crisis" as racial crisis: do *Black Lives Matter* in Europe?', *Ethnic and Racial Studies*, 41(10): 1765–82.

De Genova, N., Tazzioli, M., Aradau, C., Bhandar, B., Bojadzijev, M., Cisneros, J.D., De Genova, N., Eckert, J., Fontanari, E., Golash-Boza, T., Huysmans, J., Khosravi, S., Lecadet, C., Macías Rojas, P., Mazzara, F., McNevin, A., Nyers, P., Scheel, S., Sharma, N., Stierl, M., Squire, V., Tazzioli, M., van Baar, H. and Walters W. (2022) 'Minor keywords of political theory: migration as a critical standpoint. A collaborative project of collective writing', *Environment and Planning C: Politics and Space*, 40(4): 781–875.

Demir, I. (2022) 'Migration and methodological amnesia', IMISCOE Reflexivities in Migration Studies Blog. Available at: www.imiscoe.org/news-and-blog/sc-blogs/reflex-studies/1533-migration-and-methodological-amnesia

Dennis, C.A. (2018) 'Decolonizing education: a pedagogic intervention', in G.K. Bhambra, D. Gebrial and K. Nişancıoğlu (eds) *Decolonizing the University*, London: Pluto Press, 90–207.

Dhar, A. (2021) 'On teaching im/migration in an undergraduate classroom', *Radical Teacher*, 120 : 61–8.

Di Feliciantonio, C. (2021) '(Un)Ethical boundaries: critical reflections on what we are (not) supposed to do', *The Professional Geographer*, 73(3): 496–503.

Dittmar, L. and Annas, P. (2017) 'Introduction: toward public pedagogies: teaching outside traditional classrooms', *Radical Teacher*, 109(1): 1–3.

Dyer, S. and Demeritt, D. (2009) 'Un-ethical review? Why it is wrong to apply the medical model of research governance to human geography', *Progress in Human Geography*, 33(1): 46–64.

Edwards, R. (2022) 'Why do academics do unfunded research? Resistance, compliance and identity in the UK neo-liberal university', *Studies in Higher Education*, 47(4): 904–14.

El-Enany, N. (2020) *Bordering Britain: Law, Race and Empire*, Manchester: Manchester University Press.

Elliott-Cooper, A. (2018) 'The struggle that cannot be named: violence, space and the re-articulation of anti-racism in post-Duggan Britain', *Ethnic and Racial Studies*, 41(14): 2445–63.

Ellsworth, E. (1989) 'Why doesn't this feel empowering? Working through the repressive myths of critical pedagogy', *Harvard Educational Review*, 59: 297–324.

Elrick, J. and Schwartzman, L.F. (2015) 'From statistical category to social category: organized politics and official categorizations of "persons with a migration background" in Germany', *Ethnic and Racial Studies*, 38(9): 1539–56.

Eppley, K. (2019) 'Close reading: what is reading for?', *Curriculum Inquiry*, 49(3): 338–55.

Fahs, B. (2019) 'Writing with blood: the transformative pedagogy of teaching students to write manifestos', *Radical Teacher*, 115: 33–8.

Fanon, F. (1967) *Black skin, white masks*, New York: Grove Press.

Fekete, L. (2023) 'Civilizational racism, ethnonationalism and the clash of imperialisms in Ukraine', *Race & Class*, 64(4): 3–26.

Felman, S. (1992) 'Education and crisis, or vicissitudes of listening', in S. Felman and D. Laub (eds) *Testimony: Crises of Witnessing in Literature, Psychoanalysis, and History*, London: Routledge, 57–75.

Forced Migration Review (2019) Special Issue 'the ETHICS issue: exploring ethical questions that confront us in our work', 61, M. Couldrey and J. Peebles (eds). Available at: www.fmreview.org/ethics

Fregoso Bailon, R.O. and De Lissovoy, N. (2019) 'Against coloniality: toward an epistemically insurgent curriculum', *Policy Futures in Education*, 17: 355–69.

Freire, P. (1970) *Pedagogy of the Oppressed*, New York: Seabury Press.

Freire, P. (1973) *Education for liberation*, Melbourne: Australian Council of Churches Commission on Christian Education.

Freire, P. (1998) *Teachers and Cultural Workers: Letters to Those Who Dare to Teach*, Boulder, CO: Westview Press.

Freire, P. (1999) *Pedagogy of Freedom*, Lanham, MD: Rowman and Littlefield.

Freire, P. (2021) *Pedagogy in Process: The Letters to Guinea-Bissau* (1st edn), London: Bloomsbury.

Freire, P. and Macedo, D.P. (1987) *Literacy: Reading the Word & the World*, London: Routledge & Kegan Paul.

Funk, S., Kellner, D. and Share, J. (2016) 'Critical media literacy as transformative pedagogy', in M.N. Yildiz and J. Keengwe (eds) *Handbook of Research on Media Literacy in the Digital Age*, Hershey, PA: IGI Global, 1–30.

Gaianguest, K. (1998) 'Radical pedagogy is social change in action. Response to "Practicing radical pedagogy: balancing ideals with institutional constraints"', *Teaching Sociology*, 26: 123–6.

Gardner, J., Lenette, C. and Al-Kalmashi, R. (2022) 'Who is the host? Interrogating hosting from refugee-background women's perspectives', *Journal of Intercultural Studies*, 43(5): 621–38.

Gebrial, D. (2018) 'Rhodes Must Fall, Oxford movements and change', in G.K. Bhambra, D. Gebrial and K. Nişancıoğlu (eds) *Decolonizing the University*, London: Pluto Press, 19–34.

Geiger, M. and Pécoud, A. (2010) *The Politics of International Migration Management*, Basingstoke: Palgrave Macmillan.

Gentleman, A. (2019) 'The week that took Windrush from low-profile investigation to national scandal', *The Guardian*, 10 January. Available at: www.theguardian.com/uk-news/2018/apr/20/the-week-that-took-windrush-from-low-profile-investigation-to-national-scandal

Giroux, H.A. (1979) 'Paulo Freire's approach to radical educational reform', *Curriculum Inquiry*, 9(3): 257–72.

Giroux, H.A. (1981) *Ideology, Culture, and the Process of Schooling*, Philadelphia, PA: Temple University Press.

Giroux, H.A. (1989) *Schooling for Democracy*, London: Routledge.

Giroux, H.A. (1997) *Pedagogy and the Politics of Hope: Theory, Culture, and Schooling: A Critical Reader*, New York: Perseus.

Giroux, H.A. (2000) 'Public pedagogy as cultural politics: Stuart Hall and the "crisis" of culture', *Cultural Studies*, 14: 341–60.

Giroux, H.A. (2003) 'Public pedagogy and the politics of resistance: notes on a critical theory of educational struggle', *Educational Philosophy and Theory*, 35(1): 5–16.

Giroux, H.A. (2020) *On Critical Pedagogy* (2nd edn), London: Bloomsbury Academic.

Giroux, H.A. (2021) *Race, Politics, and Pandemic Pedagogy: Education in a Time of Crisis*, London: Bloomsbury Academic.

Giroux, H.A. (2022) *Pedagogy of Resistance: Against Manufactured Ignorance*. London: Bloomsbury Academic.

Giroux, H.A. (2023) 'Fascist culture, critical pedagogy, and resistance in pandemic times', *English Language Notes*, 61(1): 51–62.

Giroux, H.A. and Penna, A.N. (1979) 'Social education in the classroom: the dynamics of the hidden curriculum', *Theory and Research in Social Education*, 7: 21–42.

Golden, S.C. (2023) 'Toward a Grotkean pedagogy: teacher as political', *Radical Teacher*, 125: 54–61.

Griffiths, M. and Yeo, C. (2021) 'The UK's hostile environment: deputising immigration control', *Critical Social Policy*, 41(4): 521–44.

Grosfoguel, R., Oso, L. and Christou, A. (2015) ' "Racism," intersectionality and migration studies: framing some theoretical reflections', *Identities*, 22(6): 635–52.

Gruenewald, D.A. (2003a) 'The best of both worlds: a critical pedagogy of place', *Educational Researcher*, 32(4): 3–12.

Gruenewald, D.A. (2003b) 'Foundations of place: a multi-disciplinary framework for place conscious education', *American Educational Research Journal*, 40: 619–54.

Guinier, L. (2004) 'From racial liberalism to racial literacy: Brown v. Board of Education and the interest-divergence dilemma', *Journal of American History*, 91(1): 92–118.

Gutiérrez Rodríguez, E. (2018) 'The coloniality of migration and the "refugee crisis": on the asylum–migration nexus, the transatlantic white European settler colonialism-migration and racial capitalism', *Refuge: Canada's Journal on Refugees*, 34(1): 16–28.

Hadj Abdou, L. (2019) 'Immigrant integration: the governance of ethno-cultural differences', *Comparative Migration Studies*, 7: 1–15.

REFERENCES

Hadj Abdou, L. and Pettrachin, A. (2021) 'From "bogus" asylum seekers to "genuine" refugees; shifting discourses and attitudes towards Afghan migrants', University of Oxford, Centre on Migration, Policy and Society, 12 November. Available at: www.compas.ox.ac.uk/2021/from-bogus-asylum-seekers-to-genuine-refugees-shifting-discourses-and-attitudes-towards-afghan-migrants/

Hadj Abdou, L., Pettrachin, A. and Crawley, H. (2022) 'Who is a refugee? Understanding Europe's diverse responses to the 2015 and the 2022 refugee arrivals', EURAC, 23 March. Available at: www.eurac.edu/en/blogs/mobile-people-and-diverse-societies/who-is-a-refugee-understanding-europe-s-diverse-responses-to-the-2015-and-the-202

Hagen, J.J., Michelis, I., Eggert, J.P. and Turner, L. (2023) 'Learning to say "no": privilege, entitlement and refusal in peace, (post)conflict and security research', *Critical Studies on Security*, 11(2): 126–44.

Haggerty, K.D. (2004) 'Ethics creep: governing social science research in the name of ethics', *Qualitative Sociology*, 27: 391–414.

Hansard House of Commons Debate (2022) *Western Jet Foil and Manston Asylum Processing Centres*, Volume 721, Debated 31 October. Available at www.hansard.parliament.uk/Commons/2022-10-31/debates/F189CA88-FDF3-4018-905C-1CC8A1B76E28/WesternJetFoilAndManstonAsylumProcessingCentres?highlight=indulgent#contribution-E691BC11-5CF7-467B-997A-ED87A62E6642.

Hart, C. (2021) 'Animals vs. armies: resistance to extreme metaphors in anti-immigration discourse', *Journal of Language and Politics*, 20(2): 226–53.

Held, M.B.E. (2020) 'Research ethics in decolonizing research with Inuit communities in Nunavut: the challenge of translating knowledge into action', *International Journal of Qualitative Methods*, 19: 1–7.

Hesse, B. and Sayyid, S. (2006) 'Narrating the political postcolonial and the immigrant imaginary', in N. Ali, V. Kalra and S. Sayyid (eds) *A Postcolonial People: South Asians in Britain*, London: Hurst, 13–31.

Hogue, C., Parker, K. and Miller, M. (1998) 'Talking the talk and walking the walk: ethical pedagogy in the multicultural classroom', *Feminist Teacher*, 12(2): 89–106.

Holmwood, J. (2018) 'Race and the neoliberal university: lessons from the public university', in G.K. Bhambra, D. Gebrial and K. Nişancıoğlu (eds) *Decolonizing the University*, London: Pluto Press, 37–53.

Home Office (2020) 'Sovereign borders: international asylum comparisons report. Section 1: Drivers and impact on asylum migration journeys with references. Migration and borders analysis. September 2020', Free Movement Blog. Available at: https://freemovement.org.uk/wp-content/uploads/2022/11/Annex-A-Sovereign-Borders-International-Asylum-Comparisons-Report-Section-1-Drivers-and-impact-on-asylum-migration-journeys.pdf hooks, b. (1989) *Talking Back: Thinking Feminist, Thinking Black*, Boston, MA: South End.

hooks, b. (1994) *Teaching to Transgress: Education as the Practice of Freedom*, New York: Routledge.

hooks, b. (2003) *Teaching Community: A Pedagogy of Hope*, New York: Routledge.

hooks, b. (2009) *Teaching Critical Thinking: Practical Wisdom*, New York: Routledge.

Ivits, S. (2009) 'Disturbing the comfortable: an ethical inquiry into pedagogies of discomfort and crisis', MA thesis, University of British Columbia, Canada.

Jones, H. (2021) *Violent Ignorance: Confronting Racism and Migration Control*, London: Zed Books.

Joseph-Salisbury, R. and Connelly, L. (2021) *Anti-racist Scholar-activism*, Manchester: Manchester University Press.

Kainz, L. (2016) 'People can't flood, flow or stream: diverting dominant media discourses on migration', Border Criminologies Blog. Available at: www.law.ox.ac.uk/research-subject-groups/centre-criminology/centreborder-criminologies/blog/2016/02/people-can't

Kellner, D. and Share, J. (2007) 'Critical media literacy, democracy, and the reconstruction of education', in D. Macedo and S.R. Steinberg (eds) *Media Literacy: A Reader*, New York: Peter Lang, 3–23.

Kishimoto, K. and Mwangi, M. (2009) 'Critiquing the rhetoric of "safety" in feminist pedagogy: women of color offering an account of ourselves', *Feminist Teacher*, 19(2): 87–102.

Kopelson, K. (2003) 'Rhetoric on the edge of cunning; or, the performance of neutrality (re)considered as a composition pedagogy for student resistance', *College Composition and Communication*, 55(1): 115–46.

Korteweg, A.C. (2017) 'The failures of "immigrant integration": the gendered racialized production of non-belonging', *Migration Studies*, 5(3): 428–44.

Kumashiro, K.K. (2002) 'Against repetition: addressing resistance to anti-oppressive change in the practices of learning, teaching, supervising, and researching', *Harvard Educational Review*, 72(1): 67–92.

Kumashiro, K.K. (2009) *Against Common Sense: Teaching and Learning toward Social Justice* (2nd edn), London: Routledge.

Langen, N.R. (2023) 'Reaction economy: the Home Office's use of social media', Free Movement Blog, 7 June. Available at: https://freemovement.org.uk/home-offices-use-of-social-media/

Leland, H. and Harste, C. (2000) 'Critical literacy: enlarging the space of the possible', *Primary Voices K-6*, 9(2): 3–7.

Lenette, C. (2019) *Arts-Based Methods in Refugee Research: Creating Sanctuary*, Singapore: Springer.

Lenette, C. (2022) *Participatory Action Research: Ethics and Decolonization*, Oxford: Oxford University Press.

Lentin, A. (2015) 'What does race do?', *Ethnic and Racial Studies*, 38(8): 1401–6.

Lentin, A. (2020) *Why Race Still Matters?*, Cambridge: Polity Press.

Lentin, R. (2007) 'Ireland: racial state and crisis racism', *Ethnic and Racial Studies*, 30(4): 610–27.

Levitt, P. (2012) 'What's wrong with migration scholarship? A critique and a way forward', *Identities*, 19(4): 493–500.

Lichty, L.F. and Palamaro-Munsell, E. (2017) 'Pursuing an ethical, socially just classroom: searching for community psychology pedagogy', *American Journal of Community Psychology*, 60: 316–26.

Little, A. and Vaughan-Williams, N. (2017) 'Stopping boats, saving lives, securing subjects: humanitarian borders in Europe and Australia', *European Journal of International Relations*, 23(3): 533–56.

Macrine, S.L. (2009) 'What is critical pedagogy good for? An interview with Ira Shor', in S.L. Macrine (ed) *Critical Pedagogy in Uncertain Times: Hopes and Possibilities*, New York: Palgrave Macmillan, 119–36.

Maldonado-Torres, N. (2007) 'On the coloniality of being: contributions to the development of a concept', *Cultural Studies*, 21(2–3): 240–70.

Mayblin, L. (2017) *Asylum after Empire: Colonial Legacies in the Politics of Seeking Asylum*, London: Rowman and Littlefield International.

Mayblin, L. and Turner, J. (2021) *Migration Studies and Colonialism*, Bristol: Polity Press.

McCoy, S.A. (2020) 'Writing for justice in first-year composition (FYC)', *Radical Teacher*, 116: 26–36.

M'charek, A. and Black, J. (2020) 'Engaging bodies as matters of care: counting and accounting for death during migration', in P. Cuttitta and T. Last (eds) *Border Deaths: Causes, Dynamics and Consequences of Migration Related Mortality*, Amsterdam: Amsterdam University Press, 85–101.

McLaren, P. (1995) *Critical Pedagogy and Predatory Culture*, New York: Routledge.

Meer, N., Hill, E., Peace, T. and Villegas, L. (2021) 'Rethinking refuge in the time of COVID-19', *Ethnic and Racial Studies*, 44(5): 864–76.

Mernick, A. (2021) 'We the people: immigration counter-narratives in the high school visual arts classroom', *Radical Teacher*, 120: 23–31.

Miles, R. and Brown, M. (2003) *Racism* (2nd edn), London: Routledge.

Mintz, A.I. (2013) 'Helping by hurting: the paradox of suffering in social justice education', *Theory and Research in Education*, 11(3): 215–30.

Moses, M. (2022) 'Methodologically disrupting whiteness: a critical race case for visual-elicited focus groups as cultural responsiveness', *International Journal of Research & Method in Education*, 45(3): 297–308.

Mujagić, M. (2022) 'The migration as an invasion and the common European house metaphors in media discourse', *Explorations in English Language and Linguistics*, 10(1): 22–50.

Muller, M. and Bryan, N. (2020) 'W. E. B. DuBois and Paulo Freire: toward a "pedagogy of the veil" to counter racism in early childhood education', in J.D. Kirylo (ed) *Reinventing Pedagogy of the Oppressed: Contemporary Critical Perspectives*, London: Bloomsbury, 27–39.

Musolff, A. (2016) *Political Metaphor Analysis: Discourse and Scenarios*, London: Bloomsbury.

Nayel, M.A. (2013) 'Palestinian refugees are not at your service', *Electronic Intifada*. Available at. https://electronicintifada.net/content/palestinian-refugees-are-not-your-service/12464

Noterman, E. and Pusey, A. (2012) 'Inside, outside, and on the edge of the academy: experiments in radical pedagogies', in R. Haworth (ed) *Anarchist Pedagogies: Collective Actions, Theories, and Critical Reflections on Education*, PM Press, 175–99.

Ochoa, G.L. (2022) 'Learning and being in community: a Latina feminist holistic approach to researching where we live', *International Journal of Research & Method in Education*, 45(3): 246–58.

Ohtani, E. (2017) 'How can academics support migrants rights groups/cause? To begin with, forget that you are an academic', Silent Flags [Blog]. Available at: https://silentflags.wordpress.com/2017/08/02/how-can-academics-support-migration-groups-cause-to-begin-with-forget-that-you-are-an-academic/.

Pallister-Wilkins, P. (2022) *Humanitarian Borders: Unequal Mobility and Saving Lives*, London: Verso Books.

Pécoud, A. (2015) *Depoliticising Migration: Global Governance and International Migration Narratives*, Basingstoke: Palgrave Macmillan.

Pedwell, C. (2016) 'Decolonizing empathy: thinking affect transnationally', *Samyukta: A Journal of Women's Studies*, XVI (1): 27–49.

Pelkmans, M. (2013) 'A wider audience for anthropology? Political dimensions of an important debate', *Journal of the Royal Anthropological Institute*, 19: 398–404.

Philo, G., Briant, E. and Donald, P. (2013) *Bad News for Refugees*, London: Pluto Press.

Phipps, A. (2017) 'On impact', 13 June. Available at: https://phipps.space/2017/06/13/on-impact

Phipps, A. (2019) *Decolonizing Multilingualism: Struggles to Decreate*, Bristol: Multilingual Matters.

Piacentini, T. (2014) 'Everyday acts of resistance: the precarious lives of asylum seekers in Glasgow', in K. Marciniak and I. Tyler (eds) *Immigrant Protest: Politics, Aesthetics, and Everyday Dissent*, Albany, NY: State of New York Press, 169–87.

Piacentini, T. (2015) 'Missing from the picture? Migrant and refugee community organizations' responses to poverty and destitution in Glasgow', *Community Development Journal*, 50(3): 433–47.

Piacentini, T. (2016) 'Refugee solidarity in the everyday', *Soundings: A Journal of Politics and Culture*, 64: 57–61.

Piacentini, T. (2017) '"More than a refugee community organisation": a study of African migrant associations in Glasgow', in A. McCabe and J. Phillimore (eds) *Community Groups in Context: Local Activities and Actions*, Bristol: Policy Press, 192–209.

Piacentini, T. (2018a) 'Refugee and asylum seeker organisations in Scotland since 2012: reflections and future directions', in A. McCabe (ed) *Ten Years below the Radar: Reflections on Voluntary and Community Action 2008–2018*, Brimingham: Third Sector Research Centre, 36–9.

Piacentini, T. (2018b) 'African migrants, asylum seekers and refugees: tales of settling in Scotland, 2000–2015', in T.M. Devine and A. McCarthy (eds) *New Scots: Scotland's Immigrant Communities since 1945*. Edinburgh: Edinburgh University Press, 176–204.

Piacentini, T., Ohtani, E. and Clark, C. (2021 [2018]) 'Manifesto for change: critical pedagogy for teaching and researching migration in the "political now"!', National Teaching Repository. doi:10.25416/NTR.20987374.v1

Piccoli, L., Ruedin, D. and Geddes, A. (2023) 'A global network of scholars? The geographical concentration of institutes in migration studies and its implications', *Comparative Migration Studies*, 11(16): 1–16.

Quijano, A. (2000) 'Coloniality of power and Eurocentrism in Latin America', *International Sociology*, 15(2): 215–32.

Refugee Hosts (nd) 'Protestimony', *Refugee Hosts*. Available at: https://refugeehosts.org/2017/12/12/protestimony/comment-page-1/.

Reuters (2019) 'British PM Johnson says whole nation shocked by 39 deaths in truck', 28 October. Available at: https://www.reuters.com/article/us-britain-bodies-condolences-idUSKBN1X713J/.

RISE Australia (2015) '10 things you need to consider if you are an artist – not of the refugee and asylum seeker community – looking to work with our community'. Available at: https://aktiontanz.de/wp-content/uploads/2017/03/RISE-statement-on-working-with-the-refugee-community.pdf

Robinson, N. (2023) *Political thinking with Nick Robinson: The Lee Anderson One*, BBC, 4 March. Available at: https://www.bbc.co.uk/iplayer/episode/m001jylm/political-thinking-with-nick-robinson-the-lee-anderson-one

Routley, L. (2016) 'Teaching Africa, presenting, representing and the importance of who is in the classroom', *Politics*, 36: 482–94.

Sadiq, K. and Tsourapas, G. (2021) 'The postcolonial migration state', *European Journal of International Relations*, 27(3): 884–912.

Saltsman, A. and Majidi, N. (2021) 'Storytelling in research with refugees: on the promise and politics of audibility and visibility in participatory research in contexts of forced migration', *Journal of Refugee Studies*, 34(3): 2522–38.

Santa Ana, O. (1999) '"Like an animal I was treated": anti-immigrant metaphor in US public discourse', *Discourse & Society*, 10(2): 191–224.

Santa Ana, O. (2013) *Juan in a Hundred: The Representation of Latinos on Network News*, Austin, TX: University of Texas Press.

Sayad, A. (2004) *The Suffering of the Immigrant*, Cambridge: Polity Press.

Sayyid, S. (2004) 'Slippery people: the immigrant imaginary and the grammar of colours', in D. Philips and L. Turney (eds) *Institutional Racism in Higher Education*, Stoke-on-Trent: Trentham Books, 149–59.

Sayyid, S. (2009) 'Answering the Muslim question: the politics of Muslims in Europe', *e-cadernos CES*, 03. Available at: http://journals.openedition.org/eces/180

Scheel, S. and Tazzioli, M. (2022) 'Who is a migrant? Abandoning the nation-state point of view in the study of migration', *Migration Politics*, 1(1): Art 002.

Schinkel, W. (2018) 'Against "immigrant integration": for an end to neocolonial knowledge production', *Comparative Migration Studies*, 6(31): 1–17.

Scholten P. (2018) 'Research–policy relations and migration studies', in R. Zapata-Barrero and E. Yalaz (eds) *Qualitative Research in European Migration Studies*, Cham: Springer.

Scholten, P., Pisarevskaya, A. and Levy, N. (2022) 'An introduction to migration studies: the rise and coming of age of a research field', in P. Scholten (ed) *Introduction to Migration Studies*, Cham: Springer.

Schulz, S., Rigney, L.-I., Zembylas, M., Hattam, R. and Memon, A. (2023) 'Affect and the force of counter stories: learning racial literacy through thinking and feeling', *Pedagogy, Culture & Society*. doi:10.1080/14681366.2023.2173276

Share, J., Mamikonyan, T. and Lopez, E. (2019) 'Critical media literacy in teacher education, theory, and practice', in *Oxford Research Encyclopedia of Education* (Editor in Chief G.W. Noblit), Oxford: Oxford University Press.

Shor, I. (1992) *Empowering Education: Critical Teaching for Social Change*, Chicago, IL: University of Chicago Press.

Shor, I. (2019) 'Can critical teaching foster activism in this time of repression?', *Radical Teacher*, 113: 66–7.

Sian, K.P. (2022) 'Rethinking knowledge production in sociology: a critical analysis of the conceptual, the methodological and the institutional', *Social Policy and Society*, 21(1): 42–53.

Sigona, N. (2015) 'Seeing double? How the EU miscounts migrants arriving at its borders', *The Conversation*. Available at: www./theconversation.com/seeing-double-how-the-eu-miscounts-migrants-arriving-at-its-borders-49242

Sigona, N. (2022) Twitter, 3 March. Available at: https://twitter.com/nandosigona/status/1499367685624377348

Sitholé, T. (2022) 'The disease of expertise', *Zanj: The Journal of Critical Global South Studies*, 5(1–2): 30–4.

Sitholé, T., Crawley, H., Feyissa, D., Tapsoba, T.A., Meda, M.M., Sangli, G., Yeoh, S.G. and Phipps, A. (2022) 'The language of migration', *Zanj: The Journal of Critical Global South Studies*, 5(1–2): 14–26.

Sivanandan, A. (1990) 'All that melts into air is solid: the hokum of new times', *Race & Class*, 31(3): 1–30.

Sivanandan, A. (2009) 'Catching history on the wing: conference speech', *Race & Class*, 50(3): 94–8.

Smith, L.T. (2012) *Decolonizing Methodologies: Research and Indigenous Peoples* (2nd edn), London: Zed Books.

Sobolewska, M. and Ford, R. (2019) 'British culture wars? Brexit and the future politics of immigration and ethnic diversity', *The Political Quarterly*, 90(S2): 142–54.

Sobolewska, M. and Ford, R. (2020) 'Brexit and Britain's culture wars', *Political Insight*, 11(1): 4–7.

Spencer, S. (2022) 'The contested concept of "integration"', in P. Scholten (ed) *Introduction to Migration Studies: An Interactive Guide to the Literatures on Migration and Diversity*, Cham: Springer, 19–232.

Spivak, G.C. (1992) 'Can the subaltern speak?', in P. Williams and L. Chrisman (eds) *Colonial Discourse and Post-colonial Theory*, New York: Columbia University Press, 66–111.

Srilangarajah, V. (2018) 'We are here because you were with us: remembering A. Sivanandan (1923–2018)', *Ceasefire Magazine*, 4 February. Available at: www.ceasefiremagazine.co.uk/us-remembering-a-sivanandan-1923-2018/

Stierl, M. (2022) 'Do no harm? The impact of policy on migration scholarship', *Environment and Planning C: Politics and Space*, 40(5): 1083–102.

Stierl, M. (2023) 'Frontex off campus! An interview with Professor Michele Lancione', Border Criminologies Blog. Available at: https://blogs.law.ox.ac.uk/blog-post/2023/04/frontex-campus-interview-professor-michele-lancione

Stierl, M., Heller, C. and De Genova, N. (2022) 'Numbers (or, the spectacle of statistics in the production of "crisis") Europe/crisis: new keywords of "the crisis" in and of "Europe"', New Keywords Collective. Available at: https://nearfuturesonline.org/europecrisis-new-keywords-of-crisis-in-and-of-europe-part-4/

Taylor, C. (2021) 'Metaphors of migration over time', *Discourse & Society*, 32(4): 463–81.

Taylor, D. (2019) 'Far-right protesters clash with police at Merseyside hotel housing asylum seekers', *The Guardian*, 10 February. Available at: www.theguardian.com/uk-news/2023/feb/10/far-right-demonstrators-clash-with-police-at-liverpool-hotel-housing-asylum-seekers

Tazzioli, M. and De Genova, N. (eds) (2016) 'Europe/crisis: new keywords of "the crisis" in and of "Europe" – New Keywords Collective'. Available at: https://www.researchgate.net/publication/297367783_Europe_Crisis_New_Keywords_of_the_Crisis_in_and_of_Europe_-_New_Keywords_Collective_2016_edited_by_Martina_Tazzioli_and_Nicholas_De_Genova

Tejeda, C., Espinoza, M. and Gutiérrez, K. (2003) 'Toward a decolonizing pedagogy: social justice reconsidered', in P.P. Trifonas (ed) *Pedagogies of Difference*, New York: Routledge Falmer, 10–40.

Todd, S. (2003) 'Listening as attending to the "echo of the otherwise": on suffering, justice, and education', in S. Fletcher (ed) *Philosophy of Education*, Urbana, IL: Philosophy of Education Society, 405–12.

Tomaselli, K.G. (2014) 'Who owns what? Indigenous knowledge and struggles over representation', *Critical Arts*, 28(4): 631–47.

Torpey, J. (2018) *The Invention of the Passport: Surveillance, Citizenship and the State* (2nd edn), Cambridge: Cambridge University Press.

Trần, N.L. (2016) 'Calling in: a less disposable way of holding each other accountable', in M. McKenzie (ed) *The Solidarity Struggle: How People of Color Succeed and Fail at Showing up for Each Other in the Fight for Freedom*, Oakland, CA: BGD Press, 59–63.

Tuck, E. (2009) 'Suspending damage: a letter to communities', *Harvard Educational Review*, 79(3): 409–27.

Tuck, E. and Yang, K.W. (2014) 'Unbecoming claims: pedagogies of refusal in qualitative research', *Qualitative Inquiry*, 20(6): 811–18.

Vanyoro, K.P., Hadj-Abdou, L. and Dempster, H. (2019) 'Migration studies: from dehumanizing to decolonizing', LSE Higher Education Blog, 19 July. Available at: https://blogs.lse.ac.uk/highereducation/2019/07/19/migration-studies-from-dehumanising-to-decolonising/

Verduzco-Baker, L. (2018) 'Modified brave spaces: calling in brave instructors', *Sociology of Race and Ethnicity*, 4(4): 585–92.

Wagner, A.E. (2005) 'Unsettling the academy: working through the challenges of anti-racist pedagogy', *Race, Ethnicity and Education*, 8(3): 261–75.

Weckman, S. (1998) 'Doing Research with Finnish Gypsies: Advice from a Gypsy', in D. Tong (ed), *Gypsies: An Interdisciplinary Reader*, Abingdon: Routledge, pp 3–10.

Wee, K., Vanyoro, K.P. and Jinnah, Z. (2018) 'Repoliticizing international migration narratives? Critical reflections on the Civil Society Days of the Global Forum on Migration and Development', *Globalizations*, 15(6): 795–808.

Weiler, K. (2005) 'Myths of Paulo Freire', *Educational Theory*, 46(3): 353–71.

West, B., Pudsey, J. and Dunk-West, P. (2011) 'Pedagogy beyond the culture wars: de-differentiation and the use of technology and popular culture in undergraduate sociology teaching', *Journal of Sociology*, 47(2): 198–214.

Williams, R. (2015) *Keywords: A Vocabulary of Culture and Society* (new edn), Oxford: Oxford University Press.

Winter, A. (2023) 'On Gary Lineker's tweet, the politics of comparison and denial of racism', Identities [Blog]. Available at: https://www.identitiesjournal.com/blog-collection/on-gary-linekers-tweet-the-politics-of-comparison-and-denial-of-racism

Wood, L. (2017) 'The ethical implications of community-based research: a call to rethink current review board requirements', *International Journal of Qualitative Methods*, 16: 1–7.

Wood, M. (2016) 'Politicization, depoliticization and anti-politics: towards a multilevel research agenda', *Political Studies Review*, 14(4): 521–33.

Wyss, A. and Dahinden, J. (2022) 'Disentangling entangled mobilities: reflections on forms of knowledge production within migration studies', *Comparative Migration Studies*, 10(33): 1–17.

Yoon, H. (2005) 'Affecting the transformative intellectual: questioning "noble" sentiments in critical pedagogy and composition', *Journal of Advanced Composition*, 25(4): 717–59.

Zembylas, M. (2012) 'Pedagogies of strategic empathy: navigating through the emotional complexities of anti-racism in higher education', *Teaching in Higher Education*, 17(2): 113–25.

Zembylas, M. (2013a) 'The "crisis of pity" and the radicalization of solidarity: toward critical pedagogies of compassion', *Educational Studies*, 49: 504–21.

Zembylas, M. (2013b) 'Critical pedagogy and emotion: working through "troubled knowledge" in posttraumatic contexts', *Critical Studies in Education*, 54(2): 176–89.

Zembylas, M. (2015) '"Pedagogy of discomfort" and its ethical implications: the tensions of ethical violence in social justice education', *Ethics and Education*, 10(2): 163–74.

Zembylas, M. (2018) 'Reinventing critical pedagogy as decolonizing pedagogy: the education of empathy', *The Review of Education/Pedagogy/Cultural Studies*, 40(5): 404–21.

Zembylas, M. (2023a) 'The resilience of racism and affective numbness: cultivating an aesthetics of attention in education', *Critical Studies in Education*, 64(5): 411–27.

Zembylas, M. (2023b) 'The affective dimension of epistemic injustice', *Educational Theory*, 72: 703–25.

Zembylas, M. and Boler, M. (2002) 'On the spirit of patriotism: challenges of a "pedagogy of discomfort"', *Teachers College Record*, 104(5). Available at: www.meganboler.net/wp-content/uploads/2016/02/on_the_spirit_of_patriotism_challenges_o.pdf

Zembylas, M. and McGlynn, C. (2012) 'Discomforting pedagogies: emotional tensions, ethical dilemmas and transformative possibilities', *British Educational Research Journal*, 38(1): 41–60.

Zembylas, M. and Papamichael, E. (2017) 'Pedagogies of discomfort and empathy in multicultural teacher education', *Intercultural Education*, 28(1): 1–19.

Index

A

Aaronovitch, David 76
Academy of Ideas 76
accountability 27, 28, 58, 104–5, 137, 144, 151
action-oriented learning 5, 47, 56, 68, 111, 135, 136, 139, 140
active empathy 46, 59–63, 70, 96, 131, 147
activism 27, 38, 59. 61, 68, 71, 81, 83–5, 146, 154, 155
Adichie, Chimamanda Ngozi 88
'Adrift' 94
advocacy (and campaigning) 35, 59, 61, 68, 83, 103, 107, 128, 146, 152
affect in pedagogy, place of 9
affective
 experiences 27, 54, 55, 72, 90, 110
 investments 87, 160
 responses 62, 64, 131, 150
ahistoricity 16, 119
Ahmed, S. 16, 53, 55, 84
Albtran, A. 48
Aliens Act (1905) 29
alternative learning environments 51–3
Anderson, B. 41
Anderson, Lee 74
Andersson, R. 65, 105, 123, 124
Annas, P. 145
anonymization practices 49–50, 79
anti-immigrant rhetoric 24–45, 74
anti-oppressive activist pedagogy 16, 17, 21, 54, 64, 129–30, 144, 150, 161
anti-racist practices 50, 100, 120, 130, 131, 132, 156, 161
anti-racist scholar activism 79–80, 82–3
Aparna, K. 81, 82, 83
Arao, B. 69
assimilation 42–3, 111
asylum
 anti-asylum 24, 75
 'asylum seeker' as metonym 116
 migration 124
 people seeking asylum/refuge, 24, 25, 26, 28, 128, 148
 system/regime 3, 61, 68, 124

Asylum University 81–4, 96, 144
Australia 37–8, 126–30
Avalos, N. 66, 80

B

Back, L. 87, 88
Bakewell, O. 3, 122
banalization 42
Bargallie, D. 20, 99
Barnes, John 57
Benson, R. 75
Bhambra, G. 15, 30, 31
Bhatia, M. 108
Bhattacharyya, G. 61, 81, 123
Black, J. 44, 63
Black Lives Matter 99
Blaisdell, B. 3, 64, 131
 see also 'Stop the Boats'
boats (Channel/Mediterranean crossings) 26, 85, 92
Boda, P.A. 4, 7
Boler, M. 31, 46, 53–4, 55, 58, 59, 86, 91
Bonilla-Silva, E. 100
Border Forensics 128–9
borders and border controls
 border governance 3, 19, 41, 66, 86, 117
 border security 37
 border studies 122, 124
 border technologies 44, 159
 colonialism 29, 44, 45, 102
 counter-monitoring 62, 63, 67, 79, 96
 racialized border controls 28
Borrell, Josep 114–15
'both sides' arguments 2, 58, 74
Bradley, M. 106
'brave spaces' 69–70
Braverman, Suella 25, 26, 57, 115, 162, 163
Brexit 75, 116
Britain First 25
Brown, Michael 87
Browne, S. 44
Brunger, F. 48
Bryan, N. 97

INDEX

C

'calling in' 70
Cann, C. 16, 142
canonical knowledge 4, 18
'care-fullness' 112, 123, 142, 149, 150
case studies, usefulness of 34
Castle, Andrew 57
Catalano, T. 117
Charteris-Black, J. 113, 114
Christie, Gary 148
City/University of Sanctuary movement 58
civil rights movements 74, 75
civilizational racism 115
classrooms
   ethical 46–71
   political 72–96
   'political now' 2–4, 27
Clemens, K. 69
codes of conduct 47
collaborating ethically 146–8
collaborative learning 14, 59, 69, 131–9, 142, 145–55
collective action 58, 64, 133–4
Colley, H. 121
Collins, F.L. 31, 33, 87, 100
colonialism
   border logics 29
   colonial idioms 103–11
   epistemic violence 4
   ethical guidance 48
   good/bad migrant dichotomies 87–8
   and 'integration' 3
   intersection of race and history 30–40
   legacies and ties 16, 19, 47, 100, 106, 155, 156
   migration literacies 99, 100, 102
   "offshoring" 38
   in pedagogical practices 15, 159
   'political now' 27, 30–40
   racial literacies 20
   and racism 156
   refusal 126
   research ethics 50
   universities 126, 134
coloniality 30–1, 35, 45, 100, 101, 102, 104, 106, 108, 155
'colour-blind citizenship' 36
community action 58–9
community building 9, 16, 18, 141–61
community engagement 141–5
community organizations 58, 67, 110, 124, 132, 141, 149
confessional narratives 11, 12, 86–7
conflict, in classrooms 12–13, 54, 68, 70, 73, 142, 157, 158
connected classrooms 144–5
Connelly, L. 62, 79, 80, 81, 82, 134, 142, 144
conscientization 6, 7, 9, 55, 159
counter-empirics 62–8, 96

counter-metaphors 117
counter-stories/counter-narratives 3, 64–8, 88, 96, 117, 126–32
COVID-19 27–8, 124, 155
'crisis' narratives 26, 58, 63, 93, 122, 123
critical consciousness 7, 27, 53, 70, 78, 129, 159
critical dialogue 13, 69
critical inquiry 53, 79
critical literacies 17–18, 97–8
critical media literacies 8, 9, 54, 97, 98–9
critical pedagogy
   academia 124–5
   concept of 5–21
   as connected to social action 58
   connecting with communities 142, 160
   ethics/ethical imaginations 50–3
   manifestos 132–9
   migration literacies 18, 97–100
   and pedagogies of discomfort 53, 54, 64
   reconnections 159
critical race theory 99, 131
cross-border learning 81, 145, 152–8
Cuttitta, P. 101, 106
'culture wars' 2, 73–9, 98, 115, 116, 160
'Curating Discomfort' 130–2
curriculum development 2, 10–17, 23, 119, 125, 132, 137, 153–8

D

Dahinden, J. 28, 45
data, use of 44, 62–3
Davies, H. 74–5, 76
Davies, T. 38
Davis, D. 13, 19
Davis, M. 75
De Genova, N. 31, 42, 63, 111, 112
De Lissovoy, N. 100
deadly borders/politics 26, 62, 86, 128
deaths of migrants 37, 62–3, 85–6, 104
decolonizing work 4, 15–16, 47–8, 50, 66, 75, 88, 119, 129, 152
decontextualized knowledge 33, 34
defining 'migrants' 40–5
de-historicized concepts 3, 21, 29, 44
dehumanization 55, 84, 91, 93, 114, 116, 123, 161
Demeritt, D. 48
DeMeulenaere, E. 16, 142
Demir, I. 31–2
Dennis, C.A. 4, 8
depoliticization 3, 21, 41, 44, 54, 85, 94, 101, 102, 106, 108, 123, 160
de-racialization 29, 33, 40, 101, 116, 119
'deserving'/'worthy' refugees 56–7, 87
Dhar, A. 88, 97
dialogical processes 6
discomfort, productiveness of 12–15, 16, 19, 46, 53–68, 83, 130–2, 142, 148–9, 161

discomfort, ethics of 46, 53–68
'discordant communities' 142
Dittmar, L. 145
'Do not come' (Australia) 37–8
documentation, history of 44
'doing good harm' 19–20, 21, 45, 46, 61–70, 129, 160, 161
Douglass, F. 66
Dover 26
Dublin 26
DuBois, W.E.B. 30, 66
Dyer, S. 48

E

Edwards, R. 126
El-Enany, N. 29
Elliott-Cooper, A. 116
Ellsworth, E. 10, 11, 68, 71
emotions and politics 84–96
emotional responses 9, 53–68, 133, 150
empathy, pedagogies of 46, 50, 53–68, 131, 140
empire 27, 31–3, 34–5, 40, 108, 112, 131
'empowering suffering' 66
engaged pedagogy 131, 132
epidermalization of race 44
epistemic justice 18, 64, 90, 91, 129, 144, 145, 148, 150, 151, 160
epistemic violence 3–4, 33, 49, 50, 53, 62, 126, 160
equality, diversity and inclusion (EDI) 99
ethical classrooms 28, 46–71, 136–9, 143, 161
ethical collaboration 146–7
ethnic diversity 76–7
EU (European Union) 36, 54, 115, 122
Eurocentricity 26, 47, 48, 68, 83, 115
evaluation and feedback 138
exoticization 42
expert knowledge/expertise 3, 4, 10, 22, 49, 57, 59, 60, 64, 68, 79, 80, 122, 139, 142–4, 148, 149–51, 155, 157, 158, 161
extractive practice 50, 73, 127, 144, 147

F

Fahs, B. 133, 134, 135
Fanon, F. 30, 108
Farage, Nigel 25
far-right protests 24–6
feeling power 53, 54, 86
Fekete, L. 26, 115
Felman, S. 58
feminist scholarship and critique of critical pedagogy 10, 68
Ford, R. 77
Forensic Architecture 94–5
Fortress Europe 62
Fotoohi, Dylan 148
Fox, Claire 76

France 35–7, 65
Fregoso Bailon, R.O. 100
Freire, P. 6, 7, 9, 10
funding for research 73, 124, 126, 145, 153

G

Gaianguest, K. 16
garden/jungle metaphors 114–15
Gardner, J. 110
Gassama, Mamoudou 65–6, 87–8
Gebrial, D. 11, 13, 119
Geiger, M. 104
gender 10
generational markers 43, 110, 111
George the Poet 32, 64
Gilets Noirs 35–7
Giroux, H. 6, 7, 8, 9, 12, 16, 17, 50–1, 53, 55, 77, 91, 98, 120, 123, 132, 142
Glasgow 51, 130–2, 145
global migration governance 104
Golden, S.C. 2, 17
'good harm' 19–20, 21, 45, 46, 61–70, 129, 160, 161
Goodall, Lewis 74
good/bad migrant dichotomies 56–7, 87–8
Goodwin, Matthew 76
Gramsci, A. 8
Griffiths, M. 29, 34
ground rules 69
Gruenewald, D.A. 142, 143
Guinier, L. 99
Gutièrrez Rodríguez, E. 87, 116

H

Hadj Abou, L. 33, 40, 98, 108, 121, 123
Hagen, J.J. 126, 128
Hall, S. 8, 80, 116
Hamilton Mix Tape 90–1
Harste, C. 17
Held, M. 48
'helping by hurting' 64
Helping Hands Network 153
Hesse, B. 30, 111
historical context, importance of 18–19, 137–8
Hogue, C. 69
'holding knowledge' 59, 60–2, 84–96
Holliday, Zoë. 145, 147
Holmwood, J. 16, 30
Home Office 24, 35, 44, 122
hooks, b. 6, 7–8, 9–10, 12, 17, 23, 53, 54, 56, 70, 75, 86, 120, 125, 131, 142, 158
hope, pedagogy of 21, 68, 75, 120, 158, 161
'hostile environment' 3, 29, 34
'host'/'migrant' distinction 40, 42–3, 107, 108, 109
Howarth, George (MP) 24–5
human rights discourses 106
humanitarian 'assistance' 105, 107–8

INDEX

humanitarianization 37, 101, 103, 104, 105, 106, 116, 152
Hunter, J.D. 74
Hunterian Gallery, University of Glasgow 130–2

I

identity 3, 10, 16
Illegal Immigration Act (2023) 37
'imagined spatiality' 104
immigrant imaginary 42–5, 101
'Immigrants, we get the job done' 90–1
immigration processing centres 26
impact 28, 120–40
  agenda, research and policy relevance 120–4
  in teaching 121, 124–5
'inclusion' 13, 84, 99, 102, 109, 126
indigenization 83
indigenous knowledge 4, 30, 47, 50
indigenous peoples, ethically working with 47–8
'integration' 3, 42–3, 44, 82, 106–11
interconnectivity 141–61
intercultural knowledge 155, 157
interdisciplinary working 152–8
International Association for the Study of Forced Migration 48
International Governmental Organizations (IGOs) 105, 106
international migration narratives (IMNs) 20, 101, 102, 105, 121, 123
International Organization for Migration (IOM) 62, 105–6
International Organizations (IOs) 101
interruption 22, 88, 96, 119, 131, 150, 161
intersectionality 68, 108
Ivits, S. 61

J

Johannson, Ylva 85
Johnson, Boris 85
Jones, H. 56, 86, 91
Joseph-Salisbury, R. 62, 79, 80, 81, 82, 134, 142, 144

K

Kaufman, Eric 76
keywords 111–13
Kishimoto, K. 68
knowing, politics of 5, 9, 12, 87, 92–4, 113, 144, 161
knowledge
  co-creation of 154
  collaborative learning 136–9
  co-produced 50
  de-racialization 29, 33, 40, 101, 116, 119
  and discomfort 61, 97, 115, 129, 133, 146, 149
  emotions and politics 84–96
  epistemic justice 18, 64, 90, 91, 129, 144, 145, 148, 150, 151, 160
  epistemic violence 3–4, 33, 49, 50, 53, 62, 126, 160
  ethical knowledge ecologies 143
  expert/expertise 3, 4, 10, 22, 49, 57, 59, 60, 64, 68, 79, 80, 122, 139, 142–4, 148, 149–51, 155, 157, 158, 161
  'holding knowledge' 59, 60–2, 84–96
  impact and refusal 120–40
  indigenous 4, 30, 47, 50
  intercultural 155, 157
  lived and 'live' experience 4, 49, 53, 59, 60, 64, 80, 88, 89, 125, 144
  methodological whiteness 30–1
  and objectivity 9, 40, 44, 55, 62
  policy-research pipeline 16, 22, 104, 121, 122, 123, 125, 126
  politics of knowledge production 73, 79–84
  productiveness of 61
  rethinking 15, 161
  'serious' knowledge 3, 22, 23, 67, 87, 88, 110, 119
  'useful' knowledge 119, 120, 122, 124, 125, 138
  valuing knowledge 120, 127–8, 139, 149–50
  violent ignorance 56, 86, 91, 93, 144
Knowsley, Liverpool 24–6, 45, 74, 115
Kopelson, K. 17
Korteweg, A. 107, 109
Kramsch, O. 81, 82, 83
Kumashiro, K. 13, 54, 100, 113
Kundnani, A. 42

L

labour markets 122
Lancione, M. 144
Langen, Nicholas Reed 28
language
  affective 54–5
  critical literacies 17, 18, 97, 157, 159
  'culture wars' 75, 77, 78, 79, 98, 116, 117, 118, 160
  decolonizing work 129
  depoliticizing 3, 22, 41, 85, 101, 102, 106, 160
  de-racializing 101
  Hamilton Mix Tape 90
  keywords 111–13
  labels 2, 40, 41–2, 83, 101, 107, 110, 111, 114, 138
  metaphors and metonyms 90, 113–18, 138, 160
  migration literacies 97–119
  neutralized language 27, 33, 34, 41, 54, 55
  'woke' rhetoric 75, 76, 77
learning manifestos 133–6, 161

learning spaces, access to 80–4
'learning with' approaches 4, 67, 96, 125, 131, 150, 151
legislative change 28–9, 33
Leland, H. 17
Lenette, C. 3, 48, 49, 50, 59, 80, 152
Lentin, A. 20, 31, 57, 99, 108, 156
Lentin, R. 28
Lichty, L. 3, 11, 68
Lineker, Gary 57
#Linekergate 57, 59
listening 9, 12, 32, 63, 64, 69, 87, 88, 95, 150, 151
lived and 'live' experience 4, 49, 53, 59, 60, 64, 80, 88, 89, 125, 144
living syllabi 14
Love, B. 99

M

Macedo, D.P. 6
Macrae, S. 74–5, 76
Macrine, S.L. 73, 74
managerial discourse 104–5, 122, 123
manifestos 133–6, 161
manufactured illiteracy 8–9, 91, 99
marketization of academia 73, 82, 124
Maryhill Integration Network (MiN) 67, 68, 90
May, Theresa 29
Mayblin, L. 30, 31, 33, 44, 100, 106
McCoy, S. 87
McGlynn, C. 19, 56
M'charek, A. 44, 63
McLaren, P. 7
media
 coverage of Channel boat crossings 26, 58, 92
 critical media literacies 8, 54, 97–9
 critical pedagogy 8, 9
 cultural apparatus 5, 55, 76, 92, 100, 103
 'culture wars' 75, 78
 metaphors and metonyms 113–18
 political nature of 94
 'political now' 27
 reporting on Ukraine 26
 visual images/representations 94, 116, 131, 154
Mernick, A. 87
metaphors and metonyms 90, 113–18, 138, 160
 garden 114–15
 war 115–16, 117–18
 water 114, 117–18
methodological whiteness 30–1
metonyms 113–18
migrant deaths 37, 62–3, 85–6, 104
migrant rights 34–40, 68, 154
migrantization processes 39, 41, 44, 88, 91, 93, 101, 111, 119, 162

migration governance 33, 37, 43–4, 100, 103–11, 116, 160
migration grammar 18, 20, 102, 107, 123
migration literacies 18, 20, 21, 31, 88, 97–119, 126, 138, 160
migration management 29, 31, 37, 62, 102–6, 122, 126
Migration Museum 94
migration studies 30–1, 33, 41, 43, 63, 102, 114, 122, 133, 136, 146
migration-specific research ethics guidance 48
military metaphors 115–16, 117–18
Mills, C. Wright 8
Mintz, A. 61, 64, 66
Missing Migrants 62–8
moral panics 116
Mpanga, George 32, 64
Muller, M. 97
multiculturalism 42
multidisciplinary working 152–8
multilingualism 155–6
Mwangi, M. 68

N

narratives and stories 63–4, 78, 84–96, 121, 123, 126–32
 see also testimonies
Nayel, M.A. 128
neo-colonialism 108
neoliberalism 33, 56, 83, 124, 134, 144
neutrality 2, 17, 41, 47, 55, 92, 101
neutralized language 27, 33, 34, 41, 54, 55
New Keywords Collective 111
Ngọc, L.T. 70
NGO-ization 107
normalization discourses 44–5
Noterman, E. 144

O

objectivity 2, 17, 49, 52, 55, 62, 92, 101
"offshoring" 1, 38, 122
Ohtani, E. 152
Operation Sovereign Borders (Australia) 37–8
'other'/othering 3, 15, 48, 49, 50, 52, 83, 98, 108, 127

P

Palamaro-Munsell, E. 3, 11, 68
Pallister-Wilkins, P. 106, 116
Papamichael, E. 19
participatory research methods 50
passive empathy 55, 56, 58, 64, 160
Patriotic Alternative 24, 25
Pécoud, A. 20, 33, 101, 104, 105, 108, 123
Pedwell, C. 48, 49, 55
pedagogy of discomfort 16, 54, 55, 65, 134
Penna, A.N. 16

INDEX

'personal as political/political is personal' 2, 73
Pettrachin, A. 33, 40, 121, 123
Phillips, T. 76
Phipps, Ali 124
Phipps, Alison 129
Piacentini, T. 136
Piccoli, L. 43, 62, 121, 122
place 142–3
policies
  immigration policies/legislation 28–9
  policy changes in the 'political now' 33
  policy relevance 44, 120–5
  policy-research pipeline 104, 120–40
policy-relevant research 28
political classrooms 72–96
political correctness 75
'political now' 18–19, 24–45
  connecting with communities 59, 142
  legislative change 28–9, 33
  migration literacies 98, 119
  political classrooms 81, 88
  resistance 130, 135–6, 137
popular culture 8, 77
positionalities 6, 9, 10, 18, 27, 31, 47, 52, 59, 61, 141, 142, 157
post-colonial scholarship 31
power
  building literacies of 10, 14, 17, 20, 41, 78, 101, 103, 104, 121
  in classrooms 6, 11, 12, 17–18, 21, 123, 147, 150, 152, 159
  colonialism 4, 16, 29, 31, 104, 108, 110
  construction of problematic immigrants 40, 41, 42, 114
  counter-stories 67, 133, 134
  critical literacies 18
  critical pedagogy 7, 10, 12–15, 17, 125, 142
  and the curriculum 15–16, 47–8, 50, 66, 75, 88, 119, 129, 152
  'doing good harm' 19, 68
  feeling power 53, 54, 86
  grammar of migration 18, 20, 102, 104, 109, 115
  and 'integration' narratives 3
  knowledge production 15, 80, 124, 127, 128, 132
  and lived/live experiences 60, 64, 81, 89
  policy-research pipeline 124, 125
  power blind pedagogies of migration 16
  power blind/ness 42, 43, 97
  research ethics 48, 49–50, 79
  and 'safety' 12, 13, 55, 56, 60, 68–70, 71
praxis 7, 28, 50, 53, 128, 134, 136, 159, 160, 161
'problems' and 'solutions' 40–5, 54, 84–5, 101, 104, 122, 123, 160
ProTestimony 152
protests 24–6, 45, 74

proximity 100, 151, 153
public pedagogy 8–9, 50, 77–8, 98, 124, 125, 130–2, 134, 161
Pusey, A. 144

Q

Quijano, A. 30, 100

R

race-blind pedagogies of migration 16, 86, 160
racial grammar 99, 100, 102, 116
racial literacies 20, 22, 99, 100, 157
racialized hierarchies 30, 34, 57, 99, 106, 111, 155
racialized migrants 28, 29, 34–40, 66, 116–17
racism
  and academic knowledge production 3, 15, 31, 34–40, 50, 64
  anti-immigrant protests 25, 26, 74
  civilizational racism 115
  in the classroom *see also* pedagogy of discomfort 156–7
  colonialism 3, 29, 30, 156–8
  immigration legislation 28, 29, 40
  media reporting 9
  metonymic and metaphorical 90, 113–18, 138, 160
  in pedagogical practices 15, 20
  and racial illiteracy 99
  reporting on Ukraine 26, 57
'reaction economy' 28
reading the world to read the word 6, 14, 18, 123, 160
Real Message Eire 25–6
reconnections 159–60
Reed, H. 152
Refugee Hosts 152
Refugee Survival Trust 145
Refugees Deeply 95
refusal 102, 104, 119, 120, 126–32, 161
repetition, as pedagogic tool 13–14, 18
repoliticizing work 101, 113
Research Excellence Framework 124
research methods 50
resettlement 26, 56
resistance 58, 62, 67, 73, 75, 83, 84, 86, 102, 107, 117, 119, 120, 126–32, 144, 161
Rhodes Must Fall 13
rights-based approaches 38, 84, 85, 89, 106
riots 24–6
RISE Australia 93, 126–30, 136, 152
Rotherham 25, 74
Routley, L. 11
Russia 98

S

safe spaces 12–15, 69, 128, 137
'safety' 12, 13, 55, 56, 60, 68–70, 71

Sayad, A. 101, 123
Sayyid, S. 30, 42, 43, 111
Scheel, S. 41, 100, 108, 111
Schinkel, W. 107, 108, 110
Scholten, P. 2, 121
Schulz, S. 64
Scotland 67
Scott, J. 123
security studies 33, 38, 39, 93
semantic institutionalization of migration governance 20, 43–4, 97, 100, 101, 102, 111, 113, 119, 122, 159
settlement 3, 51, 101, 106, 108, 110
Shor, I. 6, 18, 41, 60
Simmons, D. 99
Sitholé, T. 4
situated learning 60–1
Sivanandan, A. 3, 40, 58, 73, 80
Skegness 25
slave trade 27, 44, 100, 131
'small boat crossings' 26, 92
Smith, L.T. 47, 48, 50, 80
Sobolewska, M. 77
social justice
  coloniality 31
  as concept 7, 9, 17
  'culture wars' 74, 78–9
  decolonizing the curriculum 15–16
  interconnectivity 160
  justice-oriented classrooms 11–12, 63–4, 132–3
  politics of knowledge production 79, 80, 120
  praxis 50, 62, 132, 134, 149, 151–2
  socially just pedagogy 8, 87, 151, 154
  third sector practitioners 145–8
  through 'doing good harm' 19–20, 21, 45, 46, 61, 68, 70, 129, 160, 161
  through refusal 120–1
social media 28, 105–6
solidarity 58, 82–5, 128–30, 154, 155
'spectating' 55, 64, 66, 84–96, 123
Spencer, S. 108
Spiderman de Mali 65
Spivak, G.C. 3–4, 49
'state thinking' 97, 101
statistics and data 44, 62–3, 123
stereotyping 3, 12, 16, 32, 39, 45, 67, 76, 78, 93, 94
Steyn, M. 13, 19
Stierl, M. 28, 40, 62, 63, 111, 121, 122, 144
'Stop the Boats' 37, 57, 115, 116
storytelling *see* narratives and stories; testimonies
structural inequalities 2, 13, 27–8, 45, 64, 100, 142
structural injustices 31, 73
subjectivities 9, 17, 31, 143
Sudan 98
suffering 63–4, 66
surveillance 44, 82, 104, 126

T

'take back control' 116
Tazzioli, M. 41, 100, 108, 111, 112
technocratic language/rhetoric 41, 86, 105, 106, 107, 128
Technocratic 'solutions' 22, 33, 86, 106, 121, 124, 125
Tejeda, C. 7, 15
testimonies 49, 64, 66–7, 87, 144, 151
third sector practitioners 145–52
Todd, S. 64, 87, 88
translocal contexts 153–4, 155, 158
transformative
  education 6, 7, 82, 143, 152, 162
  learning 70, 86, 89, 104, 135, 147, 160
  power 55, 57, 60, 67, 68, 71
trauma 70, 87
Trump, Donald 115–16
trust in classroom and research relationships 139, 141
Tuck, E. 126, 129
Turner, J. 30, 31, 44, 100, 106

U

Ukraine 26, 98, 115
'undesirable immigrant' designation 29
UNITED for Intercultural Action 62
universities
  colonial knowledge production 126, 134
  connecting with communities beyond 141–5
  'culture wars' 75–6
  ethics in 46–53
  and radical pedagogies 15–17
  research impact 120–40
  see also knowledge: policy-research pipeline
University College Dublin 48
unlearning 7, 12–15, 160, 161
US (United States) 37, 74, 87, 115–16
'us' and 'them' 31, 77
  see also 'other'

V

Vanyoro, K.P. 104, 108
Verduzco-Barker, L. 70
Vietnamese lorry deaths 85
violent ignorance 56, 86, 91, 93–4, 144
virtual learning environments (VLE) 154, 155
visual images / representations 94, 116, 131, 154
vulnerability, mutual 10, 12, 48

W

Wagner, A.E. 13
WAKA Well 105–6

Walters, W. 104
war metaphors 115–16, 117–18
'war on woke' 75, 77
water metaphors 114, 117–18
Waugh, L. 117
Weckman, S. 136
Weiler, K. 10
welfare policies 60, 116, 122
Western concepts of ethics 47, 48
'what is' to 'what if' 7, 9, 22, 50, 81, 92, 102, 109, 119, 132–9
White, Paul (Merseyside Assistant Chief Constable) 25
white supremacy 25, 77, 102
whiteness, methodological 30–1
Williams, R. 111
Windrush 34–5, 44
'witnessing' 58–59, 84–96
'wokeness' 75–6, 77
Wood, M. 101
World*ing* Classroom case study 69, 153–8
writing manifestos 133–6, 161

X

xenophobia 1, 46, 98, 114, 131

Y

Yang, K.W. 126
Yeo, C. 29, 34
Yoon, H. 9

Z

Zembylas, M. 9, 12, 15, 16, 19, 31, 45, 53, 54, 56, 58, 59, 64, 68, 86, 131

www.ingramcontent.com/pod-product-compliance
Lightning Source LLC
Chambersburg PA
CBHW051547020426
42333CB00016B/2144